SOUL SEARCHERS

The Art of Breathing

Kundalini ✦ Tibetan Reiki ✦ Aura ✦ Pranayama
Crystal ✦ Marma Gyana ✦ Mudras ✦ Asanas

R. Venugopalan

HEALTH ✦ HARMONY
An imprint of
B. Jain Publishers (P) Ltd.
An ISO 9001 : 2000 Certified Company

SOUL SEARCHERS: THE ART OF BREATHING

First Indian Edition: 2000
2nd Indian Edtion: 2001
3rd Indian Edtion: 2002
4th Indian Edtion: 2003
7th Impression: 2010

> **NOTE FROM THE PUBLISHERS**
> Any information given in this book is not intended to be taken as a replacement for medical advice. person with a condition requiring medical attention should consult a qualified practitioner or therapis

All rights reserved. No part of this book may be reproduced, stored in a retrieval system or transmitted, in a form or by any means, mechanical, photocopying, recording or otherwise, without any prior written permission of the publisher.

© by R. Venugopalan

Published by Kuldeep Jain for

HEALTH HARMONY
An imprint of
B. JAIN PUBLISHERS (P) LTD.
An ISO 9001 : 2000 Certified Company
1921/10, Chuna Mandi, Paharganj, New Delhi 110 055 (INDIA)
Tel.: 91-11-2358 0800, 2358 1100, 2358 1300, 2358 3100
Fax: 91-11-2358 0471 • *Email:* info@bjain.com
Website: **www.bjainbooks.com**

Printed in India by
Akash Press

ISBN - 81-7021-963-9

PREFACE

Currently there is a great interest among the people of the society towards the Spiritual Sciences of the East. This interest has led to the re-discovery of many of the lost spiritual sciences like Reiki, Shiastu, Marma Gyana, Crystal therapy etc. During my quest for knowing the reasons for physical sufferings, agony in life, I had met many spiritual gurus and Saints who were kind enough to guide me. As a result, I discovered the Art of Breathing and Visualisation, for cleansing the body and the soul. I have been trained in the Indian and Tibetan Tantric tradition as well as the newly discovered spiritual sciences like Reiki, Accupressure, Pranic etc.

The knowledge led me to discover various Visual techniques which were taught to the Reiki, Vajra Reiki channels. It was their demand that I should write a book which amalgamates Reiki, Crystal therapy, Pranayama and Marma Gyana and the various other techniques taught by me.

In City life people have little time for Meditating and this leads to various ailments both physical and emotional. It was always an endeavour of mine to teach in simple language and techniques which could be practiced without much physical efforts.

This book is the result of the demand of Reiki channels and my close friends and it is useful book for both new and experienced spiritually inclined people.

Through this book, I tried to cover most of the topics which was otherwise possible only by going through many books and methods. It is human nature to know more about mystic world but has no time to go through many scriptures and methods, but if it is covered in one book, the desire to know the techniques etc. increase. This book is the result of comprehensive study done by me with the blessings of may Guru and Reiki channels.

For the first time Visualisation techniques have been covered elaborately and the method of awakening the Kundalini by which the human beings can help themselves and to be good health and live in harmony.

Furthermore I would be grateful, if readers could provide their valuable suggestions for the enhancement of the book. The readers can write to me at the following address

R.Venugopalan
427, Dhruva Apartments.
Plot No. 4, I.P. Extension.
Delhi - 110 092. (India)

ACKNOWLEDGEMENTS

ॐ Sada Shivaye Namah

This book would not have been possible without the blessings of God almighty, My parents and aunties who are inspiration for my writing and

Gurus'
Aghoree Baba Pinadrik ji
Swami Sharananda ji
Lama Dzsong Rimponche
Mr. Hui Yan Tszeng
Swami Chidanand Maharaj
Matang Baba

I am indebted to the thousands of Reiki channels, who have really worked on many of the techniques explained in this book.

I also thank the Vajra Reiki channels for their continuous contact with me for their inquisitiveness to learn more and all my friends and colleagues for their valued discussion on philosophy and parasciences etc.

R.Venu Gopalan
Delhi (INDIA)
E-mail : venrudra@yahoo.com

S.C PARIJA, IRS
Director General of I.T
(Investigation)

C-II/64, Tilak Lane
New Delhi- 110001

FORWARD

Socrates said **"Knowledge is Power"** Information Technology scientists say **"Knowledge is Growth"**. Nature has been a vast reservoir of knowledge which was open to only those who were true seekers of knowledge. It is common knowledge that the Nature unfolds true sciences of life.

This book **"Soul Searchers - The Art of Breathing"** covers a wide area of knowledge ranging from Dhyana to Kundalini awakening. Asanas to Pranayama. The young author Shri R.VenuGopalan has explained in simple language techniques to gain health and prosperity through the process of awakening the Kundalini through Reiki energy, Crystal therapy, Aura healing and viewing.

I am happy to observe that the author has scientifically explained each process of technique in a simple and lucid manner making it comprehensible to the common man.

This is a tremendous successful effort of a young mind.

I commend this book to the readers and wish the author All the Best for the maiden endeavour.

CONTENTS

	Preface	3
1.	Introduction to Meditation	13
2.	**Beginners Level**	
	2.1 Alpha Level	22
	2.2 Formless Wanderer	24
	2.3 Inner Cleansing	25
	2.4 More Visual Happiness	26
	2.5 Self Introspection	27
	2.6 Self Knowledge	28
3.	**Advanced Level**	
	3.1 Freedom From The Shackles	30
	3.2 Sense of the Death	33
	3.3 Sense of the Fire	36
	3.4 Sense of the Void	38
	3.5 Soul Torturer	40
	3.6 Past Life Fantasy	43
	3.7 Dance of Ecstasy	48
4.	**Kundalini Yoga - Theory**	
	4.1 Mooladhara Chakra	61
	4.2 Swadhisthana Chakra	65
	4.3 Manipura Chakra	67
	4.4 Anahat Chakra	69
	4.5 Vishuddhi Chakra	71
	4.6 Ajna Chakra	73
	4.7 Sahasrar Chakra	76
	4.8 Important Things before awakening Kundalini Shakti	80
	4.9 Experience on awakening of Kundalini Shakti	82
	4.10 Development of Chakras in the human body	83
	4.11 Guru	86
	4.12 Path to Enlightenment	90
	4.13 Riddhis and Siddhis	93
	4.14 Visualisation and Breathing Techniques	100
5.	**Kundalini Yoga – Practical**	
	5.1 **Awaken the Giant from Sleep**	
	5.1.1 Colour Meditation	102
	5.1.2 Kundalini Awakening -Prayer	105
	5.1.3 Balancing the energies of Left and Right Nadis	110

	5.1.4	Balancing the Shakti Points	121
	5.1.5	Awakening the Mooladhara Chakra	130
	5.1.6	Awakening the Swadhisthana Chakra	134
	5.1.7	Awakening the Manipura Chakra	138
	5.1.8	Awakening the Anahat Chakra	142
	5.1.9	Awakening the Vishuddhi Chakra	146
	5.1.10	Awakening the Ajna Chakra	150
	5.1.11	Complete Awakening of Kundalini	152
5.2	Awakening the Kundalini with the Spiritual Energy of Reiki		
	5.2.1	Reiki Basics	154
	5.2.2	Reiki Ideals	159
	5.2.3	Attitude of Gratitude	164
	5.2.4	Stages in Reiki and there Importance	165
	5.2.5	Reiki I – Defination, Self Healing and Healing with Others	165
	5.2.6	Reiki II – Symbols and there relevance	182
5.2.7	Meditational Techniques with Reiki		
	5.2.7.1	Sandwich Energy	191
	5.2.7.2	Mirror Energy	192
	5.2.7.3	Distant Healing	193
	5.2.7.4	Programming the Energy	194
	5.2.7.5	Healing the Dead	195
	5.2.7.6	Reiki Box	198
	5.2.7.7	Group Healing	200
5.2.8	Reiki III A & B		
	5.2.8.1	Attunement Process	208
	5.2.8.2	Primer for Attunement	210
	5.2.8.3	Attuning	212
5.2.9	Certification		
5.2.10	Development of The Chi Energy		
	5.2.10.1	Spot Energy Technique	235
	5.2.10.2	Hum Technique	237
	5.2.10.3	Carry Load Technique	238
5.2.11	Advance Techniques for Reiki Channels		
	5.2.11.1	Healing the Past	240
	5.2.11.2	Energising the Aura	244
	5.2.11.3	Practice in Partnership	245
6. Asanas			
	6.1.1.	Savasana	249

	6.1.2.	Sukhasana	250
	6.1.3.	Vajrasana	251
	6.1.4.	Siddhasana	252
	6.1.5.	Padmasana	254
	6.1.6.	Crow Bow Asana	255
	6.1.7.	Sarva Sukha Asana	256
	6.1.8.	Tratak	257

7. Pranayama
	7.1.	Inner Invocation	262
	7.2.	Calling to the Universal Soul	263
	7.3.	Art of Breathing	264
	7.4.	Art of Breathing- Advanced	265
	7.5.	Inner Voice	266
	7.6.	Energy Burst	268

8. Aura
	8.1.	Defination, Development of various body in human being	270
	8.2.	Aura chart	283
	8.3.	**Exercise for Seeing Aura**	
		8.3.1. Flow with Me	290
		8.3.2. Check Me Out	292
		8.3.3. Advanced Check Me Out	296
		8.3.3. Watch Me	298
		8.3.4. Mirror-Mirror on the Wall	300
		8.3.5. Watching the Inner Self	302

9. Crystals
	9.1.	Healing process used by Atlantians	314
	9.2.	Choosing the Crystals	324
	9.3.	Cleansing the Crystals	325
	9.4.	Programming the Crystals	328
	9.5.	**Meditation on Crystals**	
		9.5.1. Crystal Meditation	332
		9.5.2. Crystal Ball Meditation	334
		9.5.3. Crystal Grid Meditation	337
		9.5.4. Crystal Meditation with Reiki energy	338
		9.5.5. Energy Manifestation with Crystals	340

10. Marma Gyana and Mudras
	10.1.	Marma Gyana	344
	10.2.	Mudras	356

11. Glossary
361

INTRODUCTION TO MEDITATION

The day a person gets in touch with the soul he grows beyond the sense of physicality and reaches a level of spirituality. Only thing required is to stop and ponder on the thought of attaching with the self.

- Malang Baba

In the ancient period man was more advanced than what he is now. In today's world we say that the science has made tremendous advancement, but the fact remains that the discoveries and inventions are nothing but a small percentage of the advancement made by the man in the vedic age. Development of man in the vedic age was not limited to just physical development but also mental and spiritual development. This all round development helped the man to achieve his desired goal.

This process of spiritual development was not just limited to India but it spread all over the world and more and more research was done to perfect this art of spiritual upliftment.

This art of spiritual upliftment was adopted by saints and spiritual gurus like Jesus Christ, Hui Yan Ching, Gautam the Buddha, Shirdi Sai Baba and others. Many of the mystic art was for the benefit of the body as well as soul. Performance of this mystical art was transferred to a few selected followers only. That is the reason why many of the mystic art forms were not known to world.

One of such mystical art is "The Vajra". Vajra is a Sanskrit word meaning ' Thunder ', which in turn means mystical, universal force of strength which is undefiable. Vajra is one of the oldest technique available for the development of the body and soul. The uniqueness of this technique is that it uses the forces which are inherent in the body coupled with the energy of the nature to tap the power of universe . People in Egypt, Mesopotamia have the history of using this art and many theories were also put forward on the construction of the Pyramid based on this science. This science is pure in nature and allows people to get connected with the natural forces in the most subtle manner possible. Telekinetic energy is a part of Vajra, Vajra has

Introduction to Meditation

been used by different religion around the world under different names. In China this science developed through the Martial arts and Chi energisation. In India the same was used for the development of the mystical energy points located at the back of the spine and named "Kundalini Shakti". Many of the concepts of this science have been explained in the *Rig Veda, Sama Veda, Patanjali's Yoga Sutra and Valmiki's Yoga Vashishta, Chandodaya Upanishad, Kundalini Upanishad, Keno Upanishad, Prasna Upanishad, Bhagavatam and Shiva Mahapurana, Shiva Sutra, Linga Purana.* It is a fact that this science is in sutra format which can be explained in many ways and it is only the true seekers who can find the essence of this science. This science is so vast that it covers within itself the whole gamut of other sciences.

MEDITATION is union with innerself which helps in expanding our consciousness and mingle with infinite source of light and wisdom. It is thus discovering oneself in totality. Many people think that meditation make a person introvert and uninterested in their worldly affairs. It is not so, if one balance his activities, he will find the meditation and worldly affairs compliment and enrich each other.

There are many theories on meditation, the how's and what's of which have been clearly explained the Vedas and in other great scriptures.

India has been exceptionally gifted not only with great sages, saints and rishis but also with great Vedas and Upanishads. Meditation has been practised by different people in different forms like Tantric, Aghorees, Sufis etc. Each method is different and has its own process. It has been my endeavour to bring different types of meditational process in simple way. The reader can select any of the method of dhyana and achieve success. I have not described any traditional dhyana under any headings such as Tantric, Mantric Sufis etc as certain people have preconcieved notions about these traditional dhyanas and they may not like to go through the process.

Meditation is good if done in the early morning as the mind is free from all tensions earlier and to derive the best results of meditation.

According to the scriptures it is said that the best time for doing dhyana is the "Brahma muhurat". It is because utter silence prevails in the atmosphere and has great influence on the radiation of the moon on the surface.

I have tried to bring this book under different major headings such as Meditation, Aura, Crystal, Mudra Vigyan, Marma Gyana, Asana etc and Beginners, Advanced and Kundalini Yoga under sub headings.

A person who start the process of meditation should start with beginners level as this will enhance the body's capacity to withstand the energy and to control the mind. Advanced meditation process helps the meditator to get mastery over this level by which he could free himself from material requirements and find solace in soul searching process. This stage should be attempted only after gaining good control over one of the techniques given in the beginner levels.

In the third part I have tried to explain about Kundalini Yoga, the method of awakening the sleeping serpant in two sections one which explains the theoretical aspect of the Kundalini Dhyana and second part explains the various meditations which allow the Sadhaka to raise the kundalini energy from the Mooladhara chakra to the Sahasrar Chakra.

I have tried to explain in simple language some exercises which are easy to follow and to increase the knowledge about oneself. Meditation and its practice as described in the book is necessary to develop the mind to achieve strength to face the life in totality.

According to the Shiv Mahapurana, for deriving best results in the meditation, correct posture, good surrounding is necessary.

Select a clean and comfortable place to sit which is devoid of noises and sounds. The place should be clean and comfortable in sitting. If you are not comfortable in sitting on the floor you can either place a small cushion on the floor or otherwise you can meditate sitting on a chair.

Introduction to Meditation

The place where meditation is done should be free from interference of the pets.

The place used for dhyana should not be used for any other purpose. This is important as while doing dhyana our body emits certain energy and this energy spreads in and around the place where we sit for meditation. This energy also helps one to get into the levels of meditation faster and quicker.

Avoid sitting on the plain floor for meditation, as all the energy which is generated through the process of the meditation will be absorbed by the earth. In Shiv Mahapurana, Skanda Purana and Patanjali's Yoga Sutra it is said that the meditator should not sit on plain earth but should sit on the seven layer dhyana sthal, like sitting on mat made of Kusa grass or the best insulator is said to be the Tiger skin. If the sadhaka is not able to find any of these things he/she can use thick cotton mats or woollen mats which are easily available.

Sit with back erect and in a Padmasana / Siddha asana with hands in Gyan Mudra (i.e. Index finger tip touches the tip of thumb, this mudra helps in achieving dhyana easily and faster, this is explained in detail in the Mudra section). If it is not possible to sit in the above said postures, sitting in any comfortable posture would also give the same amount of benefits. The main aim of sitting in posture is to be keep the spine erect position. It has been observed, that if a person does not sit in a correct posture and goes deep in dhyana then it is quite possible that his shoulders may stoop and may fall down.

When sitting for dhyana make sure to sit for atleast 30 minutes, in the same posture without moving any part of the body. In the beginning it may be difficult but with experience it will become comfortable.

If you like music, you can play any instrumental music which is slow and does not hamper with the flow of your process of dhyana.

Never be hasty to gain full control of senses as the mind takes its own time to open up to universal energy and slow blossoming of the heart is better than hasty blossoming as it would not be able to sustain the force and power the dhyana produces. The more a person does meditation the more his body generates energy and to sustain this energy it is important that the vessel (body) should also be strong enough to bear the energy without exhaustion or pain.

Never do dhyana when you are in emotional crisis like anger, grief etc as in this state you may give some auto suggestions which can create harm than good for the body and soul.

Never breath in and breath out as after a long run, as this will consume lot of oxygen in the body. Always take slow deep breath and slow exhalation, this will provide the oxygen required for the body.

Always have a selfless motive behind the meditation, be it total surrendering to the universal soul, be it to achieve any material or spiritual gains. This can be seen from the flg illustration:

One King was meditating with a selfish motive. After a long penance the Lord appeared before him and asked him for a boon. The king requested the lord that he wanted to ask two questions after which he would ask for the boon. The Lord agreed to the request. The king asked "My saviour, first thing, I want to clarify is whether it is true that our earth's millions and millions of years are equal to 'one moment' of the lord's time".

God laughed and said "Son it is absolutely true, now the second question".

The king asked "Lord is it also true that earth's all the billions of rupees and gold are but a particle of your lordships wealth". Lord said "it is true my son" but you may ask your boon without any hesitation.

The king said "Lord, I want the particle of your lordship's wealth as a boon".

The lord laughed and said "One moment - son" and vanished.

Introduction to Meditation

THINGS WHICH CAN HELP THE SADHAKA

❖ Meditate regularly and if possible on the same time as then the energy will get accustomed to your timing and will help you reach more deeper into the stage of meditation faster. It is quite possible that in the beginning you may not be able to get the desired results, but don't lose hope. This happens when you put standards for achievement and strive for it. Dhyana is not a competition and thus putting standards only makes the mind tense and goal oriented. Let the mind relax and work with patience, any kind of force makes the mind to work against you.

❖ Go for quiet walks, spend time with nature, and get moderate exercise.

❖ Give more attention to the subtle impressions and sensations within and around and also contemplate their meaning.

❖ Release all anger, fear, jealousy, hate, worry, etc. up to the light. Create a sacred space within and around you. This is not a easy job. Storing up anger, fear, jealousy, hate and worry and hamper your health. There are two ways of releasing them one of them is bursting out, this releases all the traumas in one go and empties you and the other is to divert your energy like punching a pillow, breathing heavily.

❖ Reduce or eliminate time for watching TV, listening to the radio, and reading newspapers. As this gets you more attached with the worldly affairs with which you as a being are not concerned with. Dhyana is a process of emptying you into nothing, if you go on filling the space with junk then the process will become endless.

Beginners

Stepping the first stone is the most difficult thing

it takes a child lot of time to balance

In the same way looking inside is also

very difficult Shaping the Physique is easy

Shaping Destiny takes the time

Nature becomes a part of you, if you

become one Come Let us take the first Step

Towards a Life full of Happiness and Love

ALPHA LEVEL

This is the first step towards understanding the body. and the flow of prana (breath) in the body. This is a 6 week course and should be done by all ,who are interested in knowing about themselves before proceeding to higher levels of meditational processes.

It is important to follow each week of the course as described in the book for receiving the full benefits of this meditational exercise.

WEEK # 1

After sitting comfortably close your eyes. Inhale deeply and exhale in a slow and steady manner. Chant Om hundred times, the speed of the count should be in symmetry with the breath. With each inhalation of breath and Om , feel the prana flowing in and with each exhalation feel the negative energy flowing out of your body. You can use fingers to count 'Om'. By the time the counting reaches 100 or before, you will reach a state where you feel lightness in the head and feel energised from inside. Sit in this position till you feel elevated. This exercise is the first step towards looking inside the self. It is not necessary to concentrate by counting Om, you can also use numbers (but they have to be repeated in a reverse manner or descendent order like 100..99..98..97..... until..1). This state of ecstasy is also known as "**Alpha Level**", whereby the mind is slowed down to a level where for the first time you will encounter with your own subconscious mind. This is the place where all the information regarding events of your whole life is stored. And programming of the mind can be done at this level in a specific manner. Most of the auto suggestion programming is done in the sub conscious mind.

WEEK # 2

This should be done only after you have full control over the Week #1 exercise. In second week also concentrate on the counting only , but on every alternate breath taken in the count should be decreased. For example

Inhale....Exhale....Inhale..100..Exhale...Inhale....Exhale....Inhale..99..Exhale... Inhale....Exhale....Inhale..98.....

Beginners Level

The same should be done with counting of "Om" or counting numbers in descending order.

WEEK # 3

This should be done after you have got full control over the Week # 1 and Week # 2 exercise. In this week, concentrate on the breath i.e. after every Inhale stop for a count of 10 and then exhale and then stop for a count of 10 before the next inhale.

WEEK # 4

This should be done after you have got full control over the Week # 3 exercise. In this week also concentrate on the breath but the pattern will be different i.e. now stop for a count of 10 after a full cycle of Inhalation and Exhalation.

WEEK # 5

This exercise will heighten your sense of your own body.

For doing this exercise stand on a floor mat with the feet apart.

Close your eyes breathe deeply and now raise your hands above your head. Now place the palms on either side of the head and make your palms feel the head by moving your finger through the hair. Now move to the face feel each feature of face. Then move to the neck feel the features of it. Same way move from neck to the shoulder plates, both the arms, chest, abdomen, lower abdomen, thighs, inner thighs, knee balls, calf muscles, upper ankle and the feet (both the upper and lower part of the feet). In the same manner move from the front part of the body to the back of the body and raise from the back of the feet to the back of the head. Regularity of this exercise will bring you closer to yourself than what you ever had known yourself.

WEEK # 6

In this week you will repeat all the exercise from the Week # 3 till Week # 4. After that sit down and close your eyes and visualise yourself as close as possible with natural surroundings.

FORMLESS WANDERER

It is a known fact that our great rishis used to protect themselves before curing others from physical or spiritual ailments. This is important because in cases where the energy which is not compatible to your energy or flows in the opposite direction of your energy, it is necessary to protect yourself. This exercise will also help you to do the cleansing process of your own body and soul.

Visualise the room in which you are sitting, the imagination should be as good as that you can see even the needle on a table as bright as you would otherwise see in plain sunlight. Once you have re-created the room as it is, locate two points in the room in an angle of 90 degree from you. Also locate a point in the ceiling at an angle of 45 degree from you. Now draw an imaginary line from the point you are sitting so that a PYRAMID shape is drawn. Imagine that each side of the PYRAMID is energised and the soothing white energy is flowing towards you and penetrating your soul and heart from the head onwards. After some time you will feel as if you are sitting in the midst of white cloud which is glowing with energy and vitality. Sit in this cloud till such a period as you would like. This cloud of energy will drain out the negative energy of your Chakras and substitute it with positive energy. This energy will help to increase your potential to sustain the unknown, to fight the power of negative force with the force of good.

It is important to know why only pyramid is drawn and not any other shape like ovals or spheres etc. The shape of the pyramid is unique as it has four sides with equidistant triangular shapes, these help in absorbing any energy which is positive in nature and reflects away any negative energy. Pyramid has inherent property to absorb any negative energy inside its sphere that is the reason why ancient Egyptian kings in the form of mummies were buried inside the centre of the pyramid.

Beginners Level

INNER CLEANSING

No dhyana is perfect without the cleansing of the soul and the body. This is a simple exercise in which you will be able to cleanse your negative karmic thoughts and activities and allow the universal bliss to flow through your body. After sitting down comfortably close your eyes and concentrate towards the centre of the eyebrow. Sit in the Gyan Mudra by joining the First finger with the thumb. Imagine all the emotions from your mind is transferring to the mother earth through your left hand and imagine positive energy flowing through your right hand . The energy on the right hand should have inflow from the universal soul. Believe in the universal soul and ask for the cleansing of the soul. It is quite possible that you may not be able to feel the sensation in the hands or you may not feel the universal energy flowing in the beginning but if do this exercise for few weeks you will automatically start to feel the energy flowing through the palms of your hands.

Do this exercise for TWO -THREE weeks and you will find a new perspective about your life and also you will get to know the real purpose of your life.

MORE VISUAL HAPPINESS

This exercise will heighten your internal capabilities to reach further into the spiritual path of progress. This type of dhyana is more fruitful if done in a group, as this exercise will heighten the true spirit in you.

Form a circle in a room / open and slowly start jumping or making movements to either sides of your body, raise your hands above your head lower it, then spread your hands across and lower it .You can do these or any other exercises you wish like. And do these exercise continuously until you feel the force letting go off the control on you. This force is nothing but your ego and all those complexes that you had carried on for years without letting those complexes leave you even for a second. At this moment you are at the best level of your own spirit. Make your spirit sore the heights of the universe itself and go on till you are physically exhausted and are on the verge of falling down.

When you are totally tired sit down silently in one place and concentrate on your breathing. Close your eyes and breath in a normal manner for a few minutes till you get a feeling of the flow of your breath inside your body. The feeling should be such that you feel each breath you inhale to flow through your body and the parts of the body it touches. When you sit and practise in this position of natural breathing for some days, you will find that you have gained strange insights onto your own self.

SELF INTROSPECTION

This exercise will heighten your internal capabilities to reach further into the spiritual path of progress. This type of dhyana is more fruitful if done in absolute silence, as this exercise will allow you to see the true person in you.

Close your eyes and breathe in a normal manner for a few minutes till you get a feeling of the flow of your breath inside your body. The feeling should be such that each breath you inhale flows through your body and it touches each part of the body. Breathing pattern is also very important as the pattern decides how much easily and quickly a person can reach the deep levels of meditative state without even trying for it.

From the childhood we have been told to breath in a manner which expands the chest and contracts the stomach which is a very wrong way of breathing. Our lungs have not been built just to breathe from the chest. The full utilisation of the lungs occurs when we breathe from our stomach, as we breathe the expansion occurs at the stomach and then the chest expands. This will allow the lungs to expand fully to its potential. This is the breathing pattern with which we are actually born You can witness this when you watch a new born child sleeping . If he/she is sleeping on his/her back you can clearly see the rise and fall of the lower back during the process of inhalation and exhalation.

When you sit in this position of natural breathing for some days, you will find that you have gained strange insights onto your own self. This knowledge will give you more power to your prana and thus rekindling the fire of life in your self.

SELF KNOWLEDGE

This exercise will heighten your intuitive capabilities of your mind to greater heights. Sit in an asana which is comfortable and do the slow breathing exercise till your mind calmed down. In this exercise you have nothing to do except to view the incoming and outgoing thoughts. Be calm and do not let the feelings or the thoughts affect you, as your role in the whole exercise is to be a spectator only. In the beginning it is quite possible that you might get carried away by the thought process, but you should strive to achieve a level of perfection where your thoughts are nothing but fragments of picture which come and go as in a movie.

This exercise may look simple but infact this exercise is important for the sadhak to reach the levels of beta and theta. In the beginning you may be able to see lot of thoughts flowing through your mind but in due course of time you will loose contact with the thought process and will be able to reach a level of no thought. This stage is not a stage of doing nothing but is stage of active meditation. In this stage the sadhak should try to do dhyana either on the breath (prana shakti)or on a mantra.

Advanced

Across the Cosmos there is light

and the aim is to make the light mine

With no exception, No Aim And No Emotion

I am trying to win the heart

of the nature to encompass me

Let the energies of the eternal life bless me

for taking the same steps taken by many before me

To help and to be helped in the work of the Nature

FREEDOM FROM THE SHACKLES

STEP #1

Sit on a comfortable chair or it is better to lie down on a hard floor. Close your eyes and keep both the hands on the sides. The feet should be kept slightly apart.

* Start taking deep breaths, inhale as much as you can hold for a two-three seconds and then release your breath as much as you can. Repeat this for ten minutes. This process allows the mind to be set on the breath you are taking.

* Relax for a minute and during this period do the normal breathing.

* For the next five minutes do the deep breathing again. With every breath inhaled visualise all the worries and tensions being caught by the breath and on each exhalation all the worries and tensions released out of the body.

* Relax for a minute and during this period do the normal breathing.

* Tense all muscles in your body and hold for a few seconds. Start with foot muscles then tense thigh muscles lower abdominal muscles, upper abdominal muscles, hand muscles, ankle muscles, shoulder muscles, neck muscles, face muscles till you reach the temple muscles. Hold this posture for a minute and release.

* Hold this posture for a minute and release. Enjoy the pleasure of it. This is the pleasure that life has given us.

STEP # 2

This stage is more effective if you have good visualisation capability. Feel a cool breeze blowing into the room. Let this cool air fill the room in such a way that you feel chillness in your bones. Visualise the

Advanced Level

chillness spreading through your body, slowing down the flow of the blood.

Feel the throbbing of heart against the rib cage slowing and slowing till you feel no more. The silence and emptiness which you feel now is very serene and spiritual. This is the moment of the blissful experience. Stay in this position for as long as you can.

Feel the emptiness transforming your physical body into a body of light. Let this body of energy flow through the air into a big cloud.

Behind the big cloud is the secret land of cosmic energy. This spiritual land is bathed in the cosmic rays from the universal soul.

Visualise a small land made of crystal and sit on this land amidst the cosmic energy. Enjoy this cosmic bath of energy. When your body has absorbed enough energy, it will float back to the place your physical body is in trance and merge with it.

Stay in this position of spiritual energisation stage for as long as you can. This will help to smoothen out the flaws in the ethric body and rejuvenate your physical body.

BENEFITS OF THIS MEDITATION

* It helps in providing breathing space in life, which is very much required for releasing all the tensions and problems in life.

* This meditation helps in understanding that the life and death are two coins of the universal energy. In nature this phase is just a part of the vast reservoir of the life you have lived and died and will live and die before reaching a level of total nirvana or eternity.

* Regular practice of this exercise will increase your mental and spiritual faculty and provide you with the true meaning of life and death.

IMPORTANT INSTRUCTIONS FOR DOING THIS MEDITATION

* Clothes of loose fittings should be worn for doing this exercise.

* This meditation should be done in a quiet place with least disturbances.

* The best time for doing this exercise is in the morning and late evenings.

* If this exercise is done before sleeping then it has been observed that the energy generated flows till the morning.

* Never do this exercise in the afternoon, as this exercise increases the body heat.

Advanced Level

SENSE OF THE DEATH

This Dhyana will heighten your sense of equilibrium with the universe and will enlighten you with the truth that what you have been doing or what you have been thriving for is nothing but pure 'maya' in its true sense.

Man has always been afraid of the darkness, afraid of the untold stories hidden in its fold. He used fire to keep the darkness at bay. This fire he used to worship as a spiritual gift from the universal lord. In the same way man is always afraid of death as it is still wrapped in a mist of untold stories. This is due to the fact that experience after death is unknown to him.

Gautam Buddha used to teach his disciples who were not afraid of death, the art of dying. It is also said that it is better to die one day than to die everyday with the fear of death. He used to send his disciples to the cremation ground where corpses were burnt and used to ask them to concentrate on the flame of the cremation fire. This concentration led to the truth that they will also be burnt similarly to reach higher life form. Regular practice of this meditation helped in understanding the karma's of this life.

PROCESS OF DOING THIS DHYANA

STEP # 1

* Darken the room in which this meditation is to be done. Spread a rug in the centre of the room and lie on it with closed eyes. Place your hands on the side of the body palms facing the sky and the feet should be kept apart.

* Start breathing slowly. The pace of the breathing should be such that every inhalation should take not more than five seconds and the exhalation should not take more than five seconds. Continue this process for ten minutes.

* Tilt your head to the right side slowly and repeat the process of breathing for ten minutes.

* Bring back your head in the centre and start breathing normally for a minute.

* Again Tilt your head to the left side slowly and repeat the process of breathing for ten minutes.

* Bring back your head in the centre and start breathing normally for a minute.

* Relax your self for a minute.

STEP # 2

This stage lets you to the first insight into the aftermath of death. The process of getting this experience is to let all your muscles relax. Start with relaxing foot muscles and then the thigh muscles lower abdominal muscles, upper abdominal muscles, hand muscles, ankle muscles, shoulder muscles, neck muscles, face muscles, temple muscles.

When you feel totally relaxed. Feel as if some force is acting inside your body which makes you feel that you are in a cage of bones and flesh and there is free space waiting for you outside this body. Feel that the cage is slowly opening its gates and allowing you to come out of it and fly in the open sky. Don't let this opportunity go by, as soon as you feel that the cage is wide open, fly to the open sky and let the cool breeze help you to reach further and further until you reach so high that you don't feel like coming down to the earth again. Let your soul dance to the tunes of the nature and feel the happiness you have forgotten for so long. This happiness will give you the strength to fight your daily battle with life and will pave your way in such a manner that you will start enjoying it. Live and breathe in this position for as much time as possible. This will release all the negative energy stored inside your body and when all the negative energy has drained out, the nature will fill it with new revitalised energy.

Advanced Level

BENEFITS OF THIS MEDITATION

* It helps in understanding the concept of death in a more clear manner.

* Regular practice of this exercise will increase your mental and spiritual faculty and provide you with the true meaning of life and death.

IMPORTANT INSTRUCTIONS FOR DOING THIS MEDITATION

* Clothes of loose fittings should be worn for doing this exercise.

* This meditation should be done in a quiet place with least disturbances.

* The best time for doing this exercise is in the night before going to sleep.

* Never do this exercise in the afternoon, as this exercise increases the body heat.

SENSE OF THE FIRE

Man from time immemorial has considered fire as a clean and mystique form of energy, which has inherent property of burning away all the bad elements. Fire can be said as the representation of Sun in its minuscule form and as the sun rays purify and keep the body and soul of life form in perfect health, fire can cleanse the soul of the person. This meditation is done better in the morning before the sunrise.

Persons who have psychological fear of fire should not do this exercise except under supervision.

THE PROCESS OF DOING THIS DHYANA

Select a comfortable place to sit and close your eyes and take deep breaths. With each inhale feel that each part of your body is getting revitalised and flowing with pure form of energy and with each exhaiation feel all the negativity flowing out of your body. Continue to inhale / exhale deeply till the time you feel a strange feeling engulfing you and all your muscles feel relaxed and deeply filled with the natural energy or the prana shakti. Now concentrate on the third eye chakra (the point where the two eyebrows meet). Visualise that a small fire is kindling in the third eye chakra, the flames of the fire is engulfing your both the eyes in such a manner that you feel that the energy of fire is relaxing you but also making you feel hot. Now visualise that the small fire is spreading to your whole face, even though you feel the heat of the fire surrounding you but you are not getting burnt by it. Let the fire take its own flow through your body in such a manner that it covers the whole body. The heat is intense and you are sweating profusely but the fire is not harming even a single hair of your body. After engulfing your whole body feel the fire entering your body through the mouth and nostrils, and now feel the heat of fire inside your body as well as outside. Every breath you inhale will allow the fire to enter your body and the flames will cleanse all the internal parts of the body. Feel the flames enter the heart region and cleanse the heart of all the negative feelings which have been accumulated over the years. The

*Advanced Level

more the flames spread the more you feel the body getting cleanse of all the negative thoughts and views. At this point, start forgiving the people who have harmed you in any way be it physical mental or emotional. If you forgive a person from heart you feel the fire is increasing. The intense heat you were feeling has transformed into the coolness as by now the flames have consumed all the negative thoughts, and you are free from all the negative emotions.

BENEFIT OF THIS EXERCISE

* Regular practice will surely get the fear of death out of your life and this will further enhance your life to greater heights.

SENSE OF THE VOID

From the ancient times our great sages had found that the universe was formed through the primordial sound 'Om' and this theory has been accepted by the scientists also.

This sadhana is a process allowing the sadhak to re-live the experience of the formation of the universe from the stages of the void.

THE PROCESS OF DOING THIS DHYANA

Select a comfortable place to sit and close your eyes and take deep breaths. With each inhalation feel that each part of your body is getting revitalised and flowing with pure form of energy and with each exhalation feel all the negativity flowing out of your body. Continue to inhale / exhale deeply till the time you feel a strange feeling engulfing you and all your muscles feel relaxed and deeply filled with the natural energy or the prana shakti.

Visualise a total dark place where nothing could be seen.

In the beginning if you feel difficulty in visualising the void then roll your eye balls to the bhu madhya (Third eye chakra) and hold the breath for a slow count of 10. When you reach the count of 10 release the breath slowly to a count of 10. Doing this process will help you to go into the void space.

Now visualise a super giant shining star in the midst of the void. The Orange light emitted by the star is so bright that you feel that the whole void is lighted up. Feel that the orange light is turning into Red and the heat of the star against your body. You hear a rumbling sound in your ears which is growing with every moment of time. After some time the rumbling sound is so loud

Advanced Level

that you feel the sound to be unbearable. Suddenly the sound stops and you feel the uncanny quietness in the space.

This quietness is abruptly disturbed by the primordial sound / big bang which blasts the star into pieces. The blast is so strong that the star pieces are thrown apart. Feel that the burning pieces are coming towards you at a fast pace.

One of the burning pieces break up into nine big pieces and other smaller pieces, which are pulled in by the gravitational pull of the bigger piece. This push and pull of the pieces make the smaller pieces revolve around the bigger burning piece. The bigger burning piece formed the sun and the smaller pieces are the planets and the satellites which revolve around the sun.

This is how our universe in the milky way galaxy was formed.

BENEFITS OF THIS DHYANA

1. Allows the sadhak to re-live the most magnificent point of time.
2. The process given in this dhyana is of basic form, it is the creative visualisation of the sadhaka which can enhance this dhyana.
3. The results derived from this dhyana is more if the sadhaka is a visual person.
4. This dhyana also helps the sadhak to enhance his visualisation.

SOUL TORTURER

This dhyana is better done under supervision as a beginner can get afraid of the things he may see, feel or hear during this exercise. Persons suffering from heart disease, blood pressure or asthma should consult a doctor before doing this exercise.

PROCESS OF DOING THIS DHYANA
STEP # 1

- Darken the room in which this exercise is to be done. Sit in Siddhasana and close your eyes. Do the 'Energy Burst' exercise as given in the Pranayama section for a period of two minutes.

- After the completion of the 'Energy Burst' do the Shavasana. Lay in the same posture for five minutes.

- Again assume the posture of Siddhasana and close your eyes. Breathe normally and with each inhalation form a internal cocoon (covering the internal body fully) and with each exhalation form a cocoon around your body. The internal cocoon will help in removing the negativity's stored in the body and the external cocoon will dispel external thoughts from interrupting the dhyana. Continue to do this process till you feel a coolness surrounding you.

- Tense all the muscles in the body and release it. Continue tensing and releasing exercise for a period of two minutes.

- Pull your anus in , hold for ten to twenty seconds and release.

- Relax every part of the body and sit for a minute.

Advanced Level

STEP # 2

Feel that energy is flowing out of your body. Feel an unknown force ripping the energy from the roots of your body without any sympathy or kindness like the butcher who doesn't feel anything while tearing the skin from the body of the goat or plucking the feathers of the live chicken before killing it. These feeling can be easily generated by imagining that you are a chicken trapped in a small cage with other chickens. The cage is so small that there is not enough space even to move a step without stepping on other chickens feet. Every chicken has different kind of look in their eyes, their eyes showed a feeling which is mix of fear and anxiety, the feeling is so strong that many of the chickens have even defecated in the cage itself. There is a particular kind of smell in the cage which is of sweat mixed with a unknown kind of fear.

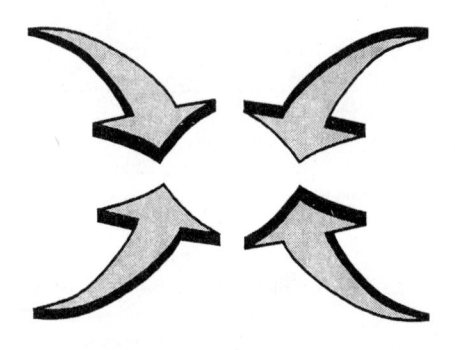

Suddenly you see a hand entering the cage and pulling out one of the chickens from the cage, and then you see the pain writhe cry of the chicken when the butcher mercilessly forces the chicken in the boiling water. When he brings the chicken out of the water, he plucks the feathers of the chicken and the blood oozing out in streams. This process continues till the chicken is plucked free of all the feathers and then you see the butcher's blade rising up and you see the fear writh face of the chicken which is nearly dead and then suddenly with a small croak everything comes to a standstill.

This is the death which we are afraid of, the chicken died because it was not afraid of the plucking of the feathers but it was afraid of the aftermath of death which it clearly saw in the eyes of the butcher.

This is evident from the fact that the chicken even near death was afraid of the butchers knife that it might cause it to die and reach a level for which it was not ready and will never be ready.

This same philosophy applies to man also. Lie in this experience for as long as you can as this feeling will bring out a special person in you.

BENEFITS OF THIS EXERCISE

* Regular practice of this exercise will generate a feeling of self confidence, removal of the fear.

* This exercise also helps in removing some of the misconceptions and phobias related to death. As a new perspective of death is provided to the sadhaka.

IMPORTANT INSTRUCTIONS FOR DOING THIS DHYANA

* This exercise may look horrible and painful in the beginning, but in reality it helps in smoothening the fear of death from your mind.

* This exercise should be preferably done in the morning or in the late night.

* At least four to five hours should elapse after intake of food before this dhyana is done.

* Jot down every feeling you get during this dhyana as you will see that the feelings change with every passing day.

Advanced Level

PAST LIFE FANTASY

This exercise should only be done after getting confidence in the mind and soul that your duty on this earth is not only to yourself but also to the entire society. The reason for this is, people love to know their past as well as future lives but are not ready to face the repercussions of their deeds in the previous lives. The karmic deeds of the person in this life depends upon the karmic deeds done by him in the previous life. If it was not so then no person will be born as a poor or rich, healthy or weak, sad or happy. It is only the karmic deeds which really changes the way we live our life. Moreover Karmic deed decide the lineage and parents. The time date and the environment in which a child is born depends upon the karmic deeds done by the person in the previous life.

This dhyana is a long one which takes you from this birth and time to the inception stage, pre-birth experiences and the past life.

If you feel that you may not be able to visualise for such a long period of time then you may record the whole dhyana word by word and concentrate on it.

This dhyana is to be done only after reviewing the risk factors which are involved like :

* *[i] during this dhyana it is quite possible that you might see some incidents and events related with your past life, which may be very distressing.*

* *[ii] in the beginning this dhyana is to be done under guidance of a teacher or a person who is well versed in handling different type of situations in dhyana.*

PROCESS OF DOING THIS DHYANA

Stage 1   Understanding Yourself

The best position for this meditation is to lie down comfortably, close your eyes and place your hands to the sides loosely. Part the legs slightly also and leave them loosely. Inhale and exhale deeply and with each inhale feel the fresh air coming into your body and releasing the tensions in the muscles. Go on breathing deeply till you find every part of your body is relaxed. After relaxing every part of the body bring the concentration to the heart. Synchronise the heart beat with the breathing pattern, i.e. to say you exhale when there is a beat and inhale when there is gap.

When you breathe with this synchronisation you will feel one with the universal soul. Go on breathing with the heart beat and pull your concentration to your mind which is the storehouse of all your memories of all your life and much more. When you concentrate on mind with synchronised breathing pattern with heart you will be amazed to know the rhythm of mind. The more synchronised you are with your heart the easier you will know the flow of mind.

Stage 2   Understanding your Life

When you have synchronised heart beat with breathing pattern and flow of mind, you will have total control over your senses. This is the moment when you are ready for travel back in time. Think of a time in past when you had achieved something great or had received some good news. If your breath is synchronised and you are pure in thoughts then you will definitely see the events one by one in front of your eyes.

Relish the moment the way you had done during that period. Now visualise the hard work and efforts you had put in for the achievement of the goal. How happy your family was with your achievement. Let this happiness carry you back to the period when you were around five years old. Visualise how you used to look, walk, talk when you were five years of age. Look how innocent you used to be free of all tensions and free like a bird. How your parents treated you, the love and affection they poured on you. Visualise how you used play with your

Advanced Level

friends. Enjoy the blissful life and let it carry you back in time when you where a toddler crawling to get control to stand up. Feel the inquisitiveness flowing through your veins in such a manner that every thing you used to hear, see or feel. Look at the chubby fat you had on your body which made you a darling of your parents as well as neighbours. Every body wanted to hold you near his / her heart. The dreams you had when you used to see other older people around you, like the way they had control over their life as well as yours. Remember how you loved to play and run around.

Run with this speed back to the period when you were a child in a cradle. How restful you used to sleep and enjoy the bliss of the natures best given gift called love. Waking up your father and mother in the middle of the night for milk, and enjoying the sleep in the morning. Many a times you feel the disturbing thoughts troubling you in the sleep, images and faces you have never seen or felt, but still felt a closeness to those images and faces. In the cradle itself see you moving your legs as if you are cycling on a path towards glorious past. Increase your speed of cycling and suddenly you feel warmth and stickiness around your body and when you open your eyes you are surrounded by lots of sticky life giving and nourishing fluids and the whole environment is dark. You are in the womb of your mother attached to her by the umbilical chord connected with your navel. All your limbs have developed and your facial features are quite visible, Now start kicking the legs in the similar pattern as you had done in the cradle and close your eyes. Go on cycling till you feel a cool and refreshing air surrounding your body.

Open your eyes and you will find yourself on the top of a hill covered with clouds or you may see yourself floating on the air at very high altitudes but in both the cases you may not be able to see the ground, however hard you may try. Look around you and you may see some numbers, figures, names, persons. Many of the things you see will feel familiar to you but you may be not be able to get connected to it. Concentrate on one of the things you see through the third eye and you may see that the figure or number have produced limbs and taking you along it to a world of your past life.

Step 3   Getting Connected

Hold on to the figures, numbers arms and recite the flowing prayer

O Lord help me to Reconnect
to the life Lived by me
To be able to see the Good & Bad Deeds
As aptly as had been done
May the Feelings be Gone when I Wake
Let all bygones be dealt with in a manner subtle
to the nature and Let it not effect me
in the life led by me now Thank you. O lord.

As soon as the prayer is over feel that the numbers have changed into a small girl child with a smiling innocent face. The smile of the child is so innocent that you will be drawn into accepting whatever the child wants. This child is your guide to your past life for that period. The child will take you into that period of your previous life which will have in store for you the solution to a problem being faced by you in this birth. Touch, feel, sense everything you see on the way. Start by requesting the guide to show all the good karmic deeds you had done during that period, then ask the guide to show all the bad karmic deeds done by. Please be patient with the guide as the scenes which may be shown to you may not appeal to you but still are a part of you which had lived through.

When you feel that the guide has shown you enough, please thank the guide for the effort she has shown you in showing the closed doors of your one of the life's you had lived through.

STEP 4   GETTING DISCONNECTED

It is important that after such a long period of meditation that you should get disconnected from guide and return back to the current life, otherwise if stay back then coming back to this life is complicated without the help of a experienced guru or a person well versed in the art of Past Life Therapy. After thanking the guide, ask the guide to take you to the realm of the sub consciousness. On reaching the sub

Advanced Level

consciousness the guide will vanish and then you start the count from 10 to 1 in a slow rhythmic manner based upon the breathing pattern. The things to be done at each count has been given in the Count Chart No. 2.1

Count	Things to Do
10	feel that your body has again entered the womb and the you are growing up.
9	feel all the limbs are growing from the body of yours.
8	feel yourself being delivered and regaining the present life.
7	feel yourself in the cradle.
6	feel yourself crawling on the floor.
5	Feel yourself growing up to the age 5
4	Feel the energy of a healthy individual flowing through your body.
3	Feel your getting mature and reaching the current age of yours.
2	Draw in Deep breaths and smell the freshness entering your body and rejuvenating your heart and body.
1	Open your eyes and feel the freshness in your life coming back.

COUNT CHART 2.1

Benefits of this meditational process :

    a. All hidden trauma and other psychological problems will burn away
    b. Connection with the guide will help you to understand the life better

DANCE OF ECSTASY

A person who dances with no sense has the insight of the true nature of the universe

From birth we have been taught to hold back our emotions and feelings. This leads to growth of insecurity in the mind of person and when he grows up leads to psychological problems like sudden anger, grief, pain etc. This exercise helps in releasing the inhibition stored up for years.

Some of the things required for doing this dhyana are

* a tape recorder with auto playback
* a dance music cassette (continuous) (if you can find a Sufi dance music cassette it better)
* a big empty room with few things

Darken the room in which you would like to this dhyana. Play the cassette at a volume in which you cannot hear any other sound except the music of the cassette.

Stand with the feet and spread out hands. Close your eyes and feel the rhythm of the music flowing from the cassette entering your senses. Release all the tension with every passing moment of the music.

Warning : Never let the body do what the conscious wants to do. Let the inner soul guide you to the music.

Start the dance, never letting the image of any dancer seen on the television overshadowing you. This dance is yours, the dance of your inner conscious. Let the body make any movement like jumping, rolling on the floor, shouting etc., do not try to curb the emotions so released.

Doing of this technique regularly will help to release all the curbed and stored emotions.

Advanced Level

SOME IMPORTANT POINTS

1) While doing this dhyana it is quite possible that your body might get tired but your mind would not allow you to stop. Let the dance of Ecstasy continue till your mind gives the permission to stop.

2) Ego, Consciousness and opening of the eyes should not be done as they will activate the conscious mind and the benefit of this dhyana will be lost.

3) Benefits of this Dhyana :

   a. This dhyana will release all the curbed emotions

   b. When the emotions are released things like tension, irritation etc. will also be released

WARNING : People suffering from Asthma, Heart problems, High Blood Pressure should consult a doctor before doing this dhyana.

Kundalini Yoga

Human Body is the perfect specimen of machinery, which has evolved over a period of millions of years, to reach the stage, which is now. If we look at history then we will find the ascent of man only covering a small minuscule period of the total time. But the inquisitive nature of man has made him into a fine specimen of advanced growth and thinking. Man from the beginning was very much interested in finding out more about the riddle of life and also in knowing more the nature itself so as to control and harness its power. This quest lead him to the worship of the nature and then to the tantra for controlling the nature itself.

Nature never hides anything from the people who are desirous to learn the true things of life. As Lord Krishna said to the great warrior Arjuna that like a tree draws its energy from the roots and sustains the whole plant to become a tree, the same way our body is like an inverted tree with the brain acting as the roots of the body and drawing energy from the universe and developing the body from that of child to that of a grown up person.

In each person the same level of strength is there to draw the energy from the nature but how many of us try is of utmost importance. A person who allows maximum time for material things will not be able to gauge the depth of the sea; while a person who works and strives towards the spiritual path to achieve th right kind of path and goals will be able to reach the sea and also able to gauge the depth of it. As in India, people of other countries like Sumeria, Egypt, China, and Mesopotamia were doing deep research in the field of unriddling the science of human body. Even though the languages were different but the concepts drawn by these ancient cultures were very similar to that of India.

As per this science each human body is engulfed with the ethric energy field called Aura and this auric field is energy pattern of the body. Depending upon the energy field the colour of the aura changes to show the level of the energy. As per the scriptures we have 14 Lokas which is very pertinent for the life of person. The list of the Lokas are given in the figure 1.1 A. As per the figure we can see that a person starts the life from the Bhu Loka and he has two options either to

Kundalini Yoga - Theory

deceit life to reach the Patal loka or strive to get to the Satya Loka which is the abode of the universal soul.

Sri Krishna while explaining the complexity of life and karma to Arjuna has said that a single karma can be either a sin or can be a deed, which is pious. On being asked how by Arjuna, the lord replies that if a person kills a person for his own benefit alone then this is sin but if a person kills another person for the benefit for others then this is a work of piousness.

14 LOKA'S	Indri	God
Satya Loka		
Tapo Loka	Chaksurindriya	Surya
Janar Loka	Granaindriya	Ashwini Kumar
Mahar Loka		(Nasika)
Rudra Loka (Swah Loka)	Shrutri indriya	Dhik (Ear)
	Jiva	Varuna (Ras)
Vishnu Loka (Bhav Loka)	Tavak	Vayu (Touch)
	Hastindriya	Indra
BHU LOKA	Charahindriya	Vishnu
Atal Loka	Vaani	Saraswati
Vital Loka	Guhindriya	Prajapati (Anand)
Nital Loka		(Shristri)
Gambhist Loka	VAYUGUDA(Ansu)	VAYU
Mhatal Loka		
Sutal Loka	The First Five are the Gyanindriyas and the Last Five are the Karamindriyas	
Patal Loka		

DIAGRAM NO. 1.1A

KUNDALINI

Kundalini is derived from the word "Kundala" meaning coiled. This power is symbolised by the sleeping serpent with the tail in its mouth. Lord Shiva had explained this secret of Kundalini to Mata Parvati for the benefit of the people and also explained the process of awakening the energy thereof. Maa Kundalini has been worshipped for a long period of time. Many rishies have called Kundalini by many names like Kundli, Kula Kundalini, Nagini, Tapasvini, and Bhujagana. Like the Tri- Shakti who have assigned the duty of destroying, creating and supporting. Lord Shiva is said to be the destroyer, Lord Brahma as the creator and Lord Vishnu as the protector.

As per our scriptures, in the beginning there was nothing, no sound, no land, no earth or anything but a huge void. Due to cosmic destiny there was a big bang and the first word was heard OM. This Om is considered as the "pranava mantra" and the sadhak who meditates on this mantra will be blessed with the darshan of the Omkareshwar. Lord Shiva for the creation of the universe awakened Lord Vishnu from his chir-nidra. From the navel of Lord Narayana, Lord Brahma was born seated on the Lotus flower with four heads showing the four Veda's and the four varnas. He first created the ether and fire and from the combination of fire and akasha (ether) water was created. Earth was created from the combination of all the four tatva. As per the scientists also in the beginning there was nothing, after that there was a big bang (**Sabda**) and then there was light (**Tejas**) and the universe began to spread very fast. Out of the big bang, galaxies were formed and stars were born, our milky way is one such galaxy and sun is one of the mid sized stars. Many pieces got broken up from the sun to form the planets and due to the gravitational pull of the sun they revolved around the sun. In the beginning the planets were very hot and due to the hot air (**vayu**) and pressure they cooled down to form water (apa). One such planet, which cooled down was earth (**dharti**). And then from the combination of all the tatvas life was created on the earth.

Kundalini Yoga - Theory

S.No.	Elements	No. Guna's	Guna Tatva
1	Akash (Ether)	1	Sabda
2	Vayu (Air)	2	Touch
3	Agni (Fire)	3	Speed, Tejas (light)
4	Apa (Water)	4	Taste
5	Earth	all the above gunas	

From the Homo erectus to Homo Sapiens, man was inquisitive enough to develop his latent powers. The brain of the human is of particular structure which is unique in nature and it is fact that even after so much development of science man has not been able to fully understand the concept of the brain. The rishies and munies of the ancient times had developed the science, which could fully explore the brain.

This can be proved by many of the spiritual feats showed by the great rishies like telekinetic abilities, telepathic abilities etc. More about the Siddhies have been provided in a tabular format later in this section.

BRAIN

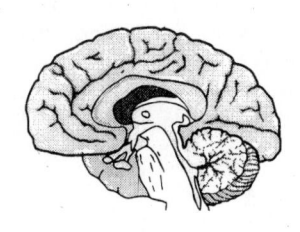

The most complex and important structure in our body is brain, which is the main important part of our body that can be compared to a Central Processing Unit (CPU) in a computer. In the same manner brain also acts like controlling and processing centre for the whole body. The brain consists of the forebrain, the mid brain and the hindbrain. The shape of the brain is very much like an apricot. The brain is divided into two sides 'The left' and 'The right'.

CENTRAL NERVOUS SYSTEM (CNS)

Body has more than 3½ lakh nadis (Shiv Samhita, Gorak Samhita) and these are spread all over our body in a very complex manner. In scientific terminology we can call them as nervous system of our body. The elaborate net of the nerves serves two purposes one to transmit the information received from the brain to different parts of the body and also to receive and pass the messages from the different parts of the body to the brain. The combination of various veins and nerves combine together form the Nadis.

The CNS contains nerve centres for all sensations and activities. Membranes called meninges cover the brain and the spinal cord. The cavities of the cerebral ventricles inside the brain and the cavity meninges contain the cerebrospinal fluid.

CEREBELLUM: Cerebellum receives impulses from the semicircular canals and from stretch receptors in muscles and joints. It uses information from these sources to maintain muscle tone and thereby a balanced posture and it also contains muscles during activities like walking, riding, running etc.. The *pons* is a bridge of nerve fibres that connect the lobes of the cerebellum. Transmission of impulses across this bridge ensures a co-ordination of muscular movements on the two sides of the body.

Above the cerebellum is located the **cerebrum** which is the largest part of the human brain. Its shape like a walnut (dome shaped made-up of two parts). The cerebrum consists of grey matter, which forms the outer layer, and the layers, which are whitish in colour, form the inner layer of the nerves.

The grey layer is called the Cerebral cortex. This is an important layer as it is concerned with the following senses of the body:

PHYSICAL SENSES	EMOTIONAL SENSES
Vision Touch Hearing Taste Smell	Control of Voluntary Movements Reasoning Emotional Activities Memory

The cortex has separate block for each senses and these blocks receives impulses from different parts of the body and are stored here. These sensory blocks help in activating and controlling the sensory activities.

There are other cortex area are called motor areas which control the bodily movements of the muscles like limbs, abdomen, neck etc.

Medulla oblongata is the lowest part of the brain, that is the part which merges with the spinal cord is called the medulla oblongata. This region is concerned with unconsciousness processes including the regulation of the blood pressure, body temperature and rates of the heartbeat and breathing. It performs these tasks through connections with the autonomic nervous system. The medulla also contains the mass fibres, which connect the brain and the spinal cord.

Spinal Cord is a tubular structure and a downward continuation of the brain. The whole of the spinal cord is covered by meninges like the brain and is housed in the neural canal within the vertebral column. The spinal cord has two enlargements; one is the cervical region where the nerves to the upper limbs originate and the other in the lumbar region where the nerves to the lower limbs originate. Running through the centre of the spinal cord is the central canal of the vertebral column; this is a continuation of the ventricles of the brain and contains the same cerebrospinal fluid. Spinal cord plays a very important role in the structure of the body by acting as the reflex centre and also conducts the impulses to and from the brain. On this spinal cord is situated the mystic chakras which control the flow of the other small and minor chakras. Spinal cord also acts as an adhara for the body. As humans stand erect the spinal cord is also upright this helps in rising the Kundalini from the Mooladhara chakra to the Sahasrar chakra without any interference, in cases of animals the spinal cord is mostly vertical in position which does not allow the kundalini to rise from the Mooladhara to the Sahasrar in a uniform manner.

The cranial nerves originate from the brain and the spinal nerves emerge from the spinal cord. The neurones which carry an impulse from the Central Nervous System to the muscle or a gland is called the motor nerves. In man there are 12 pairs of cranial nerves which emit from the brain and supply to the head. There are 31 pairs of mixed nerves, which intervene with the internal organs, body walls and the limbs. Each spinal nerve originates into two roots called *dorsal root* and *ventral root which* join together to form the spinal nerve. The rate of travel of a nerve impulse is 50 to 100 metres per second.

Automatic nervous system lies outside the central nervous system. This system looks after the heart beat, working of the stomach, digestive system, intestines etc.

There are two sets of nerves, which are totally opposite in action and activity.

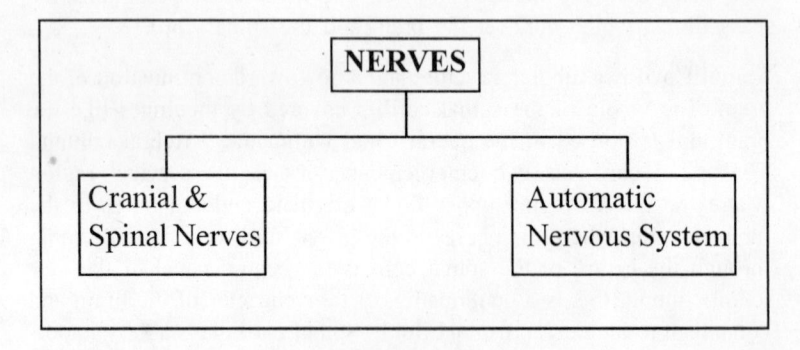

```
                    ┌─────────┐
                    │ NERVES  │
                    └────┬────┘
              ┌──────────┴──────────┐
      ┌───────┴───────┐     ┌───────┴───────┐
      │ Cranial &     │     │ Automatic     │
      │ Spinal Nerves │     │ Nervous System│
      └───────────────┘     └───────────────┘
```

Kundalini Yoga - Theory

Sympathetic Nerves: These nerves start from the two chains of sympathetic ganglia's situated on the either side of the spinal column,

Parasympathetic Nerves: These nerves start from the brain and the spinal cord.

The sympathetic nerves in Kundalini Tantra is known as Surya nadi (Sun nerve) or *Pingala nadi* and the Parasympathetic nerves as the Chandra Nadi (Moon nerve) or *Ida nadi*. Ida nadi starts from right testicle and Pingala from the left testicle. The breath from the left nostril is cool and thus Ida flows through it and Pingala nadi, which flows from the right nostril, is hot in nature. In Yoga when there is requirement of increasing the body temperature the Sadhak will control the flow of the Ida nadi and increase the flow of the Pingala nadi. Bastika also increases the flow of the pingala nadi. That is why after doing yogic exercises it is necessary to do Shavasana which helps in making the Ida flow, which is cool in nature and pale in colour.

In many of the scriptures the flow of the Ida and pingala is termed as that of flow of the pious river Ganga and its tributary Yamuna. Between the Ida and Pingala nadis another nadi flows which is called as the Sushmana. This nadi is crimson red in colour. Through this nadi the mysterious river Saraswati flows. In centre of Sushmana nadi there exists Vajra nadi, which in turn has Chitrni nadi in its centre. Vajra nadi is the source of the energy for our body. Chitrni nadi is the spiritual nadi, which can only be seen by people, who have cleansed their body, mind and spirit, the size of this nadi is ten thousandth part of the thread in a cobweb. In the centre of this Chitrni nadi exists the Brahma nadi. Brahma nadi flows from the beginning of the Mooladhara chakra to the Sahasrar chakra. Through the Susumna nadi rises the Kundalini energy like a serpent and pierces through the Mooladhara Chakra to the Sahasrar chakra also said as Brahmadvara to Brahmarandhra.

These three nadis (Ida, Pingala, Sushmana) meet each other at Mooladhara Chakra (Mukta Triveni) and Ajna Chakra (Yukta Triveni).

The serpent sleeps in the Mooladhara chakra when dormant in a state of 3½ coils representing the three gunas (Sat, Raja, Tama) and the half represents the ahamkara of the person. It is important for the sadhak to first cleanse all the tamasic and rajasic gunas to reach the fullness of the sattvic guna.

This can also be said as the path of the Shakti The flow of the Ida and Pingala can be known from the fact that the flow after every 2 ½ hours the flow of prana changes its swara.

When Ida nadi is flowing then milk, water and liquid foods should only be taken and no heavy jobs should be done. While when the Pingala nadi is flowing then travelling and other hard work can also be done.

Other than Ida, Pingala, Sushmana Nadis some of the major nadis are *Gandhari, Hastijivha, Kuhu, Saraswati, Pusha, Shankhini, Pyasvani, Varuni, Alambuja, Vishvodhari, Yashaswini.*

Gandhari nadi is situated in the right eye and Hastijivha nadi is in the left eye

Pusha is in the left ear and Yashaswini in the right ear.

Alambuja nadi is situated in the mouth and the Kuhu nadi is the Linga

Shankhini nadi is situated at the kidney.

Ida and Pingala nadi meet at six places in the spinal region and the places where the nadis meet there exist the major chakras Mooladhara, Swadhisthana, Manipura, Anahat, Vishuddhi, Ajna.

Kundalini Yoga - Theory

MOOLADHARA CHAKRA

Mooladhara chakra is the most important chakra of the body located two fingers below the testis and two fingers above the anus, this chakra is four fingers in width and rotates in the right direction. In females this chakra is located near the opening of the uterus. In the anatomical diagram 1.1 B you can see the male and female genital organs and also see the exact position of the Mooladhara Chakra.

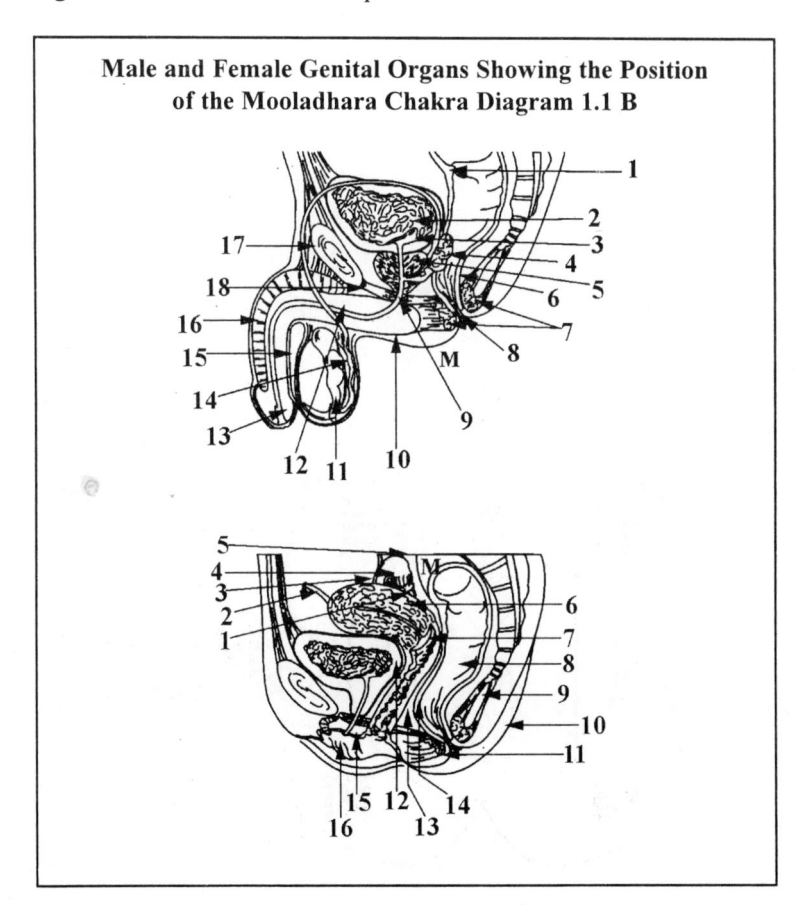

Male and Female Genital Organs Showing the Position of the Mooladhara Chakra Diagram 1.1 B

DESCRIPTION OF THE DIAGRAM 1.1 B

Sagittal Median Section through the Male Genital Organ : 1 Prostata, 2 Vesica Urinaria, 3 Ostium Ureteris, 4 Intertinum Tenue, 5 Vesicula Seminalis, 6 Rectum, 7 m.Sphincter ani externus, 8 Anus, 9 Urethra (Pars membranacea), 10 m.bubocavernosus, 11 Bulbus penis, 12 Testis, 13 glans penis, 14 plecus pampiniformis, 15 Corpus spongiosum penis, 16 Corpus cavernosum penis, 17 Symphysis pubica, 18 Diaphragma urogenitale

Median Sagittal Section through the Female Genital Organ: 1 lig. teres uteri, 2 lig. ovarii proprium, 3 tuba uterina, 4 ovarium, 5 uterer, 6 uterus, 7 labium posterius uteri, 8 rectum, 9 m. sphincter ani externus, 10 Anus, 11 m.sphincter ani externus, 12 labium anterius uteri, 13 muscles of the urogential diaphragm, 14 muscles of the urogential diaphragm, 15 Vagina, 16 muscles of the urogential diaphragm, 17 labium minus pudendi, 18 labium majus pudendi, 19 Urethra, 20 Clitoris, 21 Symphysis pubica, 22 Vesica urinaria

M- MOOLADHARA CHAKRA

Kundalini Yoga - Theory

Mooladhara derives the name from **Moola** meaning **root** and **adhara** meaning **Base**, this chakra forms the base of the spine and also the other chakra's of the body.

The basic ability to smell comes from this chakra. Mooladhara has the quality of earth. This quality of the chakra gives it the colour red with four nadis sprouting out of it like the petals of a flower. In its dormant state this chakra is facing downward towards the earth and when awakened blossoms like a sunflower.

The square in this chakra represents the earth quality, which is pale yellow in colour and is energised by eight spears on its sides (two on each corner). Each nadi is symbolised by the swara VAM (वं), SHAM (शं), SHAM (षं), SAM (सं) respectively with the Bij word LAM (लं) in the centre. The main granti working on this chakra is Brahma granti with Bhu Loka as its abode.

In the centre of this chakra is a bright silver coloured triangle representing the sexuality. In the centre of this chakra is lord of the three world the Adi-Antha prabhu Lord Shiva in form of a golden Shivalinga, the Linga being enveloped by a giant sleeping snake in a three and half coils.

This snake is the Kundalini shakti in its three and half coiled shape in dormant state. When the shakti is awakened, it moves like lightening speed and with a Hissing sound, penetrating the mooladhara chakra to cross the five other chakras to reach the bliss.

Airavat the white elephant with seven trunks is the cosmic animal in this chakra. Such a huge and fast animal represents the energy required for upholding the awakened Kundalini. Lord Indra sits on Airavat with his Vajra in the right hand. Lord Indra represents the various Indriya's (smell, taste, sense, feeling etc.). Lord Indra has been depicted as a wayward king of the devata who used to take pleasure in women, wine and luxury. In the same way the indriyae in the body of a person is wayward and tries to pull man away from the reaching the spiritual bliss by giving him the greed of all the worldly pleasures. Only the sadhak who can control the indriyae can reach the tenth door

(Dasham Dwara) or the Sahasrar Chakra. The other indriyae represented by the 2 nostrils for smelling and breathing, 2 ears for hearing, 2 eyes for seeing, 1 mouth for the taste, anus for throwing the waste products out of the body and genital organ for the reproduction purpose. The basic knowledge of this chakra is through smell, which is done through the nose. The physical part of the body, which responds to the chakra, is the anus

The adhipati devata of this chakra is four-handed Lord Ganesha with Lord Brahma and his Shakti Savitri (tantric tradition this shakti is worshipped as Mother Dakini). Ganesha means 'Gana' and 'Isha', the lord of attendants as he stands in guard on the mouth of the chakra wherein the Kundalini is lying in a dormant state. In Hindu scriptures it is said that before worshipping any devata, Lord Ganesha is to be worshipped and after getting his blessings only a sadhaka can cross this dwara (door). Lord Ganesha is the guardian of the Chakra and stops anybody who is not eligible for the entry. And all the leela's (miracle) of the lord are in the form of a child so is the behaviour, i.e. like a child lord Ganesha is playful and when pleased removes all the obstacles in the way for the rise of the kundalini by the sadhak. When the lord Ganesha is pleased then the Mother Kundalini is also pleased and helps the sadhak in all possible way.

The person who concentrates on chakra will be blessed with health and happiness and all the earthly needs. Below this chakra lies a triangle yantra from where Susumna arises from the centre of the triangle and from the left rises the Ida nadi and from the right the Pingala nadi.

Kundalini Yoga - Theory

SWADHISTHANA CHAKRA

Swadhisthana is a two word **Swa** and **Adhisthana** meaning under ones own control. Swadhisthana chakra is situated two fingers above the Mooladhara chakra and is vermilion red in colour. This chakra is responsible for all the urinary, excretory, reproductive system and water related needs of the body. Physically the chakra is located on the base of the spinal column with the pubic bone.

As we know by the scientific laws that the earth is covered by 75% water and the rest is land in the same manner our body also contains 75 % of water. This chakra is responsible for the correct maintenance of the water level and also to maintain the correct viscosity of the blood. This chakra is having Brahma nadi and also controls the water status of the body. The main vayu of this chakra is vyana. This chakra has six nadis in the form of petals arising out of the chakra with the swara BAM (बं), BHAM (भं), MAM (मं), YAM (यं), RAM (रं), LAM (लं) attached with the bija word VAM (वं) in the centre. The loka of this chakra is Bhuvarloka and the tatva is apa (water).

The shape of the base chakra is half- crescent moon, flowing downward like a crocodile diving deep into the river. The lord of the chakra is Lord Vishnu sitting on Garuda at the entrance of this chakra, with Goddess Saraswati (in tantric tradition Goddess Saraswati is worshipped as mother Rakini who is having four hands, three eyes and in the fierce pose. The three faces of the goddess Rakini represent the three phases of time past, present and the future). The goddess Saraswati is considered the mother of all knowledge the sadhaka who meditates on this chakra will be blessed with the knowledge of the past present and the future and is freed from all the lust, anger, greed and other materialistic attachments. The main reason for this is that this chakra represents the hidden knowledge and true science. The sloka given below aptly represents the essence of this chakra.

Asato Ma Sadgamaya
Tamso Ma Jyotirmaya
Mrityur Ma Amritagamaya

(Oh lord take me from the wrong ways to the good ways

Oh lord take me from the darkness to the light of knowledge

Oh lord take me from the darkness of death to the nectar of life)

This chakra stores within itself the karmas of the person. Every single activity of the person is stored in the Swadhisthana chakra. When a person is taken into Past Life therapy through hypnotic trance then the brain accesses this chakra to retrieve the information. This is the reason why this chakra is regarded as a blockage to the awakening of the Kundalini. Thus when the kundalini awakens the sadhak faces lot of problems both psychologically and physically.

This chakra also tests the sadhaka by tempting him the luxuries of life and the sadhak who has the will power to restraint from the offer is allowed to control this chakra. Lord Jesus and Lord Buddha also had to face the temptation during their sadhana.

Kundalini Yoga - Theory

MANIPURA CHAKRA

This chakra is also called as the Navel chakra as the position of this chakra on the physical body is the navel. The name of this chakra is derived from two words 'Mani' and 'Pura' meaning Jewel and Place, thereby meaning the place where jewels are found. The Tibetan mantra

Om Mani Padme Hum is for this chakra where Mani Padme means 'jewelled lotus'.

This is an important chakra for the awakening of the kundalini as this chakra represents the dynamism and energy in the body. This chakra is responsible for the correct working of the digestive system, small and large intestines, appendix, pancreas, duodenum, stomach and liver.

Navel chakra is dark greyish in colour with ten nadis forming the petals with the swara / word DAM (इं), DHAM (ढं), NAM (णं), THAM (तं), DHAM (थं), DHAM (दं), DHAM (धं), NAM (नं), PAM (पं), FAM (फं) and the tatva bija being RAM (रं). The ferocity of this chakra can be compared to that of Agni (Fire), and the power can be compared to that of RAM. This chakra is blood red in colour and the chakra moves up like a RAM with full force and vigour.

The Adhipati devata of this chakra is Three eyed Rudra with his shakti Lakshmi. Rudra is fair in colour and covered with ash (symbolising the beginning and end of the world). His two beautiful eyes are partially opened looking inside the self and the third eye partially closed representing the knowledge and power. In the tantric tradition Shakti Lakshmi is worshipped as Mother Lakini who has three faces (representing the three lokas - Naraka, Bhu sthala and Swargaloka) and three eyes in each face representing the Trikala Gyana.

This chakra has Swarga or Swah loka. The tatva of this chakra is Agni. As in the body you can see that the agni helps in maintaining the body temperature, and helps in the digestion process.

The actual awakening of the Kundalini starts from the Manipura chakra only; the reason for this is because Mooladhara and Swadhisthana represent the animalistic tendencies of the human body. Till the time Manipura chakra does not get purified and awaken, the Kundalini cannot rise fully. Manipura chakra works as the energy point for the awakening of the Kundalini energy.

Meditation on this chakra helps in removing all the physical diseases. Awakening of this chakra also gives the power to the sadhaka to heal others. In awakened state this chakra provides heat and energy to the body.

Some Siddhies received from awakening of this chakra: full knowledge of the body both ethric and physical, control over the fear of fire and death.

Kundalini Yoga - Theory

ANAHAT CHAKRA

Anahat means endless love and pacification. The physical part of the body where the chakra is located is heart. This chakra is responsible for the correct working of the lungs and the heart. This chakra is deep red in colour and from this 12 nadis flow out like petals of a flower with the swara / word as KAM (कं), KHAM (खं), GAM (गं), GHAM (घं), DAM (ङं), CHAM (चं), CHHAM (छं), JAM (जं), JHAM (झं), JHAM (ञं), TAM (टं), THAM (ठं) with the bija word YAM (यं).

This chakra has the speed of a black deer and it runs fast in an angular direction. The loka of this chakra is Maha loka and has Vayu mandala as the base. The Adhipati lord of this chakra is Three eyed Ishan Rudra with his shakti Kakini. The lord is having three eyes and the third eye closed to symbolise the love and forgiveness, which the lord bestows upon the sadhaka who meditates on this chakra. This love can be compared to a mother, who forgives the child even if the child has committed some crime. Shakti Kakini is Four handed who is beautiful to look at and gives out love and compassion to whomsoever required. The granti, which flows through this chakra is Vishnu granti. This granti represents the emotional attachment, which a person has with his family, friends and relatives. This chakra relies on the touch concept physical or psychological.

Meditation on this chakra makes the sadhaka humble, noble and knowledgeable. When this chakra awakens it bestows the sadhaka with a radiance of spirituality. Such a person has large followers who believe him as a guru.

Once a person awakens Anahat chakra he crosses the limits of the animalistic tendencies and reaches the levels of human. The other three chakras Mooladhara, Swadhisthana and Manipura are related with the animalistic status, while from the Anahat chakra the sadhaka transforms himself into a Yogi. Saints who have followed the path of bhakti yoga have opened up the chakra with ease.

Women easily open up this chakra while males easily do the ajna chakra.

Some of the Siddhies achieved on awakening of this chakra are: Total control of the senses, the power to do Parkaya Pravesh.

VISHUDDHA CHAKRA

Vishuddhi chakra is located in the throat where the collarbones meet. This chakra is responsible for the correct functioning of the throat, vocal cord, upper lungs, mouth and nose.

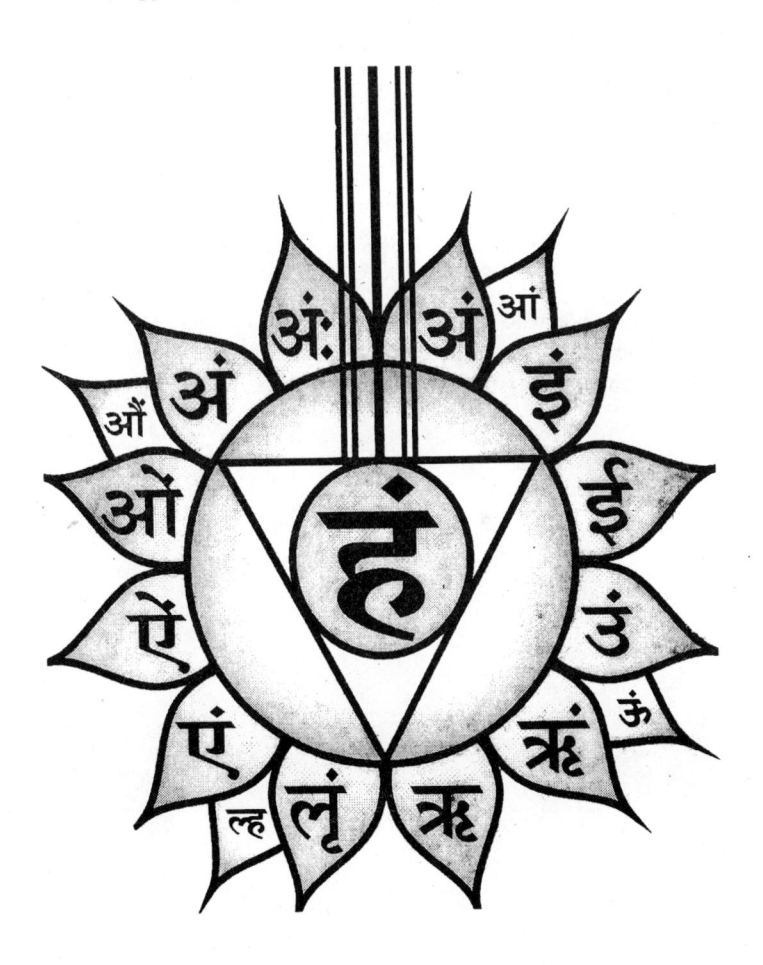

This is deep Blue in colour with 16 nadis in the form of petals AM (अं), AAM (आं), IM (इं), EEM (ई), UM' (उं), UUM' (ऊं), RSH' (ऋं), REEM' (ऋं), LRIM' (लं), LREEM (ल्हं), EIYM (एं), EEIYM' (ऐं), OM' (ओं), AUM' (औं), AM' (अं), AH (अः) attached with the bija word Ham' (हं).

The bija word is ivory white in colour. This chakra represents the akash tatva or the ether and the loka of this Janar loka.

The Adhipati lord of this chakra is Sadashiva as bindurupa with his shakti Shakini. Goddesses Shakini is beautiful to look at with four hands, five faces with three eyes on each face, in her four arms she holds the bow, arrow, spear and ankush. Sadashiva in the bindurupa represents the energy of the panch mahabhuta shakti (Sagyojata. Vamadeva, Agorha, Tat purusha and Ishan)

The Sadhaka who meditates on this chakra gets the ManoVanchit Siddhi (the siddhi he desires). The sadhaka attains the power of controlling people with speech and writing.

AJNA CHAKRA

The exact location of the Ajna chakra is behind the head where the spinal cord meets the brain. On the physical plane the location of the chakra is between the two eyebrows. Physically speaking this chakra is responsible for the correct functioning of the eyes, ears and nose. This chakra is very difficult to open as it forms the barrier between this world and the abode of Lord Shiva. Only a sadhak who has been able to gain control over the tamasic and rajasic pravartis will be allowed access into the world beyond. Once this chakra is opened up, then the nature opens up its gates and allows you to meet the universal soul, in its full form. This chakra in itself combines and harnesses the energy of the sapt lokas and also holds the key to the beginning of the nature and the meaning of the soul. This chakra resides on the Tapoloka or the realm of mind. This chakra has two petals / nadis with the swara HAM (हं) and KSHAM (क्षं) with the bija word AUM (ॐ). The bija mantra AUM itself is formed of the three syllable A (अ) + U (उ) + M (म), representing the past, present and the future. Aum itself represents the eternal knowledge. He who finds the meaning of the AUM finds the lord.

The Adhipati lord of this chakra is Sadashiva with his shakti goddess Hakini who has 6 faced, 3 eye on each face and 6 arms sitting on white lotus. As per the scriptures when the time for the end of the world (Kalayuga) comes Lord Shiva does the fierce dance of **tandava** and assumes the form of Nataraja (lord of the dance) to destroy the creation. In the same way the Lord destroys the tamasic and rajasic tatvas of the sadhak to increase the sattvic tatva of the person. Ajna means 'command' , this is not the command given by the Guru but by the universal soul. The lord only allows the true sadhaka to reach this plane Guru in physical form only acts as a medium for the same.

Soul Searchers The Art of Breathing

Kundalini Yoga - Theory

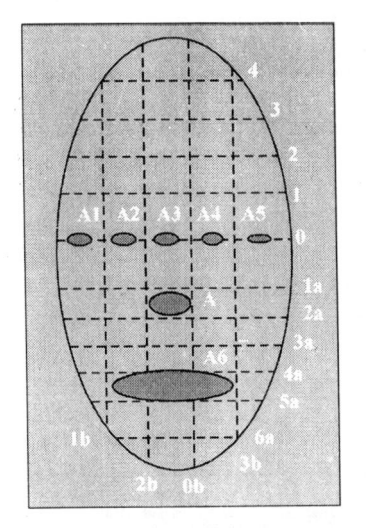

If you look at the diagram of the human face you can see the point where the 0 and 0b intersect is the centre of the face. The line 0 is the centre of the face and from the left edge of the face to the right edge of the face on the line 0 if partitioned at equidistant parallels then we will be able to draw five eyes equal eyes i.e. A1, A2, A3, A4, A5. If we join the A1 and A2, A4 and A5 we will get the two eyes and the A3 is the point where Ajna chakra is located. Perpendicular to the point A is the nose and if the distance between point 2a and 6a is equally divided in three parts i.e. 3a, 4a, 5a then between the points 4a and 5a mostly where the mouth is found. If a straight line is drawn from the point 0 on the either sides then the beginning of the ear is found and on the straight line on the point 2a then the lower part of the ear is there. This is nature's wonder as mostly in all the cases the positioning of the body parts are nearly as shown above.

SAHASRAR CHAKRA

Sahasrar is actually not a chakra but the energy of the universe itself. Sahasrar means thousand petalled lotus. This chakra does not have one colour but has many unique and beautiful colours. This chakra is where the Shakti Devi Kundalini meets the Shiva or the union of the Shakti & Shiva takes place. Kundalini when awakened travels from the Mooladhara to reach the Sahasrar and this causes the eternal bliss. This chakra symbolises the awakening of Shiva from the Shava awastha of the mundane physical body to take the form of the ArdhNareshwar i.e. Shiva on the right part of the body and Shakti on the left part of the body. Lord Shiva represents the surya energy and the shakti represents the moon energy. Lord Shiva is the lord of the death and without death new life cannot be formed and this new life cannot be created without the Shakti. This culmination of the Lord Shiva with Shakti shows the tradition of Adi-Antha prabhu i.e. the God of beginning as well as the end.

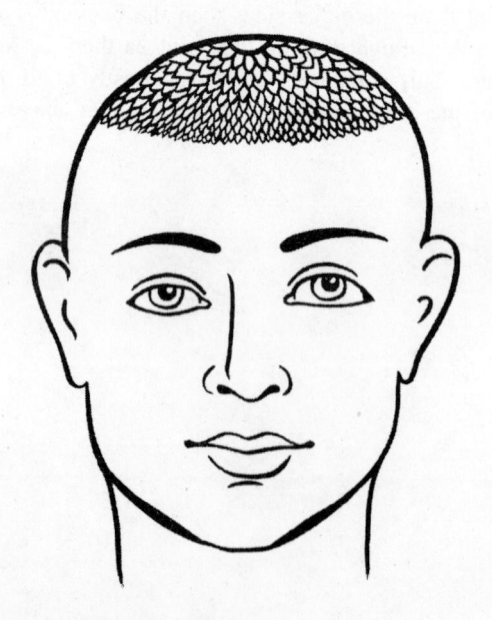

Kundalini Yoga - Theory

Due to this reason only the sahasrar chakra is called the fountain of nectar, the nectar of spiritual and universal knowledge. When a sadhaka reaches this stage he achieves the knowledge of the past present and the future.

When a Sadhaka reaches the crown chakra there is no night, no day, no present, no past, no future, no life, no death, no sound, no birth, no pain, no agony, no happiness, no sorrow, no relatives, no guru only a void of eternity. This void is the only truth and nothing is beyond it.

The sadhak reaches the zenith of fantasy and spiritual upliftment when the kundalini rises from the mooladhara chakra to the sahasrar chakra. The experiences of the rising kundalini vary from person to person. The experience is so spiritual that it is not possible to explain the feeling in words, it can only be experienced.

After the kundalini raises it does not stay in the sahasrar but again comes down to the mooladhara chakra. The rising and falling of the kundalini is a natural phenomenon after it has risen once. Like a diver dives into the ocean to find the pearl hidden inside the oyster shell and after finding it brings it back to the surface in the same way regular meditation helps in the accumulation of the sattvic guna. As in the case of a diver he cannot stay in the water for long and has to come out of the water to take breath, in the same way kundalini comes back to its own coiled form near the mooladhara chakra. The sadhaka goes on living the karmic life as done by him except that now he is nearer to the universal soul. Thus gets detached from the material life and travels in the eternal blissful life understood by few who have been able to achieve the same level of spiritual growth.

Other than the frequently discussed above Seven chakras there are some secret energy points which actually store the essence of the universe.

Between the Anahat and Swadhisthana chakra there exists the energy point of the sun itself. This is the energy point golden in colour and spins in the clockwise direction. This energy chakra controls the sudden awakening of the kundalini power from the Mooladhara chakra. This energy point is also referred to as the Sun chakra, the controller of the temperature of the body. This centre also stores the nectar of life development.

Near the joining of the throat chord there exists the shir sagar of life. This energy centre is triangle in shape with smooth tips. As per the Shrimad Bhagwata it is said that Lord Vishnu resides on this ocean of milk floating on the Seshnaga. The colour of this chakra is silvery white which changes colour with the emotions. This chakra controls the emotions of the person. This chakra is called as Shir chakra (Chakra of Ocean).

Kundalini Yoga - Theory

Just above the ajna chakra there is small oval energy centre which is house of the nectar of the cosmic energy itself. When the right time comes Guru gives the key for the nectar of cosmos. When the nectar flows out the spiritual bliss felt by the sadhaka is equivalent to the awakening of the kundalini. This chakra is called as the Lalata chakra.

Near the soft upper palate exists the Lalana chakra, which controls the vocal chord of the physical body. Other than the above major chakras there are more than 800 minor chakras in the body which work as per the instructions given by the major chakra.

Locations of the 109 main minor chakras on the physical plane of the body are:

∗ The eye holes	∗ Joints of the fingers with the Palms of both the hands	∗ Centre of the feet
∗ Sides of the temple	∗ Thumbs of both the hands	∗ Toe nails of the feet
∗ On both the sides of the cheek.	∗ Palms of both the hands	∗ Hind part of the feet
∗ Nasal holes	∗ Finger tips	∗ Near the calf muscle
∗ The mouth	∗ Sides of the Abdomen	∗ Back of the thigh muscle
∗ Near the vocal chord	∗ Lower sides of the abdomen covering the liver and kidneys	∗ Base of each buttock
∗ Collar bones	∗ Near the hip joints	∗ Each cartilage of the spine
∗ Shoulder joints	∗ Centre of the thighs	∗ Hind part of the back of the skull
∗ Near Elbow joints	∗ Knee joints	∗ Back of the head
∗ Both the wrists	∗ Ankle Joints	∗ Back of both the ears

SOME IMPORTANT THINGS TO BE KNOWN BEFORE AWAKENING KUNDALINI

A new entrant in this kundalini dhyana will have to keep many of the following things in mind before proceeding further:-

1. Never be hasty for doing the dhyana as this is the energy of the nature itself and should not be played without proper care and dedication.

2. Follow the steps as given in the dhyana fully to awaken the kundalini.

3. Many times you may feel that the dhyana is not giving you any results, it may be due to the following reasons :

    a. You are putting too much stress on your mind for achieving the benefits.

    b. Never bring forth your ego while doing the dhyana. Pray or worship the way you have been doing. And your belief will bring in the results.

Most of the time the arousal of the kundalini is a blissful experience. There is no experience in this world which can be compared with the awakening. Kundalini awakening is a spiritual experience, but the force with which it uncoils itself is very powerful. The force can be somewhat compared to the blast off of a rocket. People without the basic knowledge of the nature of Kundalini shakti should not tread on the path of arousal.

* Sadhaka who tries to awaken the kundalini in a haste can cause himself some irreparable damage including psychic difficulties (trouble) and problems in the family and at work. This is due to the fact that more and more people find that in today's society based on materialistic values, cannot make them happy. Many want to reach something genuine within themselves, something eternal and imperishable. In this quest they do experiments with cosmic knowledge and expanded

consciousness without knowing about the dangers of obtaining powers without proper guidance.

* Sadhaka should take guidance from a person who has been through the process of Kundalini-arousal, with expanded consciousness and increased creativity.

* Kundalini arousal occurs sometimes as an unintentional side-effect of yoga, meditation, healing and psychotherapy. Other factors can be : Births, celibacy, deep sorrow, high fever and drug intake. But Kundalini arousal can also occur suddenly without apparent cause. The secret purpose with yoga and meditation actually is to release the Kundalini force. When Kundalini reaches the brain, it is said to be stimulating the unused braincells, so that higher state of consciousness is gained.

* When Kundalini arousal takes place it is important to meditate even more. But caution should be taken so that too much pressure is not given to the mooladhara chakra. Healing therapies like Sparsh chikitsiya, Pranic healing, Reiki can help people with the arousal. Earth is a very good place to be linked with during this period of time like walking, gardening etc. with bare feet.

* Bathing and wearing of clean clothes during the period helps to calm the body energy down.

* Try to follow the period of arousal by keeping quiet during the day.

* Some precautions to be taken during this period of time

    * Avoid getting in contact with people who have negative feelings in mind as it can cause conflicts and also cause psychological disturbances to you.

    * Avoid stressing your body physically or mentally for no reason.

SENSATIONS EXPERIENCED DURING THE AROUSAL OF KUNDALINI

* Burning heat or ice-cold currents moving up and down the spine.
* Feeling of snake wriggling up the spine from the mooladhara to the vishuddhi chakra.
* Moving pains throughout the entire body, but no stress being felt on the joints or muscles.
* Tingling feelings are felt in the spine, abdomen and the head.
* Strain or stiffness in the neck or headache.
* Vibrations and restlessness is felt in the legs, arms, palms and feet.
* The pulse is found to rise with extra alertness in the body.
* There is comparative raise in the sensitiveness for sound, light, smell.
* Mystical experiences, cosmic glimpses are felt during this period of time.
* Many revelations are also bestowed upon the sadhaka.
* Leviathan experiences and Parapsychological abilities are bestowed upon during this period of time.
* Every minute of life is seen in a different view of light.
* Light-phenomena inside or outside the body during this period.
* Sleeplessness and deep depression.
* During this period of time there is feeling of staying aloof from the crowd.

Kundalini Yoga' - Theory

DEVELOPMENT OF CHAKRAS IN A HUMAN BODY AND KARMA

From the time of inception till birth the child is bestowed with the energy of the universe itself, it is a miracle that the development takes place inside the womb with the only source of food energy and oxygen being the umbilical chord.

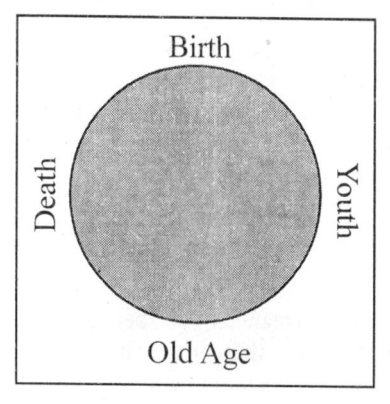

The development of the child in the womb is in dark with the body fluids around it. The development of the child in nine month's carries with it lot of activities, which help in deciding the psychological and physical development of the child. Before we discuss about the inception we have to know how the child gets incepted in a particular womb only.

Birth of a child is a moment of joy for everyone in the family. The child so born is not the result of the union of human beings, but has wider perspective to it.

We will start with the death, as death can only be the starting point of birth.

Death has evoked a sense of dread in the minds of people for ages. People who have had near death experience have become petrified with the images they had seen while they were dead. The images they saw were of them being carried away by strange people with hoods on heads, being tortured by the strange beings.

When a person dies he leaves his physical body through the following passage :

* If the person has attained siddhi and has become one with the lord then his soul leaves the physical body through the crown chakra. Such people think and work with their heart, they are the people who are said to have achieved the nirvana or mukti. Such people escape the cycle of birth and death.

* A materialistic person who has lived a life of sexual gratification and other earthly requirements cannot cross the Base chakra. Even at the deathbed such a person will not able to recall anything except the things for which he had a craving. Such type of people think and work with their mind, the soul of such a person will leave the body through the base chakra. When such a person dies, his soul has difficulty in leaving the physical form (body).

* A person who has maintained a balanced life, between the spiritual path and the worldly requirements will have a peaceful death. Such type of people think with their heart and work with their mind, the soul of such people will leave the body through the heart chakra.

When a person dies he carries with him the karmic deeds done by him in the current life with the deeds committed by him in the previous lives. As per Hindu scriptures, it is said that a soul gets the body of man after passing through the eighty four lakh births in various forms of life. The body of human is bestowed to him for seven births, so that he can praise the lord and cleanse himself of the sins he has done. Even after the seven births if he is not able to cleanse himself then he goes back into the cycle of births.

Whatever sin/piousness he has committed he has to repay the same in the next birth. In accounting form this concept can be understood very fast. If a person does a good deed the asset of the soul increases, while he commits a sin his asset is reduced by the same amount. Till such a time he has got a balance in either of the sides, the person will be part of the cycle of life and death. He achieves mukti only when

Kundalini Yoga - Theory

both the sides have no balance. The form in which the soul will enter in the next birth is predestined. After the death the soul travels in the space till such a period it finds the body suitable for it. The parents are also destined depending upon the karmic deeds of them.

If a person dies due to an accident, killed or any other unforeseen circumstances cuts short the life, then the soul of the person roams till it finds a suitable body. This suitable body is mostly related to the person who was the cause for the death of the person so that he could repent for the deeds.

After understanding the concept of death now we will move towards the life. The life begins with the divine spark of pure sabda of love. This sabda creates an environment of the five tatva which helps in creating the foetus from the energy. In the foetus the life is given with the destined soul from the Sahasrar chakra, in this stage the sex of the child is destined. As the time passes the various chakras get activated from the energy received from the sahasrar chakra. The physical part of the body develops as the time passes and starts working in the womb itself. This is the stage when the child in the womb fights to severe ties with his previous life. During the last stage of development of the foetus in the womb the mooladhara chakra activates and gets connected with the sahasrar chakra. When the child is delivered, the child cries due to the grounding of the Mooladhara chakra. Children who donot have grounding of the mooladhara chakra and have defects in other chakras due to his karmic deeds suffer from various diseases.

GURU (MASTER)

**Gurur' Brahma Gurur' Vishnu Gurur' Devo Maheshwarah
Gurur' Shakshat Parahbrahmah Tasmaye Sri Guruve Namah**

Gurur' Brahma : Guru is like the creator of the universe Brahma. He is the one who creates the qualities of shishya (student) in me.

Gurur' Vishnu : Like Lord Vishnu supports and maintains the life on the universe, the same way guru shows the path of enlightenment. Like a friend guides through the path, like a mother caresses and loves, like a father scolds and guides to achieve the goal.

Gurur' Devo Maheshwara : Lord Shiva is the god of destruction, he destroys all the evil so that the new life can be created. In the same manner guru also destroys all tamasic and rajasic guna to fill with sattvic guna.

The above sloka aptly explains the role of guru in the life of a sadhaka. Without an able guru and a able shishya no dhyana can be successful. The relation between the guru and shishya is like an child and a mother. Like mother who takes the tiny hands of the child and tells the child who his father is, as the child alone is not so strong enough to face the father. The same way the guru takes the hand of shishya and shows him the path to the Lord Shiva, a shishya alone may not be able to face the celestial bliss of the lord. When a shishya finds such a guru he is not in control of himself but becomes only a toddler who wants to walk but cannot do so.

Vivekananda did not become Vivekananda till he met Swami Ramakrishna Paramhamsa and the day he was initiated he was nothing but the image of his Guru.

In today's city life, it is very difficult to find such a guru and also to find such a shishya. Any sadhaka who is very much interested to find the guru also should know the following :

Guru is one who knows more about the shishya than the shishya himself knows.

Guru is one who is a mother, father, sister, brother, friend and guide to the shishya.

Guru is one who knows all the answers to the queries of the shishya.

Guru is one who takes the shishya towards the total bliss.

Guru is one who initiates the shishya to ask questions. This question answer session inculcates the habit of finding the true reason of doing a particular thing and also keeps the shishya from blindly following the path without asking questions. This is important as in the Vedic tradition lot of things, which were done, had some scientific meaning and were not just done for the sake of doing. This also helps the guru to judge the development of the student. This path is not followed by the gurus of modern age who tend to get influenced the western thoughts and discourage the shishya from asking questions.

Guru is one who does not exploit the shishya for personal gains but gives the shishya some of his energy for the spiritual development of the shishya.

Guru is **not** one who preaches austerity and lives in luxury. In today's world lot of people are there who preach about austerity in living but travel in luxurious cars, travel by planes etc. They do the preaching and collect huge sums of money and live a life of rajasic tatva and claim to be sattvic in nature.

Guru never claims to be one to be worshipped but stays a worshipper of the lord. He who wants himself to be worshipped is nothing but a person who is full of ego and worshipping such a person will only increase the negative energy of the person and also increase the bad karma in the shishya. Guru's who dress themselves as Goddess, Krishna, Shiva to be worshipped are nothing but people with high ego value. Following such gurus will cause destruction to the sattvic guna in the body.

A true **Guru** is one who is above ego, pride and sentiments, when he gives shaktipata to a shishya he only thinks of himself as a medium and this also happens only at a time when the shishya as well as the guru are ready for the ecstatic experience. He never feels pride in claiming to do shaktipata, as he knows he is nothing but a madhyam or a medium and not the source of the energy. Such a guru can be called a Sadguru.

Never consider the age of the **Guru** as a factor of ego for learning. Remember the idiom "Child is the father of man". A child can teach more things to a person than even a very learned person about the realities of the nature. When Sage Sankaracharya, Saint Gyaneshwar gave the true knowledge to the world they were very young.

Never believe in a **Guru** who claims to give shaktipata to a huge number of people at one time. It is not possible to do, as the main reason being that every person has different energy levels and different sustainability. If we assume that a Guru is able to give shaktipata to a number of people at the same time without taking into consideration the requirement of the shishya then he/she is endangering the life of the person. When a Guru gives shaktipata to a shishya then he/she is transferring a part of his/her energy to the awaken the Kundalini shakti.

If the guru should have the above qualities then the shishya also should have the following qualities :

Shishya should respect the guru. It is said that if a shishya faces the guru, parents and the god, then the shishya should first give respect, to the guru then to the parents and then to the Lord. It is the guru who transforms a normal person into a sadhaka and becomes the medium for meeting the God, thus guru is the one who gives him the second life. Without the parents he wouldn't be born.

Shishya should always be interested to ask questions and should continue the debate till he gets the satisfactory answer.

Shishya should practice and remember the things taught by the guru.

Shishya should propagate the knowledge gained by him to his colleagues, friends and relatives after getting permission from the guru. This will help the shishya as he will remember the knowledge and also will try to improvise on it, to propagate the knowledge he gained.

Shishya should experiment and find new things so that he is able to gain sufficient knowledge to guide other.

PATH OF ENLIGHTENMENT

There are many paths to the enlightenment, some of them are mentioned here. The sadhaka can take any of the methods mentioned under to achieve the path of enlightenment, but care should be taken that the method is suitable to you and you are guided by an able master to achieve the correct path. Each method requires full faith and devotion to the lord without which it is not possible to achieve the full benefits of the method.

Blessing of the Guru, Parents, Lord is required for attaining anything.

HATHA YOGA

Through rigorous practice of the physical exercises. In this method each chakra is activated one by one and on achieving expertise on opening of one chakra the sadhaka moves on the next chakra. This is very tough process and can take years and years of practice to awaken the kundalini. Gurus who are expert in the Hatha yoga are very few in the city. The city life also does not provide the sadhaka with sufficient time to practice the art without getting deviated.

TANTRA AND MANTRA YOGA

Through the attainment of siddhis from the practice of the Tantra and Mantra. This requires rigorous changes in the life styles and the path to be followed is not very easy. This is pure science of the nature and the achiever of this science gets enlightenment in this life only and moves out from the cycle of birth and death forever. As already been discussed this science was given to the world by the Lord Shiva himself. More of this science will be discussed later.

SHAKTIPATA

Through the blessings of a Guru. In this ritual the knowledge of the Guru is transferred to the suitable shishya (disciple) through a process called shaktipata.

Shakti means energy and pata means the fall. When this energy passing takes place the sleeping kundalini in the shishya opens up instantly and passes through all the chakra to reach the sahasrar chakra. This same knowledge was given by Sage Vishwamitra to Lord Shri Ram and his brother Lakhsman. This same attunement was given by the Swami Ramakrishna Paramhamsa to Shri Vivekananda. This is the most spiritual experience a shishya can get as he transients all the physical realms in a flash of a moment. For this kind of experience both the Guru and shishya should be of comparable stature.

BHAKTI

This is the most simple yet most difficult form of dhyana to achieve the lord. Simple in the sense that the sadhaka does not do anything but believes in the lord completely, i.e. to say that he sacrifices his ego, self esteem, physical and mental body at the celestial feet of the lord. But doing this is very difficult as only one in a million can achieve this feat. Bhakt Meera, Bhakt Soordas, Goswami Tulsidas, Sant Gyaneshwar, Sant Tukaram are some of the great saints of this tradition.

KARMAYOGA

Karmayoga is the art of doing the work with full faith and devotion. The idiom that Work is God, fits this sadhana. Work does not mean only the job assigned to the person officially but also means the job assigned to him by the life like family responsibility.

A person should look after his parents in the old age, take the responsibility of a wife and children without any grudge or discomfort. A true karma yogi is one who does away with his responsibility without wanting anything in return. In Gita also Lord Krishna has said that no yoga is greater than the Karmayoga and those who do this without any selfishness will merge with me.

DHYANA

Dhyana is a very important method in awakening the kundalini. This becomes easier if the sadhaka can combine the dhyana with pranayama. Many sages have awakened their cosmic energy with the help of dhyana. In dhyana a sadhaka gets into a stage of paramdhama where he is in a situation of full bliss.

REIKI *(Universal Energy)*

Rediscovered only in the middle of 19th century. Originally developed in India, later went to Tibet and was used by the Tibetan saints for thousands of years. As time passed this science of healing and energisation was lost in the dunes of time. Discovered by an enthusiast Dr. Usui from an old scripture from Tibet written in Sanskrit and Tibetan language. The process of receiving this science is through a process of initiation. There are now many forms of Reiki today. The traditional Reiki as taught today has the following stages :

1. Level - I Allows the user to do hands on healing
2. Level - II Allows the user to do distant healing also.
3. Level - III Allows the user to initiate other people to become the Reiki channels.

There are other higher levels of this science which will be told at a later period.

Generally people use this science for healing only but this energy is also acquired through the initiation of the chakra or the kundalini awakening.

A true Reiki channel will utilise this power of healing to awaken his kundalini fully and also allow the spirituality engulf him rather than follow the path of material tendency.

Other than the methods given above there are other ways of achieving the enlightenment.

DEPENDING UPON THE SPIRITUAL GROWTH THE SADHAK CAN GET THE RIDDHIS AND THE SIDDHIS

1. ANIMA

Concentrating all the energy and prana in the body to one place so as to achieve the power of reducing the size of the body to any level or to the level of an atom. The Adhipati Goddess of this siddhi is Indrani. This siddhi was used by Lord Hanuman when he reduced his body size to that of an atom to find Mata Sita in Lanka. The tatva of this siddhi is Fire.

2. MAHIMA

The power of increasing the size of the body. This happens when the atoms in the body are made to be packed in such a manner so that there is enough space between without losing out to the structure of the atom. Lord Sri Krishna used this power when he showed his Viratroopa to Arjuna in the battlefield of Kurukshetra and also by Ram Bagat Hanuman when he assumed a huge body for crossing the sea to reach Mata Sita in Lanka. The Adhipati Goddess of this siddhi is Vaishnavi. The tatva of this siddhi is Fire.

3. LAGHIMA

The power of making the body light as air. This siddhi gives the sadhak the power to travel in air anywhere and in the golden age of our vedas it said that many sages had this power of travel from one place to another. Sage Narada had this siddhi and because of which he used to travel from Vaikunt the abode of Lord Vishnu to the Mt. Kailash the abode of Lord Shiva. The Goddess of this siddhi is Brahmini. The tatva of this siddhi is Ether.

4. GARIMA

This is the siddhi of concentrating the energy and prana in the body in such a way so as to make the part of body as heavy as mountain. The tatva of this siddhi is Earth. For achieving this siddhi Goddess Kaumari is to be pleased. Angad had used this siddhi when he challenged the courtiers of Ravana to remove the foot from where he placed and he would withdraw from Lanka with Sri Ram without any fight. Courtiers of Ravana could not move even an inch of Angad's feet.

5. PRAPTI

When a sadhak concentrates all his prana and energy in the body to convert the energy and prana flowing the universe to any material thing which he wants to achieve. This siddhi empowers the sadhak to convert the energy around the space into the material things. The Goddess of this siddhi is Narasinghi. The tatva of this siddhi is Ether.

6. PRAKAMYA

When a Sadhak achieves the power to control the ageing process and also maintains the chirayu youth he is said to be a Prakamya Siddh. The goddess of this siddhi is Varahi. The tatva of this siddhi is Earth, Fire, Wind, Water and Ether i.e. the power of Panch Tatva

7. VASITVAM

When a sadhak achieves the power to control men, women, animals then he is said to have achieved the Vasitvam siddhi. For achieving this siddhi the sadhak concentrates on the prana energy of the man, animal, women or anything to be controlled and then converts his prana energy to match with that of them. After matching his prana the siddha overcomes the energy of the person, animal and takes full control of the thing or person. The siddha worship Goddess Maheshwari to bless them with this power.

Kundalini Yoga - Theory

8. ISHATVAM

When a person achieves so much energy that he can create a Brahmand of his own then he is said to be the ishatvam siddha. Sage Vishwamitra had created a second Swarga (Heaven) for the King Trishanku when he was denied the passage to the heaven with his own physical body. These siddha are destined for the dominion of the universe either in this life or next as per his karmic deeds. The Ishatvam siddha worships Goddess Bhairavi.

9. DOORSHRAVAN

This siddhi helps the sadhaka to hear any voice or speech done even at distant place

10. DOORDARSHAN

This siddhi helps the sadhaka to see things or events happening at any place in all the three worlds. This power was used by Sanjay to explain the happenings at the Kurukshetra war to King Dhritrastra.

11. MANOJAVA

This siddhi helps the sadhaka to achieve the strength to travel at the speed of the mind. The speed was compared as the speed of the Maruti (air). Sage Parshuram, who could travel any distance, achieved this siddhi, just by the power of thought.

12. KAAMAROOPA

This siddhi helps the sadhaka to assume any shape of body as desired by him. Lord Hanuman used this siddhi when he changed into a brahman at Kishkindha parvat to check if it was Lord Ram coming to meet the King Sugriva and not any enemy sent by King Vali (brother of King Sugriva).

13. PARAKAAYAPRAVESH

This siddhi allows the sadhak to achieve the power to enter the body of a dead or alive person for a temporary period leaving one's own body. This siddhi was used by Sage Sankaracharya to enter the body of the King of Kashmir.

14. SWACHICHANDAMRUTYU

This siddhi gives the sadhaka the power to die at the moment decided by him. This siddhi was achieved by the great warrior Bheesma, and he lay on the bed of arrows for the whole period of the mahabharata war and decided to die at the time when Arjuna came to him for blessing for winning the war.

15. SAHAKRIDANU DARSHANAM

This siddhi allows the sadhaka to see the sports of gods in heaven and also allows him to participate in the games played by the gods.

16. YATHAASANKALPA SIDDHI

This siddhi allows the sadhaka to achieve whatever he desires at whatever place desired.

17. AJNAAPRATIHATAAGATIH

This siddhi allows the sadhaka to move anywhere without any obstruction

18. TRIKALDARSHI

This siddhi allows the sadhaka to know the past, present and future events. Many of the sages of the ancient India had this power to view the past, present and the future.

19. ADVANDVAM

This siddhi allows the sadhaka to control the pleasure, pain, heat, cold, death, life in a very common manner. This siddhi allowed the sadhaka to concentrate on the dhyana towards the Lord and did not allow to diver his attention towards his physical traumas. Many of the sages of the ancient India could meditate on rocks, cold water, fire, difficult postures for ages together due to this siddhi.

20. PARACHITTAADYABHIJNATAA

This siddhi allows the sadhaka to read the mind of the other person and also helps the sadhaka to control the dreams of the person.

21. PRATISHTAMBAH

This siddhi helps the sadhaka to stop the effect of fire, wind, water, weapon, poison and the sun on the body. This siddhi is similar to the siddhi 19.

22. APARAAJAYAH

This siddhi helps the sadhaka to achieve victory over whatever goals set by him. The controller of this siddhi allows the sadhak to be always victorious. Many of the Kshatriya kind of ancient used to meditate to get this siddhi as this allowed to expand their kingdom and also to make their kingdoms prosper.

23. SARVAGYA

This siddhi allows the sadhaka to gain knowledge of any material or things in this universe.

24. VAKASIDDHI
This siddhi allows the sadhaka to achieve strength to control any person with the power of speech.

25. KALPVRIKSHATATVA
This siddhi allows the sadhaka to achieve the Kalpavriksha the eternal tree of the Gods. It is said that any thing can be asked from the tree and the tree will fulfil the desire of the sadhaka.

26. SHRISTI
This siddhi allows the sadhaka to have the power to create another universe or any material as desired by him.

27. SANHARASAMARTHYA
This siddhi gives the sadhaka the power of killing. The sadhak of this siddhi was bestowed with celestial weapons for bringing success in war.

28. AMARTVA
This siddhi allowed the sadhaka to achieve chirayu (eternal life). This achiever of this siddhi is said to carry the celestial pot of amrit (amrit kalaṣa) in the navel. King Ravana was bestowed with siddhi, and he died only when the bow of Lord Rama pierced the navel making the amrit flow down.

29. SARVA NYAYKATVA
This siddhi gave the sadhaka the power over the law of the nature.

30. BHAVANA SIDDHI

This siddhi gave the sadhaka the power to control any person or living being with the power of emotion.

31. PRATYAKSHAM AND AP-PRATYAKSHAM

This siddhi allows the sadhaka to make himself vanish from the sight of anyone and also bestows to him the power to resume the original body when required.

32. MAYA SIDDHI

This siddhi allows the sadhaka to gain control over the power of illusion. This siddhi allows the sadhaka to create illusion of any size and proportion. In the scriptures we can see that most the daityas had the power of maya with which they used to get more advantage over the devatas.

VISUALISATION AND BREATHING TECHNIQUES

Man has a unique ability, which no other animal has, and that is visualisation this power is so strong that he can create a universe of his own with that.

Visualisation and breathing techniques is a complex process of imagining a process and then actively participating in the process. For this purpose only in the Beginner's section and Advance section lot of visualisation and breathing techniques have been provided.

For any visualisation technique to be successful it is important to have full information regarding the process, techniques and equipments required. As of now we know the basic of the chakras and their physical location in the body.

Awaken the Giant from Sleep

COLOUR MEDITATION

Colour meditation is a very good method of de-voiding yourself of the negative feelings from your mind as also to heal others. In this method, we concentrate on different colours and on each colour the visualisation and the methodology is different. This exercise can be done at any period of time, but be warned that this exercise should not be attempted while passing through any of the emotional phases like anger, stress, tension etc.. As the emotional phase can also affect the process of meditation, thereby giving a totally different result than expected.

METHOD OF DOING THIS DHYANA

This method is best done if done sitting on Siddha asana with the fingers in Gyana Mudra. Close your eyes and concentrate on the third eye Chakra (Ajna Chakra).

Inhale and exhale deeply for a few minutes till a time that you feel lightness in the head and coolness in the body. Visualise a white luminous light coming down from the sky and entering through your crown chakra (Sahasrar chakra) and surrounding you from all sides to form a large cocoon. Feel that every cell in your body is getting re-energised and rejuvenated by this universal light of life. This white light contains all the qualities of seven basic colours of the nature.

The process of meditation is to break each individual colour from the universal white light and use individual colours and rejuvenating qualities for healing the physical and ethric bodies.

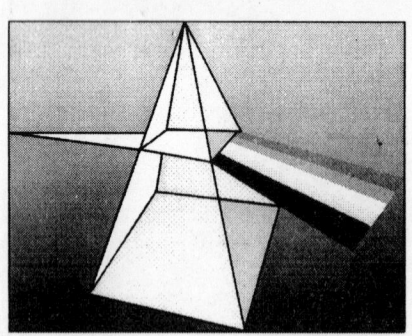

Begin with the visualisation of the **VIOLET** colour, the colour of serenity. Feel the violet colour flowing out from the universal white light and

Kundalini Yoga - Practical

covering your body forming a second layer to the body. Feel the serenity and spiritual coolness of the light.

This colour is cool in nature and is very suitable for curing diseases related with the heat like small pox, rashes, sun burns, high fever etc..

This colour also helps in connecting with the higher self.

Visualise that the Violet colour is breaking down to form the **Indigo** colour. This colour has similar attributes of the colour violet but is hotter in nature than the colour violet and works on the ethric body. Let this colour form the third layer to the body. Indigo colour helps in calming down a person in a fit of anger and also solves problems related with the bowel.

After the Indigo colour, visualise the colour **BLUE** covering your whole body in such a way that the view from your eyes also looks blue. This colour is very important as this represents the energy of the ether i.e. the energy of the sky. This colour is cool in nature and helps in curing diseases related with skin and reproductory senses. This colour also helps in reducing the pulse rate, increase the appetite, lowers the body temperature. This colour forms the fourth layer to the body.

Visualise the colour **GREEN**, this is the colour of the nature and provides for the goodness of the health of the person. The Green colour should be visualised in such a way that the whole world surrounding you is made of green colour which draws the impurities from the atmosphere and converts them into pure form before it reaches your body. Stay in this cool atmosphere till you feel the energisation taking place in your body. This colour will form the fifth layer of the body. This colour is helpful in reducing the allergies, heart, bowel and intestinal problems.

Visualise the cool **YELLOW** emerging from the layers of cosmic energy surrounding you. This colour is good for curing diseases which are related with cold like common cold, nausea, low blood pressure etc. This colour is related with the creativity and the reception of knowledge. This colour will form the sixth layer to the body.

Now visualise the colour **RED**, dark red like the colour of the blood. This is the colour of anger, lust, needs, wants and all the other physical requirement. This colour is hot in nature and creates heat in the body, this colour is useful for removal of cold diseases (coughs, cold, nasal blockages), increasing the appetite. This colour forms the seventh layer. Feel the pulse beat increasing against your skin. Imagine that all the heat generated burns of all the anger, lust, needs, emotions and any other negativity related with the earth energy.

At this moment your whole body is engulfed in seven layers of cosmic energy. Stay in this blissful experience for as long as possible. Each energy level will automatically cure you of any negativity and diseases.

Lastly, visualise that the inner layer of the universal energy changes the colour of the blood red into **VERMILION RED** and forming a layer. This colour is having both the qualities of the red and also the white and thus it has the dual nature of coolness and heat. This is a very good colour for therapeutic use and also this colour is the colour of the Mother goddess. Imagine this colour taking the form of mother goddess and take the blessings of the mother and relieve all your agony and pain under the blissful feet of the mother. Regular practice of this method helps you to build better visualisation power and also will help in cleansing your chakras.

BENEFITS OF DOING THIS DHYANA :

* you will find a new perspective about Prana Shakti
* you will get to know the real energy of your life.

KUNDALINI AWAKENING-PRAYER

The process for kundalini awakening is more spiritual process rather than the mechanical process. So it is important that you should have full faith and dedication towards the universal lord and should be humble enough to bow down to the universal energy for granting the energy for the awakening the kundalini.

Process for praying for all the chakras

Sit comfortably on a chair or on the floor, close your eyes. Fold your hands in a posture of namaskar and the tips of the fingers should touch the chest, the thumbs should be crossed (right thumb over the left thumb). Bend your head a little towards the chest and pray

O Lord. O Saviour.
I bow to thee,
the lord of the seven world
I bow to thee
Giver of happiness and wealth.
I bow to thee
Like a tree laden with fruit
make me humble
Let my small endeavour be
a step for future
O Lord. O Saviour
Never let go off my hand
Bless me
Like a flower blossoms from bud
So, should I
Let the 'I' in me be the 'I' in you
flowing through the veins
Lead me from the falsehood
to the truth
Lead me from the darkness
to the light
O Lord. O Saviour

Soul Searchers The Art of Breathing

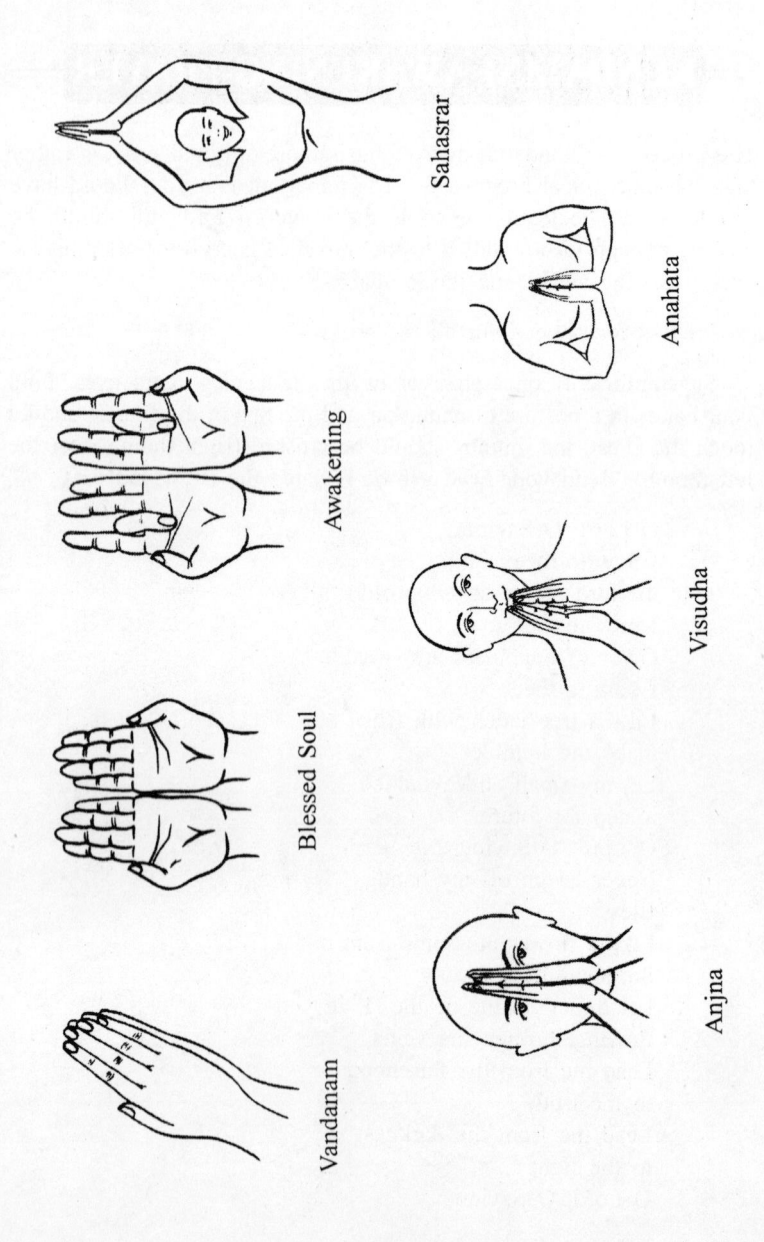

- Sahasrar
- Anahata
- Awakening
- Visudha
- Blessed Soul
- Anjna
- Vandanam

Kundalini Yoga - Practical

Give peace to the world
Give peace to my parents
Give peace to my friends
Give peace to my relatives
Give peace to my.

You may also recite the prayer you normally do. The method of praying doesn't mean that each word is repeated monotonously, but has to be inculcated in the life also and each words meaning should be absorbed.

Keep the eyes closed and take folded hands above the head and pray.

O Lord of the Tri gunas,
Bless with the Shakti that I may achieve
what, I strive for.
O Lord like the thousand petals
let, I be bestowed with thy blessing
Let my body, soul be near thee
enjoying the eternal bliss
of the supreme life.

Bring the folded hands over the third eye chakra and pray

O Lord of time
let the past, present and future
be one with me
neither the past nor the future
trouble me
O Saviour help me
to gain control over the life

Bring the folded hands over the throat and pray

O Lord of the speech
I bow to thee
Let the words of wisdom flow
from the ocean of speech

> O Saviour help me
> to undo all the problems made by me
> to make happiness
> to make life a true heaven on earth.

Bring the folded hands over the heart and pray

> O Lord of the knowledge
> let I be bestowed with the knowledge
> of the good from the bad
> of the spiritual from the evil
> of the karma from the dharma

Bring the folded hands over the navel and pray

> O lord of the land of jewels
> I bow to thee
> let I be bestowed with health
> so I may be able to bow to thee
> love may flow like and ocean
> encompassing everyone on the way.

Bring the folded hands over the Mooladhara and pray

> O lord of the land of Birth and death
> I bow to thee
> let I be bestowed with happiness
> of flowering
> your land with the blossoms of life
> O Saviour help me
> to get earthed and lead a life of truth

Sit in this praying position till a time you feel comfortable. These prayers if truely inculcated in life will make your life like a tree laden with fruits. It is beneficial if the following ideals are also inculcated in day to day life also.

INTENTION IS THE MOST IMPORTANT THING FOR OVERCOMING ANY EVENTS EVEN THE FEAR OF DEATH

For any meditation it is important that the sadhak should have very strong intention. Without any intention and determination sadhaka may not be able to achieve the levels of dhyana for the full awakening of the spiritual energy. Intention, practice and faith go hand in hand. In the diagram the colour red represents the intention of the sadhak, green represents the practice and blue represents the faith. All the three are complementary to each other and even if one of them is weak, the entire chakra will be broken and the chances of awakening the spiritual energy will be remote.

I sincerely hope that the sadhak by now has the basic knowledge about the science of Kundalini. The following exercises will help the sadhaka to awaken the spiritual energy and allow the naga power to travel from the adhar chakra to the crown chakra.

BALANCING THE ENERGIES OF THE LEFT AND THE RIGHT NADIS

Balancing of the right and the left nadis are important before we begin with the kundalini awakening process.

Even doctors have agreed that our left brain controls the activities of the right part of the body and right part of the brain controls the left part of the body.

When the right nadi is more active compared to the left nadi then the person has more of male tatva and when the left nadi is active the person has more of feminine tatva. This means that when the left part of the brain is working more, the person is very creative, more caring, emotionally weak and when the right part of the brain is working then the person is very strong headed, egoistic, less attached to relations, weighs every options before deciding anything. In the same way anger, bursts of violence, sadistic tendencies, shadowing internal fear etc. are caused with the over working of the right brain and emotional outbursts, agony, sympathy, love, affection, tenderness etc. are due the left part of the brain working. When both the parts of the brain is working simultaneously then the person is balanced in himself.

PROCESS OF DOING THIS DHYANA

PRIMER FOR THE EXERCISE

This exercise must be done for finding more about your body and the variation in the energy levels.

Locate a comfortable place and sit down with closed eyes and hands resting on the knees in gyan mudra. Inhale and exhale very fast for a count of 30 i.e. inhale.. exhale .. inhale .. exhale. After doing the process sit silently and watch the breath flow through your body.

Raise your left and right hands upto your shoulder palms facing downward. Inhale deeply and hold the breath and slowly lower your left hand approximately one to two inches away from your body keeping the right hand in the same place. When you lower your left hand over the knee try to feel the changes in the temperature from the shoulder height to the knee. Now release the breath and simultaneously bring the right hand down in the same way done with the left hand. Repeat the same process until you come to know every variation in the body temperature from the shoulder height to the knee.

The **second step** is to inhale deeply and hold the breath and move the hands up and down in the front from the shoulder height to a height of one inch above the knee. The flow of the hands should be as if you are in a trance, slow and methodical. This step helps to crisscross the body from the shoulder height to the knee and also allows to know the speed of variation in the temperature of the body.

The **third step** is to inhale deeply and hold the breath and move the hands sideways from the left shoulder to the right shoulder. And slowly lower the flowing hands towards the knee. This step helps to analyse the whole body from the shoulder height to the knee.

In both the steps i.e. second and the third, when you feel the tiredness creeping into your body stop the movements of the body and release the breath and sit in the same posture with normal breathing pattern.

The **fourth step** involves doing all the steps from one to step three. The process of doing the exercise should be such that you become one with the process and every movement takes you a step further in understanding the basic culture of your body.

The above four steps should be done at different time in a day to clearly know the variation in the body temperature.

All these four steps if done with determination and dedication can reveal which side of your body is more warm than the other. Other than the warmness and coldness of the body these exercise reveal the following things :

1	Flow of the breath in the body from the throat to the lower part of the body.
2	Understandings of the movements of the muscles with the activities of the brain are known.
3	At different period of time the variation in the flow of the hands can be judged. The smoothness and flow of the flow is not there if the right side of the brain is active and working.
4	If done in silence you can hear the rhythmic change in the heartbeats when the flow of hands changes from sideways of the body to up and down of the body.
5	Continues practice of the above exercise in understanding the changing pattern of the aura.
6	Show the variation in the energy levels in the left and right part of the body. These variation can be in the form of temperature, vibrations , tingling sensations etc.

Repeat the above exercises in front of a mirror with open eyes. This will help you to understand more about the energy circles in and around the body.

After a period of time you will automatically sense the variation without going through all the four steps. At that period you may not have to do the above steps.

Kundalini Yoga - Practical

CAN I DO THE SAME WITH ANOTHER PERSON

Yes, it can be done. But only after getting to know your own variation. If you start of with another person directly then the inferences drawn by you may be totally wrong.

Process of doing it another person:

Both the person should sit opposite to one another in the same posture and start with the step one.

After both the persons have completed the first step. One person becomes the source and the other becomes the analyst.

The source should close his eyes and sit in a prayerful mood with his back towards the analyst at a distance of ten to twelve inches.

The analyst should do all the four steps to find which side of the body is active at that period of time.

If Left Side of your body has more variation than the Right side

When such a situation arises, then the body scanning should not done as in such case the emotional aspect of the giver will play a important role in determining the energy pattern of the other person. This can lead to wrong conclusions.

In such a situation, hold your breath for a few seconds and after that do the **ENERGY BURST** exercise mentioned in the pranayama section. Then proceed again from the steps one to four given in the beginning of this exercise.

If Right Side of your body has more variation than the Left side

Raise your left-hand upto the crown chakra of the source keeping the right palm on the heart chakra. The palms should face the crown chakra and move the palms in a circular motion on the crown chakra. Try to sense any vibration from the crown chakra. If you donot feel any vibration at the crown chakra lower the left hand to the mooladhara chakra or the base of the spine and move the hands in a circular movement. In normal cases you can find some tingling sensation in the mooladhara chakra as most of the people are just restricted to the earthly requirement of the body.

Vibration from the crown chakra is most visible when the person has started moving up from the earthy requirements to the spiritual upliftment.

Vibration on the Crown Chakra is sensed : In such case remove the right hand from your heart chakra and place the hand over the heart chakra of the person (one to two inches away from the body) , keeping the left hand over the crown chakra. Slowly move the left hand from the crown chakra to the ajna chakra or the back of the head. Do the same circular motion on the back of the head. In the same manner move the left hand from the back of the head to the back of the neck (Vishuddhi chakra) and repeat the circular motion of the hand.

The circular motion should be done to find the variation in the body temperature and at the chakra you feel a sensation of pulling-pushing, cool air, tingling in the centre of the palm move the right hand over the place. This means that at that particular period of time the energy movement is more at that particular chakra. Most of the time when I have used this method the energy transmission was more at the heart chakra with concentrated energy transmission from the Vishuddhi chakra.

Vibration on the Mooladhara Chakra is sensed : In such case remove the right hand from your heart chakra and place the hand over the heart chakra of the person (one to two inches away from the body) keeping the left hand over the mooladhara chakra. Slowly move the left hand from the mooladhara chakra to the swadhisthana chakra or the tip of the spine. Do the same circular motion on the tip of the spine. In the same manner move the left hand from the tip of the spine to the back of the navel (Manipura chakra) and repeat the circular motion of the hand.

The circular motion should be done to find the variation in the body temperature and the chakra, you feel a sensation of pulling-pushing, cool air, tingling in the centre of the palm move the right hand over the place. This means that at that particular period of time

Kundalini Yoga - Practical

the energy movement is more at that particular chakra. Most of the time when I have used this method the energy transmission was more at the heart chakra with concentrated energy transmission from the manipura chakra.

After you have sensed the variation in the energy flow compare the energy flow with your own body. And feel the differences, in the beginning the feeling may not be so easy to get but with regular practice with the many people can yield you the desired results.

After attaining good sensory receptiveness in the hands we will start with the exercise for balancing the nadis.

Balancing the Energies of the Left and the Right Nadis

We will start with exercise for one's own body first and then explain the process of doing the same with other person.

With One's Own Body

Right side of the body has more variation than the left side of the body

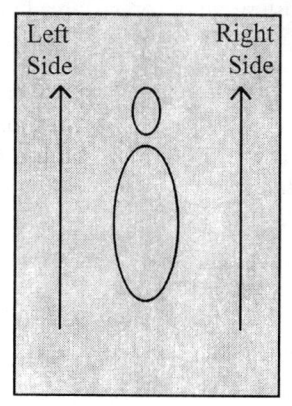

With eyes still closed raise your left and right hands upto your shoulder, the left palm facing downward and the right palm facing upward (both the palms should be cupped). Inhale and exhale deeply for a few times till you find the rigidity from the body is released. Finally take a deep breath visualising that the breath is bringing with it a divine white cloud inside your body. Visualise that from the crown chakra divine pure energy is entering passing through the third eye chakra, throat chakra and finally settling down in the heart chakra. You feel as if your whole body is engulfed in the white divine energy. The coolness spreading throughout your body relaxing every muscles and cells. Visualise the above process with every breath you inhale.

Slowly lower your left hand approximately one to two inches away from your body keeping the right hand in the same place. When you lower your left hand over the knee try to feel the changes in the temperature from the shoulder height to the knee. Now release the breath and simultaneously bring the right hand down in the same way done with the left hand. Repeat the same process until you come to know every variation in the body temperature from the shoulder height to the knee.

The **second step** is to inhale deeply and hold the breath and move the hands up and down in front from the shoulder height to a height of one inch above the knee. The flow of the hands should be as if you are in a trance, slow and methodical. This step helps to criss-cross the body from the shoulder height to the knee and also allows to know the speed of variation in the temperature of the body.

The **third step** is to inhale deeply and hold the breath and move the hands sideways from the left shoulder to the right shoulder. And slowly lower the flowing hands towards the knee. This step helps to analyse the whole body from the shoulder height to the knee.

In both the steps i.e. second and the third, when you feel the tiredness creeping into your body stop the movements of the body and release the breath and sit in the same posture with normal breathing pattern.

The **fourth step** involves doing all the steps from one to step three. The process of doing the exercise should be such that you become one with the process and every movement takes you a step further in understanding the basic culture of your body.

Doing it with another person :

Kundalini Yoga - Practical

Right side of the body has more variation than the left side of the body

While doing the balancing with another person the second person should sit in the opposite side of the first person. Ask the person to be balanced to sit in a meditative posture with the hands in the namaskar position.

The difference between you and the person should be from six inches to twelve inches.

After sensing the vibration on Crown chakra or Mooladhara chakra the following method is used to balance the nadis.

Vibration on the Crown Chakra is sensed : After sensing the variation in the energy in your body and the energy transmission of the source the following procedure is to be used :

* From the earlier method discussed, you will be able to find out the levels of vibrations from the Vishuddhi chakra compared with the lower and the upper chakras.

* Place the right hand over the heart chakra of the person (one to two inches away from the body), and place the left hand over the crown chakra. Pray in the following manner **"Oh Lord, let the energies get balanced. Both the surya nadi and Chandra nadi be in same level of energy flow."**

* Slowly move the left hand from the crown chakra to the ajna chakra keeping the right hand over the Vishuddhi chakra. Close your eyes and visualise the sun on your third eye chakra. Feel the heat increasing in the third eye chakra, the sweat trickling down the sides of the face. Visualise the heat energy flow from the third eye chakra to the right hand.

* In the same way visualise the moon on the third eye chakra. Feel the coolness spread through your body. Visualise the flow of the cool energy from the third eye chakra to the left hand

* Now the right hand is hot in nature and the left hand is

cool in nature. Place the left hand on the left shoulder tip and the right hand over the right shoulder tip of the other person.

* Let both the hands drop down towards the mooladhara chakra as if flowing down a slow smooth river fall. Pray while the hands falls down :

   Om Agni shanti
   Om Varuna shanti
   Shanti, Shanti, Shanti
   Om Rudra Shanti
   Om Shakti Shanti
   Shanti, Shanti, Shanti

This mantra should be repeated continuously till both the hands reach the mooladhara chakra. When the hands reach the Mooladhara chakra, move both the hands to the shoulder tips, and repeat the mantra given above in the same manner. This process should be done for three times.

* Breath in through the mouth as if drawing the energy of the universe itself. Visualise a white spiritual flowing inside your mouth. Touch the tongue on cranium and slowly come close towards the lower back of the neck and blow out with full force on it. Repeat the same process on the heart chakra, swadhisthana chakra, manipura chakra and mooladhara chakra.

* Place the right hand over the mooladhara chakra and the left hand over the spine. Do the spiralling on the spine from the top of the body to the bottom of the spine with the left hand. Do this process for three times. This will release the knots in the nadis.

Kundalini Yoga - Practical

Vibration on the Mooladhara Chakra is sensed :

After the sensing the variation in the energy in your body and the energy transmission of the source the following procedure is to be used:

* From the earlier method discussed, you will be able to find out the levels of vibrations from the Anahat chakra compared with the lower and the upper chakras.

* Place the right hand over the heart chakra of the person (one to two inches away from the body) , and place the left hand over the crown chakra. Pray in the following manner

"Oh Lord, let the energies get balanced. Both the Surya nadi and Chandra nadi be in same level of energy f low."

* Slowly move the left hand from the mooladhara chakra to the swadhisthana chakra keeping the right hand over the Manipura chakra. Close your eyes and visualise a crimson diamond on your third eye chakra. Feel the energy and heat emitting from the diamond and spreading throughout the area of the third eye chakra.

* Visualise a land mine of diamonds and sparkling emeralds in the manipura chakra. The manipura chakra is so bright that it is dazzling your eyes. Place the left hand near the left buttock tip and the right hand near the right buttock tip of the other person.

* Raise both the hands towards the Ajna chakra as if a furious volcano is erupting. Say the following prayer in a fast way:

Om Agni urvaha
Om Varuna urvaha
Urvaha, Urvaha, Urvaha
Om Rudra urvaha
Om Shakti urvaha
Urvaha, Urvaha, Urvaha

This mantra should be repeated continuously till both the hands reach the Ajna chakra. When the hands reach the Ajna chakra, move both the hands to the Buttock tips, and repeat the mantra given above in the same manner. This process should be done for three times.

* Breath in through the mouth as if drawing the energy of the universe itself. Visualise a white spiritual flowing inside your mouth. Touch the tongue on the palate and slowly come close towards the lower back of the neck and blow out with full force on it. Repeat the same process on the mooladhara chakra, manipura chakra, swadhisthana chakra and heart chakra.

* Place the right hand over the mooladhara chakra and the left hand over the spine. Do the spiralling on the spine from the bottom of the body to the top of the spine with the left hand. Do this process for three times. This will release the knots in the nadis.

SOME SPECIAL TIPS :

It is not necessary to say the mantra as mentioned above, if it is difficult. In the above cases where the vibrations are felt at the Crown chakra the healer can breathe in slowly as a calm cool breeze and in the case where the vibration is felt at the Mooladhara chakra the healer should breathe in very fast like a hurricane. This method may not be hundred percent powerful as with chanting mantra, but can still work wonders.

Never do the balancing, when you have woken up, come from work or exercise as at that moment your true energy cannot be accessed.

Never do the balancing in the afternoon or in the late nights as in the former the energy is totally heated up and in the later the energy is zapped.

Kundalini Yoga - Practical

BALANCING OF SHAKTI POINTS

Mantras play an important role in balancing the shakti points. Every mantra if uttered in a proper way can help in creating a resonance, which can help in creating an aura of spiritual energy thereby balancing the points. This is an important exercise, which helps in balancing the various body energy points with the chakras involved.

Instructions for doing this exercise

* This exercise is effective if done in the early morning with an empty stomach, it can also be done in the evening

* Atleast 4 hours should lapse after the intake of the food.

* The exercise should not be done during periods of tension, anger, depression etc.

* Never do fast movements during this exercise. The flow of the hands should be like that of the dew drops settling on the petals of the flower.

* All the sounds in this exercise should be created with depthness in sound

* The movements of the hands should be smooth.

* The movement from one position to another should be done after uttering the sound.

For doing this exercise stand with the feet apart slightly on a cotton rug. Close your eyes and pray

> O lord, help me for doing this exercise
> Let every step taken by me help me
> to heal me both physically and mentally
> balance all the shakti points
> balance both the left and right nadis
> balance the auric energies
> balance the spiritual energy
> thank you O lord Thank you.

Bow down with reverence and spread your hands in front of you (palms facing the sky).

Inhale deeply and exhale deeply for a few minutes and feel the tension flowing out. When you feel every muscle of your body is relaxed, inhale deeply and start with the syllable given in the chart with the palms touching the particular part of the body. Every syllable should be repeated with full faith and depth, the depthness should be from the heart and not from the throat alone.

Sl. No.	Utterance of the Sound	Position of the hands	Significance of the hand positions
1.	A' (अ)	Both the hands should be on the forehead	This hand position helps in balancing the third eye chakra and other minor nadis flowing to it.
2.	Aah' (आ)	Both the hands should be on the mouth and face.	This hand position helps in balancing the third eye chakra, throat chakra.
3.	E' (इ)	Place the right hand on the right eye. The centre of the palm should be on the eyelids.	—Same as 1.—
4.	Eeh' (ई)	Place the left hand on the left eye. The centre of the palm should be on the eyelids.	—Same as 1.—

Kundalini Yoga - Practical

5.	Oo' (उ)	Place the right hand on the right ear. The centre of the palm should be on the earlobes.	Balances the minor chakra located near the ears.
6.	Ooh' (ऊ)	Place the left hand on the left ear. The centre of the palm should be on the earlobes.	—Same as 5.—
7.	Rh' (ऋ)	Place the right hand on the right nostril. The centre of the palm should be on the sides of the nostril.	Balances the minor eye chakra, minor chakra located near the cheeks.
8.	Rh' (ऋ)	Place the left hand on the left nostril. The centre of the palm should be on the sides of the nostril.	—Same as 7.—
9.	Lrih' (ऌ)	Place the right hand on the right cheek.	Balances the minor chakra located on the cheek.
10.	Aey' (ए)	Place the left hand on the left cheek.	—Same as 9.—
11.	Aaey' (ऐ)	Place the right hand over the upper lip.	Balances the minor chakra located on the cheeks and the major chakra of throat.
12.	O' (ओ)	Place the left hand over the lower lip.	—Same as 11.—
13.	Ouh' (औ)	Part the lips and place the right hand over the lips to cover the upper teeth.	—Same as 11.—
14.	Am' (अं)	Part the lips and place the left hand over lip to cover the lower teeth.	—Same as 11.—

15.	Amh' (अ:)	Touch the tongue over the palate.	This balances two major chakras located on the third eye and the throat, and it also balances the minor chakras located on the cheeks.
16.	K' क	Touch the ring fingers of both the hands to the tip of the tongue.	This balances the minor chakras located on the shoulders and also the third eye chakra.
17.	Kh' ख	Spread the right hand in front and turn the palm into fist.	Balances the minor chakras located on the knuckles and the elbow.
18.	G' ग	Hold the right wrist with the left hand.	—Same as 17.—
19.	Gha' घ	Spread the left hand in front and turn the palm into fist.	—Same as 17.—
20.	Dm' ड.	Cup the fingers of the right hand with the left hand.	Balances the minor chakras located on the centre of the palm and the finger tips.
21.	Ch' च	Cup the fingers of the left hand with the right hand.	—Same as 20.—
22.	Cha' छ	Wave both the hands in the air, as if saying bye-bye.	This balances both the minor chakras located on the knuckles, palms, finger tips and the shoulder.
23.	Ja' ज	Hold the left wrist with the right hand.	—Same as 17.—
24.	Jha' झ	Move both the hands up and down.	—Same as 22.—

Kundalini Yoga - Practical

25.	Tr' ञ	Cup the fingers of the left hand with the right hand.	—Same as 17.—
26.	Ta' ट	Place the right hand over the right thigh.	Balances the minor chakra located on the hands with the chakras on the knees. Mooladhara chakra also gets the balancing energy.
27.	Tha' ठ	Place the right hand over the right knee.	—Same as 26.—
28.	Da' ड	Place the right hand over the right knee	—Same as 26.—
29.	Dha' ढ	Place the right hand over the base of the right feet.	Balances the minor chakras located on the base of the feet.
30.	Na' ण	Cup the fingers of the right feet with the right hand.	—Same as 29.—
31.	T' त	Place the left hand over the left thigh.	—Same as 26.—
32.	Th' थ	Place the left hand over the left knee.	—Same as 26.—
33.	D' द	Place the left hand over the left knuckle.	—Same as 26.—
34.	Dhha' ध	Place the left hand over the left base of the feet.	—Same as 29.—
35.	Na न	Cup the fingers of the left feet with the left hand.	—Same as 29.—
36.	Pa प	Touch the right hand over the right buttock and with the left hand touch the right side of the stomach.	Balances all the chakras in the legs like the minor chakra located on the knee, ankle, base of the feet.

37.	Fa फ	Touch the left hand over the left buttock and with the right hand touch the left side of the stomach.	—Same as 36.—
38.	Ba' ब	Place both the hands over the spinal column.	Balances the minor chakras located near the spinal column
39.	Bha' भ	Place the right hand over the navel and cover the right hand with the left hand.	Helps balance the minor chakras located near the navel chakras.
40.	Ma म	Place both the hands on both the sides of the stomach.	Balances the minor chakra of near kidney, liver, spleen.
41.	Ya य	Place the right hand over the heart and cover the right hand with the left hand.	This helps in balancing the thought processes in the mind.
42.	Ra' र	Place the right hand over the right hip. Place the left hand over the left hip.	This helps in balancing the minor chakras located near the kidney, liver, spleen.
43.	La' ल	Place the right hand over the left shoulder.	—Same as 42.—
44.	Va' व	Place the left hand over the right shoulder.	Balances the minor chakr as located on the tips of the shoulders

Kundalini Yoga - Practical

45.	S' श	Place the right hand over the front of the heart and place the left hand over the back of the heart.	—Same as 44.—
46.	Sha' ष	Place the left hand over the front of the heart and place the right hand over the back of the heart.	This helps in balancing the flow of the heart and also the minor chakras located on the right feet.
47.	Sa' स	Cup both the hands and place it on top of the heart.	This helps in balancing the flow of the heart and also the minor chakras located on the left feet.
48.	Ha' ह	Place the left hand over the navel, the fingers should point towards the right shoulder. Place the right hand over the left hand the fingers should point towards the floor.	This helps in balancing the energy points related with past life traumas.
49.	Ksh' क्ष	Place the right hand over the navel, the fingers should point towards the left shoulder.	Controls the phobias, traumas, psychological problems
50.	Gya' ज्ञ	Place the left hand over the right hand the fingers should point towards the floor.	——Same as 49.——

After finishing all the 51 syllables, breath in deeply again and sit down with closed eyes and mediate on the third eye chakra.

> O lord, thank you to helping me to do this exercise
> bless me lord that I donot move away from you
> every breath should be one in name of you
> thank you O lord Thank you.

Bow down again in reverence for finishing this exercise.

We have two bodies
One the Conscious and
the other Cosmic. Normally we
use only the Conscious and believe
it to be the complete form
of ourselves. It is only
through the process of meditation
that both the bodies merge to
reach the Cosmic consciousness.

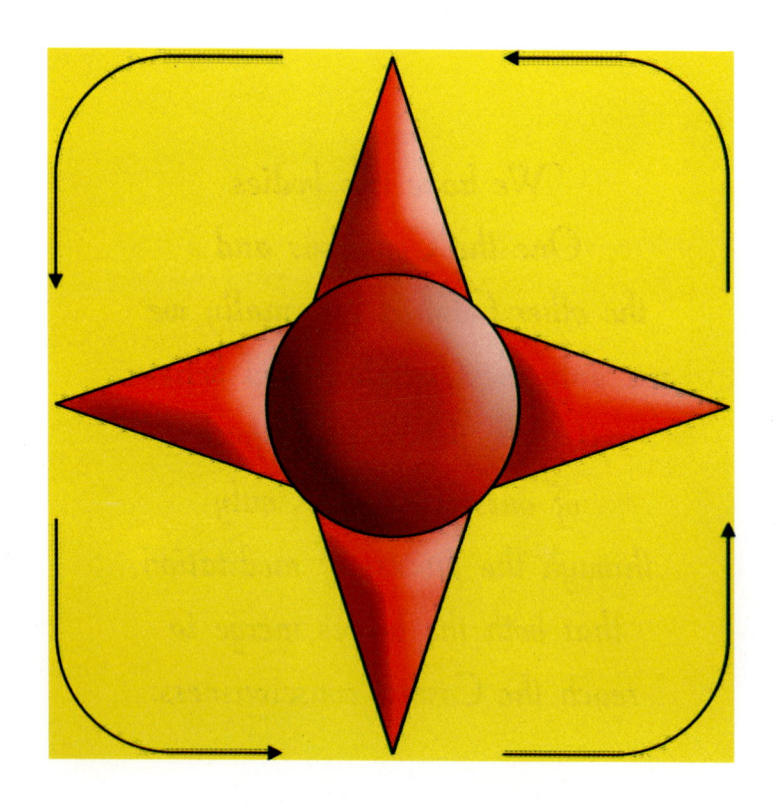

Molladhara Chakra

MOOLADHARA CHAKRA

Week # 1

Darken the room in which you want to do this meditation. Switch on a neon red light if you cannot find red colour bulb then cover a white bulb with red colour transparent sheet.

Sit with closed eyes on a rug facing the bulb. Breathe normally for few minutes feeling that every part of the body is getting relaxed. Feel that the whole body is being engulfed by the red light of the bulb. Continue to breathe normally, place the hands in gyana mudra on the knees.

- Inhale and exhale deeply for a count of 100. With each inhalation and exhalation feel all the tensions flowing out and the body being energised from the flow of the breath.
- Relax and breathe in normally for a period of two minutes. You may slowly count upto 120 for the two minutes.
- Inhale deeply and pull the anus up towards the base of the spine. The tongue should touch the palate.
- Concentrate on the location of the Mooladhara as has been shown in the genital diagram in the theory section of Kundalini Yoga.
- Contract all the muscles of the perineum and hold the breath for half a minute. Release the muscles and the breath. Repeat the process four times. This will help in understanding the sensation of the Mooladhara chakra.
- During the rest of the process, the breathing should be deep.
- Visualise the diagram on the location of the Mooladhara chakra. Feel the four nadis rotating in the direction as shown in the diagram. The speed of the rotation of the chakra increases slowly. As the rotation gains the speed, feel the warmth spreading throughout the genital area.

- ❖ Mentally visualise the Bija mantra LAM (लं) in the centre of the diagram. VAM (वं) on the right nadi, SHAM (शं) on the nadi facing down, SHAM (षं) on the left nadi and SAM (सं) on the nadi facing upwards.
- ❖ Feel the bija mantra flowing from the base of the spine to the Sahasrar chakra. The flow should be like the serpent preparing for attack.

  ✶ It is quite possible that during this last process the breathing may become heavy and deep. When this process takes place, the breathing should be forced to become normal.
- ❖ Go on repeating the name LAM and feel it flowing to the centre of the chakra. Visualise the nadi mantra Vam and visualise it flowing to the right nadi. Repeat the same process with SHAM on the nadi facing down; SHAM on the left nadi and SAM on the nadi facing upwards. Repeat this process four times.
- ❖ Contract all the muscles of the perineum and hold the breath for half a minute. Release the muscles and the breath. Repeat the process four times.
- ❖ Repeat the name 'Mooladhara Uthana' three times, concentrating on the Mooladhara chakra.

If this sadhana is done properly then after a week you will feel tingling sensation in the region of Mooladhara, representing the awakening of the chakra.

INSTRUCTION FOR DOING THIS SADHANA:
- ✶ This sadhana should be done empty stomach.
- ✶ The best time for doing this sadhana is Brahma Muhurata
- ✶ This sadhana should be continuously done for seven days, if there is break then the whole process should be repeated from the start.
- ✶ If you have problem in visualisation of the chakra then the diagram can be concentrated upon.

It is only by thinking deeply about what we really are within that we can find answer to the question 'Who am I?' It cannot be found by external vision or observation, but only by entering into conscious unity with our innermost reality.

Ramana Maharshi

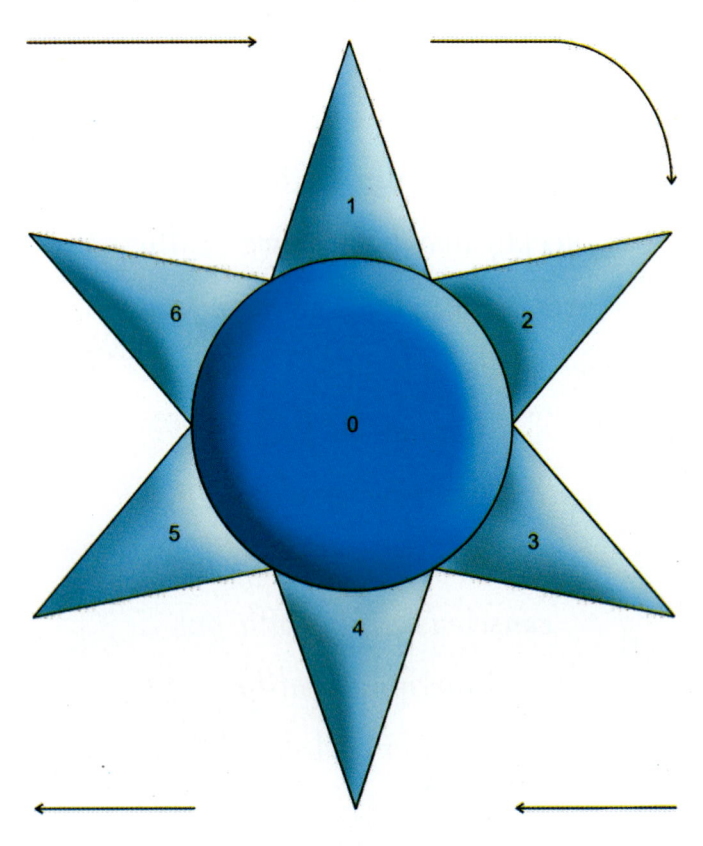

Swadisthana Chakra

SWADHISTHANA CHAKRA

Week # 2

The best time for doing this sadhana is in the evening just before sunset. Sit facing the west direction in Siddhasana.

- Start with the 'Energy Burst' exercise as given in the Pranayama section.
- Relax for a minute or two after the 'Energy burst' exercise. Sit again in Siddhasana facing the west direction.
- Place the right hand on the pubic bone and place the left hand on the Heart chakra. Pubic bone is the physical location of the Swadhisthana chakra.
- Mentally repeat the name 'Swadhisthana Uthana' three times, concentrating on the Swadhisthana chakra.
- Inhale and exhale deeply concentrating on the Swadhisthana chakra for two minutes. With each inhalation feel the energy flowing in the body and with each exhalation feel negative energies flowing out.
- Place both the hands on the knees in gyana mudra and close your eyes.
- Visualise the above diagram on the location of the chakra. Feel the six nadis rotating in the direction as shown in the diagram. The speed of the rotation of the chakra increases slowly. As the rotation gains the speed, feel the coolness spreading throughout the pubic area.
- Mentally visualise the bija mantra VAM (वं) on the centre of the chakra. Visualise the nadi sabda BAM (बं), BHAM (भं), MAM (मं), YAM (यं), RAM (रं), LAM (लं) and feel them flowing to the points 1,2,3,4,5,6 respectively.
- Contract the anus and hold the breath for a period of one minute.

- ❖ Repeat the above two processes for five times.
- ❖ Mentally repeat the mantra five times

Asato Ma Sadgamaya
Tamso Ma Jyotirmaya
Mrityur Ma Amritagamaya

(Oh lord take me from the wrong ways to the good ways
Oh lord take me from the darkness to the light of knowledge
Oh lord take me from the darkness of death to the nectar of life)

- ❖ Mentally repeat the name 'Swadhisthana Uthana' three times, concentrating on the Swadhisthana chakra.

After a week of dedicated practice of this sadhana, you may feel tingling sensation in the Swadhisthana chakra indicating the opening of the chakra.

IMPORTANT INSTRUCTION FOR DOING THIS SADHANA:

- ❖ This sadhana is very cold in nature and may cause drop in the body temperature.
- ❖ If the climate is cold then before doing this sadhana the sadhaka should place his feet in a bucket of warm water mixed with salt. This will help in reducing the negativity of the person. The water should be disposed off to open earth.
  - ✳ The used water should not be used for any other purpose.
  - ✳ Arthritic patients can benefit from this process.
- ❖ This sadhana should be continuously done for seven days, if there is break then the whole process should be repeated from the start.
- ❖ If you have problem in visualisation of the chakra then the diagram can be concentrated upon.

Ordinary people speak for hours on various topics of religion but implement little of it in their life while the sage speaks little and imbibes the concept of religion in life.

Upanishad

Manipura Chakra

MANIPURA CHAKRA

Week # 3

This sadhana is best done in the afternoon, facing the eastern side. This sadhana can also be done in the outside during the winter season.

- ❖ Sit in Siddhasana with the hands on knee in gyana mudra.
- ❖ Do the 'Art of Breathing- Beginners Pose'
- ❖ Relax your body for a period of five minutes.
- ❖ Do the 'The Art of Breathing for Advanced Students'
- ❖ Relax for a period of five minutes.
- ❖ Place your right hand on the navel region and the left hand directly behind the navel region. This is the place of the Manipura chakra.
- ❖ Inhale deeply and exhale. Hold for ten seconds and repeat the process for ten times concentrating on the Manipura chakra.
- ❖ Mentally chant 'Om Mani padme Hum' for Seven times.
- ❖ **Place your hands back on the knee in the gyana mudra.**
- ❖ Mentally visualise the diagram on the physical location of the Manipura chakra, rotating in the direction as shown in the diagram. Feel the chakra rotating slowly and gaining speed with each passing moment. When the speed increases the body gets very warm.
- ❖ Visualise the bija mantra RAM (रं) in the centre of the chakra. Visualise the nadis sabda DAM (डं), DHAM (ढं), NAM (णं), THAM (तं), THAM (थं), DHAM (दं) DHAM (धं), NAM (नं), PAM (पं), FAM (फं) flowing to the numbers 1,2,3,4,5,6,7,8,9,10 respectively
- ❖ Hold the breath for a minute and repeat the above process for ten times.

- Mentally chant 'Manipura Uthana' for three times.

If this sadhana is done correctly, then you will feel tingling sensation in the navel chakra.

IMPORTANT INSTRUCTIONS FOR DOING THIS SADHANA:

- This sadhana should be done on the empty stomach or after a gap of five hours between the meals.
- This sadhana increases the body temperature. In summer season, the sadhaka can do this sadhana with a bucket of lukewarm water mixed with salt or a bucket of lukewarm water mixed with one drop of sandal oil.
- This water helps in cooling the body temperature. After the sadhana is over the water should be given to the plants.
- If this sadhana is done a group then the benefit is manifold.

Warning this sadhana should not be done in open during the summer season as this can over heat the body.

Trying to be human in
nature is very difficult
and it is further more
difficult to
maintain it.

Swami Nityanandji

Anahat Chakra

Kundalini Yoga - Practical

ANAHAT CHAKRA

Week # 4

Sit in a comfortable position with folded hands. Close your eyes and breathe in normally.

- ❖ Bring your awareness to the chest and feel the expansion and the contraction of the chest with each breath. Continue with this awareness for a period of five minutes.
- ❖ Do the 'Inner Voice' technique.
- ❖ Relax for a minute or two.
- ❖ Do the 'Self Introspection' technique.
- ❖ Sit in siddhasana and place the hands on the knees in gyana mudra.
- ❖ Place the right hand on the chest and the left hand on the lower part of the chest.
- ❖ Visualise the diagram on the heart region and feel that the chakra is rotating in the direction shown. The speed of this chakra is slow and moves in angular direction.

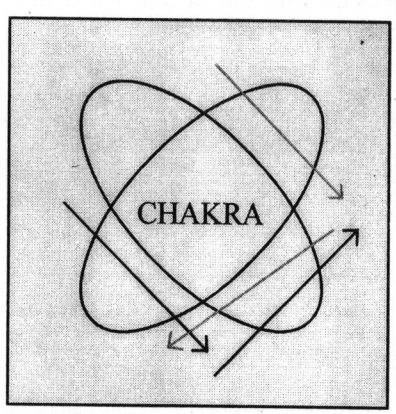

- ❖ Visualise the bija mantra YAM (यं) in the centre of the chakra and feel that the bija mantra is emitting golden light which is completely engulfing the whole chakra. Visualise the nadi swara KAM (कं), KHAM (खं), GAM (गं), GHAM (घं), DAM (डं.), CHAM (चं), CHHAM (छं), JAM (जं), JHAM (झं), JHAM (ञं), TAM (टं), THAM (ठं)

at 1, 2, 3, 4, 5, 6, 7, 8, 9, 10, 11, 12 positions respectively in the diagram. Feel that the nadi swara is also emitting the golden light, which is spreading throughout your body. Repeat the process for five times.

- ❖ Mentally chant 'Anahat Jagratey' seven times bringing the awareness to the heart chakra.
- ❖ Lower your hands from the chest and sit back in the Siddhasana with hands in gyana mudra.
- ❖ Do the 'Self Introspection' technique.
- ❖ Relax for a period of two minutes and repeat the mantra 'Anahat Uthana' three times.

Regular practice of this technique will awaken the Anahat chakra. When this chakra awakens you will become humble, noble, and knowledgeable and there is radiance of spirituality.

IMPORTANT INSTRUCTIONS FOR DOING THIS SADHANA:

- ❖ This sadhana should not be done during the periods of emotional stress like anger, jealousy etc.
- ❖ There should be no break during the whole sadhana.
- ❖ This sadhana should be done with full devotion and dedication and can be continued even later than the seven-day duration.
- ❖ This sadhana can be done even during attending Satsangs, mass prayers etc.

Life is the most complex subject to learn, few who master it rule the World.

Vishuddha Chakra

VISHUDDHA CHAKRA

Week # 5

This sadhana is best done before the sunset.

For doing this sadhana you would require the following things :
* 7-8 gm. of sandal powder
* Rose water (three tablespoon)
* Natural perfume (few drops)
* Two candles

Mix the sandal powder with rose water and perfume to form a fine paste.

- ❖ Sit down in Siddhasana facing the north direction. The spine should be erect and hands on knee in gyana mudra.
- ❖ Do the 'Inner Invocation' technique and relax for two minutes.
- ❖ Use the right hand first and the middle finger to draw the following symbol in front of you and place the two-lighted candle in the front of each knee.
- ❖ Place both your hands over the symbol in such a way the central symbol is fully covered by your hands.
- ❖ Chant 'Vishuddhi Jagratey' seven times, concentrating on the symbol.
- ❖ Move your right hand to the lump of the throat region while keeping the left hand on position 'a'. Massage the throat region with the right hand by moving the hands up and down. When the right hand moves up the left hand should move from the position 'a' to 'b','c' and vice versa.

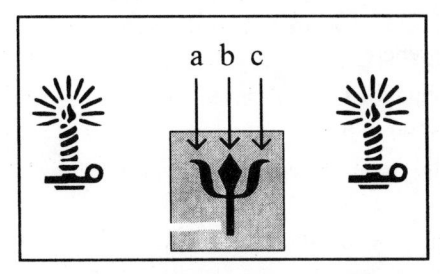

- ❖ Repeat the above process seven times concentrating on the throat region. This is the physical location of the Vishuddhi chakra. If this process is done properly then you will feel the smell of sandal emitting from the throat chakra.
- ❖ Bring both the palms near the lighted candle in such a way that the centre of the palm feels the warmth of the candle-light. Chant 'Vishuddhi Jagratey' seven times, concentrating on the symbol.
- ❖ Close your eyes, sit in gyana mudra, and mentally visualise the chakra as given in the diagram on the throat region. Visualise the chakra rotating slowly in the direction given.
- ❖ Visualise the bija mantra HAM' (हं) in the centre of the chakra radiating pure white energy. Visualise the nadi swara AM (अं), AAM (आं), IM (इं), EEM (ईं), UM' (उं), UUM' (ऊं), RSH' (ऋ), REEM' (ऋं), LRIM' (ल), LREEM (ल्हं), EIYM (एं), EEIYM' (ऐं), OM' (ओं), AUM' (औं), AM' (अं), AH (अः) on the positions 1, 2, 3, 4, 5, 6, 7, 8, 9, 10, 11, 12, 13, 14, 15, 16 respectively radiating pure white energy.
- ❖ Mentally chant ' Vishuddhi Uthana' seven times and repeat the above process seven times.
- ❖ Open your eyes and repeat the 'Inner Invocation' technique'.
- ❖ Relax for two minutes by breathing normally.
- ❖ Inhale deeply and hold the breath and chant 'Vishuddhi Uthana' seven times and forcefully exhale from mouth in such a way that both the candlelight's are blown out.

IMPORTANT INSTRUCTIONS FOR THE PRACTICE OF THIS SADHANA :

- ✶ Never use bright clothes for doing this sadhana.
- ✶ This sadhana should never be done in the afternoons.
- ✶ Never do this sadhana during emotional stress.
- ✶ Pregnant Women should not do this sadhana.

*Nature in folds holds the
true science of life.
A science so incomprehensible,
inexplicable and so
dynamic in nature that
few have been able to
unfold the mysteries of it.*

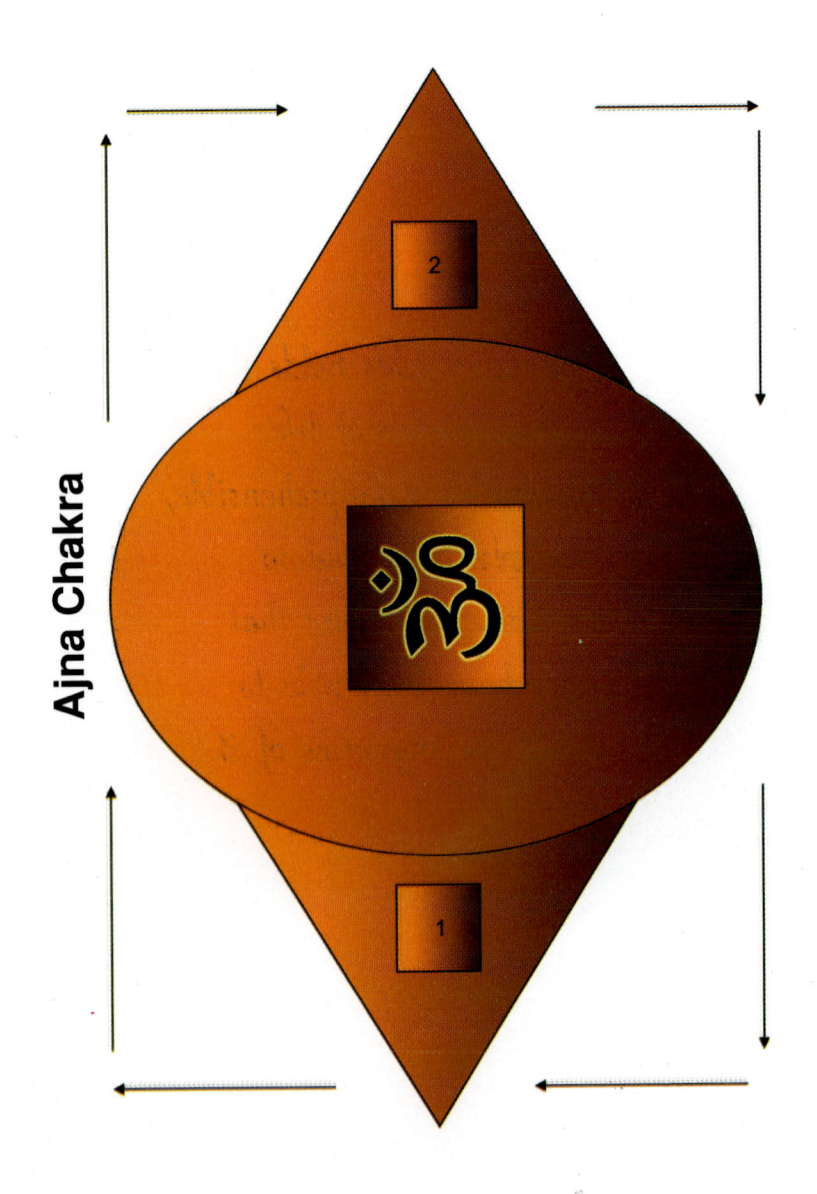

Ajna Chakra

AJNA CHAKRA

Week # 6

This sadhana is best done late in the night or Brahma muhurata.

- Sit in siddhasana with hands in gyana mudra on the knees
- Do the 'Inner Invocation' exercise
- Relax and breathe normally for two minutes
- Do the 'Calling to the Universal Soul' exercise
- Relax and breathe normally for two minutes
- Do 'Tratak – The way of the Yogi' exercise, relax for two to three minutes.
- Sit back again in Siddhasana with hands in gyana mudra on the knees.
- Focus on the centre of the eyebrow and chant the mantra 'Om' for hundred times without any thoughts creeping into mind process.
- Close the eyes and still keep the concentration on the bhu madhya chanting the mantra 'Om' for five minutes.
- Feel the vibration of the mantra 'Om' spreading throughout the body.
- Relax for a minute or two.
- Mentally chant the mantra 'Agya Jagratey' seven times.
- Visualise the chakra between the eyebrows and feel it rotating in the direction shown. The speed of the rotation is fast and flows inwards as shown in the diagram.
- A sadhaka can also place the first and the middle finger on the centre of the eyebrow and visualise the chakra.

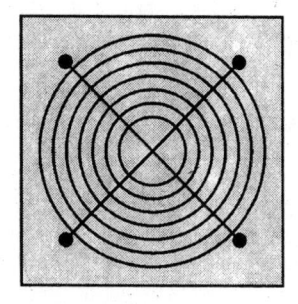

- Visualise the bija mantra AUM (ॐ) on the centre of the chakra. Visualise the nadi sabda HAM (हं) and KSHAM (क्षं) on the positions 1, 2 respectively.
- Chant the mantra 'Agya Uthana' seven times and repeat the above process ten times.
- Mentally chant 'Om' repetitively during the whole process.
- Repeat the 'Inner Invocation' technique.

When this chakra awakens, the sadhaka may go in trance for hours together.

IMPORTANT INSTRUCTIONS FOR DOING THIS SADHANA:
* This sadhana should be done only after the sadhak attains full control over the other techniques.
* There should not be any lapse in the exercise mentioned in the sadhana. If any break happens in the sadhana then the whole process has to be repeated from the beginning.

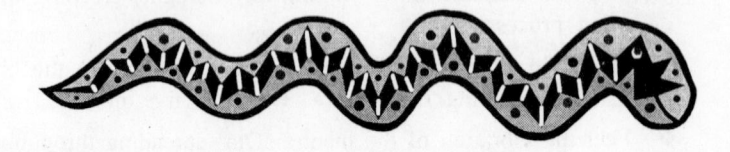

COMPLETE PROCESS OF KUNDALINI AWAKENING WITHOUT ANY BREAK

This whole process takes the whole day. A sadhaka should do this process only after attaining proficiency in the individual chakra awakening process.

Start with the process given for awakening Ajna chakra as given above.

Proceed with the awakening of the Mooladhara chakra, Swadhisthana Chakra, Anahat chakra, Vishuddhi chakra as given in the above section.

Awakening the Kundalini With the spiritual energy of Reiki

Reiki – A true knowledge of life

CONTENTS

- ✓ Reiki Basics
- ✓ Stages in Reiki and their importance
    - ✓ Reiki I
    - ✓ Reiki II
    - ✓ Reiki III A
    - ✓ Reiki III B
- ✓ Attunement process for Reiki I
- ✓ Attunement process for Reiki II
- ✓ Attunement process for Reiki III A & B
- ✓ Certification for the Degrees
- ✓ Some Do's and Don'ts
- ✓ Meditational and healing Techniques have been provided in each of the stages

Reiki

Is the purest form of gods love

Handed over to us for the benefit of the world

Never requiring paying for it

Except with a bow of head with reverence

Smoothening out the curves of life caused by us

Removing all the obstacles for our furtherance

By the affectionate touch of the universal hand

Requiring no specific belief in

the Supreme Being or reiki itself

always there to help, with the love of a mother

harnesses the power of the universe itself

with no individualistic pride for the power

A science so spiritual that it becomes a diva for the world

Asking nothing in return except love for everyone.

> Reiki heals the body and the emotions, bringing them into balance and promoting health, happiness, prosperity and long life.

Reiki pronounced as Ray- Key was a science of healing and spiritual upliftment known to this world around 3000 years back. This science was very much used by the Tibetan monks for doing physical, auric and spiritual healing and development. This science was slowly forgotten and it was only in the middle of the 19th century that this science received a new life in the form of Reiki. As we have stated earlier that there is an unseen energy, flowing through our body, this energy is the basis for us being alive and kicking. This energy was discovered thousands of years ago by many spiritual saints and traditional medicinal practitioners; this becomes evident from the following names given by them for the energy:

Ch'i in Chinese

Prana in Sanskrit (India)

Bioplasmic energy

Ka in Egypt

Jesod of Jew cabalists

Baraka of Sufis

Mana by Kahunas

Other names given to the unseen energy are fifth power, delta source, megalith etc.

(N.B. this list is just a sample and not a complete one)

This rediscovered science has even made scientists to experiment to verify the healing powers of this energy and now even they are understanding the deep rooted secret of the immune system and the method of healing.

Reiki is a very simple and amazing thing to learn. This science has not exploited to its fullest, as in the current scenario this science has become popular only for the healing properties of this science.

Spiritual Energy of Reiki

Dr. Mikao Usui is the person who rediscovered this beautiful science from the secret land of Tibet, which was used by ancient India for the spiritual upliftment, and healing of the people. This science was kept secret and was only known to a handful number of people who were very much involved in the realm of spirituality. This science was lost in the vast dune of time. Dr. Usui was a Dean at a Christian missionary college. The students who used to study there were very much excited by the healing done by Jesus. They used to ask Dr. Usui the method of doing the healing as was done by Jesus Christ. Frequent probe by the students created a sense of wanting in the mind of Dr. Usui and he resigned from the post of the dean to look for the science of healing. He had traveled far and wide learning English, Chinese, Tibetan, Sanskrit languages and researching the scriptures for finding the answer to his quest. During the quest, he received his Doctorate in Theology. He had started visiting Buddhist monastery and became a full time student there learning the ancient arts. After doing continuous study for long one day, he accidentally found a Sanskrit text from a Buddhist sutra showing the whole process of attaining the siddhi of healing. Following the text he meditated and prayed on the holy Mt. of Kuriyama and got the initiation after 21 days. This energy he called Rei-Ki meaning the universal energy.

REI - SPIRITUAL WISDOM/ UNIVERSAL
Ki - The Life Force/ Energy

Dr. Usui after getting the enlightenment travelled to different places teaching this spiritual art. Before he left for the other world, he had passed on the flag to Dr. Hayashi and Hawayo Takata who carried this tradition of the Guru – Shishya parampara.

Dr. Usui in the beginning had trained the beggars with whom he lived with and later realised the fault, which he had committed by not teaching them to be grateful and have gratitude for the spiritual art. This resulted in making the beggars having the same kind of attitude towards life, which they had before learning Reiki from Dr. Usui. Those beggars did nothing from there own side to improve their life. Dr. Usui decided from that day to teach only those people who came to him asking for the spiritual energy. He created the ideals, which a student of this science should follow to achieve success in the path he has decided to take. These ideals are not to done or recited as a stanza but has to be imbibed in the life. These ideals should be a part of you.

WHO WILL BELL THE CAT............

This is very famous fairy tale about a wheat storage house, which was inhabited by mice. These mice used to enjoy the foods, which was kept in the storage house. All the mice had grown big and fat because of the free availability of the food.

The owner of the storage was unhappy due to heavy loses he was incurring because of the mice's. One day he brought a cat and left it in the storage house. The cat was very happy to see so many easy preys. In a few days the cat killed and ate many mice. This caused panic in the whole community of the mouse, they called up emergency meeting.

The agenda of the meeting was to decide how the pursuit of the cat could be stopped or avoided.

One young mouse came up with an idea that they should bell the cat. The sound of the bell will forewarn them of the arrival of the cat, this in turn will give sufficient time to the mice's to hide.

This idea of belling the cat was appreciated by all, but none of the mice volunteered to tie the bell around cat. Day after day, this idea was considered but still no one volunteered. The cat went around killing the mice's one by one.

In the end there were no mice in the storage house, the cat swelled up and the owner was very much happy.

Like the cat, our indriyae (senses) eat away our natural thoughts and, we only think of taming the cat. The doers only succeed, for every success there is a flood of failure. **Never let the cat eat you.**

Spiritual Energy of Reiki

REIKI IDEALS

The ideals are both guidelines for living a gracious life and virtues worthy of practice for their inherent value.

Just for Today:
I will let go of anger.
I will let go of worry.
I will give thanks for my many blessings.
I will do my work honestly.
I will be kind to my neighbour and every living being.
Just for Today, I will let go of anger.

Anger is a precious jewel, so precious that it should be safeguarded then only will it serve us. This does not mean to suppress the anger but to use for beneficial purposes. Always divert anger for others and not for you alone.

Just for Today, I will let go of worry.

Worry destroys the equilibrium of the nervous and endocrine system of the body thereby leaving you in a distressed condition.

Just for Today, I will give thanks for my many blessings.

You as a human being are not born to a couple but actually, you are outcome of the prayers and rituals of the generations, which made your soul to be a part of the dynasty or clan. From the time of birth till now, you have been blessed by your parents, relatives, friends, gurus and so many people you come in contact with. With so much blessings being showered, we must be thankful to all those people.

Just for Today, I will do my work honestly

Honesty in work does not mean the work done at office, but means the dedication and honesty shown by you for doing your moral duties at home for your parents, relatives etc. When a work is done with full honesty and dedication then you will feel happiness and fullness in the heart.

Just for Today, I will be kind to my neighbour and every living being.

A man is rightly said to be a social animal. He requires help in every moment of time and changes the nature with those living around him. Love is something so divine that the more it is distributed the more it grows. Kindness here does not mean sympathy but means the softness in the heart for others.

These ideals are to be repeated every day and should be imbibed in the life and you will definitely find a new person from inside you.

PLEASE DON'T KILL ME....

In ancient times, Bradamuni had an ashram near the river Krishna. He had attained the siddhi of trikaldarshi. As per his visions, he was to leave his body in a short period and he was going to be born as white pig in a gutter before attaining nirvana.

This vision troubled him, he was at disbelief that after attaining so much through tapa and dhyana he was going to be born as a filthy pig and that too in a gutter.

This thought troubled him all the time. After thinking a lot, he called his favourite disciple Madhav and told him all about his vision. He also gave instructions, as to where he will be born and what will be the verifying marks on his body. The disciple was also sad, his guru after attaining siddhies was going to be born as a pig.

Then out of the blue the muni asked for his gurudakshina, he said "Dear Madhav, what, I saw will happen and there is nothing you or I can do. Since, I have not asked any gurudakshina (fees) till now, I would to ask for it now".

Madhav bowed down at the feet of his guru and said "Guruji, I am indebted to you for life for the knowledge provided to me. If possible, as a gurudakshina I would like to take the birth of the pig, so that you can get mukti (freedom) from the cycle of birth and death".

Muni was overwhelmed by the love of the disciple, he hugged him and said "Son, it is I who sinned for which I only have to repent. As a gurudakshina I would like a favour from you and that is when I am born as a pig in the next birth, you should search for me and after finding me, you should kill me. This will save me from eating and living in the filth of the gutter."

Madhav agreed to the gurudakshina. On the destined day the muni left his body and Madhav became incharge of the ashram. He went in the direction as told by his guru, and found a cute little white baby pig in a filth. The pig was white in colour but it was rolling on the filth with great joy and happiness. Madhav bowed down to the little pig and said "Guruji, it is I Madhav who has come to fulfill your desire. It really pains me to see you suffer like this. Bless me so that I have the power to kill this body of your with one blow". Saying this Madhav took out a long sharp knife with one hand and took hold of the pig with the other hand.

Suddenly the pig yelled out "Who said, I am suffering. I am really enjoying this life. Please do not kill me. I take back my wish and you are free from my debt". Madhav had a divine realisation and left the pig to enjoy its life.

NATURE AND HEALING PROPERTIES OF REIKI

Reiki channels who have been using Reiki energy for sometime have found that Reiki is bipolar in nature. It follows the concept of Kundalini in tantric Indian tradition of Ardh-Nareshwar i.e. the culmination of both the male and female energy the union of Shiva and Shakti. The crown chakra is representing the male energy and the root chakra representing the female energy. The moment these two energies are balanced, you will find peace at heart and if there is some imbalance in them then Reiki balances both the energy points by finding a proper combination for them.

Reiki is simple and pure in nature itself, that is why many people can give Reiki healing to one individual patient and the energy gets automatically adjusted to the need of the patient.

Reiki acts on the aura, physical and emotional level and is thus a holistic system of healing. This process makes Reiki a very strong force with a gentle touch for healing of any kind of diseases and injuries like multiple sclerosis, heart disease, cancer, skin problems, cuts, bruises, broken bones, headache, colds, flu, sore throat, sunburn, fatigue, insomnia, impotence, poor memory, lack of confidence, psychosomatic problems etc. This does not prevent from continuing with the medical treatment, Reiki can help the medication to act at the required area and give relief to the patient.

Other benefit of Reiki when added with the medication
- Helps in providing relief faster.
- Heals the cuts or bruises faster.
- Side effects of the medicine are reduced as also reduce the feeling of tiredness is not there.
- In cases of burns the feeling of relief can be felt if Reiki is given with the medication.

LIFE'S LIKE THAT...

In a city, there lived a brahman Shanker with his wife Mohini. Mohini used to abuse Shanker. This was known to the whole city. Shanker never rebuffed her and did whatever possible to make her happy.

One day his neighbour asked him the reason for his wife's behaviour and his calmness in such a sickening atmosphere. Shanker laughed and said "In the last birth, I was a dhobi (washerman) and she was my donkey. I used to load her with many bundles of clothes. One day in a fit of anger, I loaded her with so many bundles' that she died of the burden. Now she is born as my wife and, I have to carry the burden of hers till, I am able to repay for all the troubles caused by me to her".

The neighbour realised the meaning of what Shanker said and bowed down to him.

Spiritual Energy of Reiki

HOW DOES REIKI DO THIS....

We have explained earlier that our body is like a machine, which works in perfect condition due to the correct functioning of seven major chakras and the related nadis. In addition to the seven major chakras, there are other minor chakras which function as per the instructions received from the major chakras. When a child is born at that moment the crown and navel chakras are very much active and act as sources for the assimilation of the information. During this period the child is closer to the nature and is away from the world we know of. As the child grows up, he is drawn into the fold of the worldly affairs and the contact with the nature fads away. As the time goes by the child losses his internal voice and the problems start accumulating. These problems are nothing but obstacles as created by the person himself. These obstacles interrupt the flow of the life energy in the chakras and the nadis. This in turn affect the auric energy flowing around our body, this energy acts as a safeguard against the diseases, when the auric energy gets depleted the diseases starts to manifest in the physical form of the human being.

(For a detailed description of the Kundalini, refer to the section on Kundalini)

The man made obstacles in the life are mainly jealousy, anger, attachment, desire, needs and wants. When a Reiki channel does the healing session he balances the chakras and removes the obstacles so that the healing is faster, by re-energising the chakras and the nadis. Reiki first heals the auric body then heals the emotional and physical bodies.

Reiki has been used only for healing physical and emotional diseases, but if we look at the diagram, we can see that the Reiki is something more beyond the physical and emotional healing.

ATTITUDE OF GRATITUDE

For any healing, it is important that there has to be a sense of gratitude, towards everything, because a person gets the power to heal from the universal soul, from the nature and from the karmic deeds. The person who wants to heal is nothing more than a medium for the universal energy to flow. Thus, it is important to say the attitude of gratitude before beginning the Reiki or any other healing treatment. You can use the attitude of gratitude as given here or develop an attitude of gratitude of your very own.

I thank myself (name............) for being here
I thank the cosmic that is Reiki for being here
I thank my parents (names............) for being in my Life
I thank my Guru (name............) for being in my life
I thank my God (name............) for always being in my life
I thank my all the Reiki masters for there loved blessing

In case of treating others:
I thank (name(s)...............) for being here
I thank their soul and body for being here

This is very much important as the more humble a person the better prospects are there for him to rise both materially and spiritually.

A SITTING IS A SITTING....

Meditation means silencing your mind, but before that you should be aware of the surroundings. Meditation is not a silent zone but an active process. Sitting in one place without any thoughts is not easy. Rather it should be said that when we normally sit we do not sit alone and not on the buttocks but rather we sit with whole lot of thoughts and images. These images and thoughts go on hampering the natural process of sitting, causing lot of physical problems like piles, bed sores etc.

When sitting, sit and do nothing. Nothing to be seen, viewed, thought, talked or even discussed.

Sit and be conscious about it. Awareness of the sitting should be like awareness of breathing.

Spiritual Energy of Reiki

STAGES IN REIKI AND THEIR IMPORTANCE

The traditional form of Reiki is taught in stages. The different stages of degrees of Reiki are
 Reiki I
 Reiki II
 Reiki III A
 Reiki III B

(All the above stages require an attunement by the Reiki master.)

Originally Reiki consisted of only Three stages, the Reiki IIIA and Reiki IIIB were separated only recently.

Some teachers teach Reiki in five stages, the last being the stage of Reiki Grand Master.

ATTUNEMENT

Reiki is a science bestowed upon the channel by the Reiki Master. The Reiki Master through a process called attunement transfers this spiritual science. Attunement process opens the crown, heart, and palm chakra for receiving the spiritual energy for healing.

Once a person is attuned to Reiki, he becomes a channel for Reiki for the entire life. This energy never depletes and can be used by the practitioner even after gap of years.

Detailed description of the 'Process of Attunement' is given later in this section.

REIKI I – THE FACE OF TRUE KNOWLEDGE

This is the first level of attunement whereby the Reiki channel is asked to heal the physical body. Body, is something we are generally familiar. Reiki allows a gradual transgression from the material world to the spiritual world by making ourselves more aware of the strength of the body, which could treat and heal. It may not be possible for a beginner to sit in deep meditation without cleansing his body and soul, which is aptly done by the 'Hands on Healing' process.

After a student is initiated into Reiki –I, he will be able to do Self Treatment &Treat Others.

In Reiki -I the student does the healing with physical touch. He is taught 25 hand positions, which cover the whole body including the major and minor chakras. For healing others, the student uses the same 25 hand positions.

The channel should start by healing himself. By using the hand positions all the accumulated negative thoughts and energies are dispersed by making you a more balanced person. This will also balance the chakras, nadis and repair the damage on the auric level. 21 days of regular practice of hands on self -healing will repair the auric energies, which in turn will balance the emotional and physical bodies. 21 days represent your penance and dedication for doing the practice of hands on self-healing. The hand positions are to be kept at one part of the body for a minimum period of three minutes for getting the full benefit of the spiritual energy.

PROCESS FOR DOING SELF–HEALING TREATMENT FOR REIKI I

Some things are to be understood before the process of hands on healing begins.

- Do the Reiki healing in a quiet comfortable and airy room.
- Avoid wearing the following things while doing the hand positions :
  * Spectacles, Watches
  * Ties, Vests/Jacket
  * Belts (Leather), Shoes
  * Jewellery, Scarves
  * No Crystals or any gems of any type
- Wear comfortable clothes so that there is no restriction in the movement of the hands.

❖ Hand position is to be kept on the body as shown in the diagram for a period of 3 minutes. In the beginning, one may find difficulty in checking with the time. This can be resolved by using a bell cassette for it, the recording of this cassette is done such a way that after every 3 minutes a bell sound is heard, allowing the student to change the hand position. Moving or swaying with the music, while doing the hand positions are allowed.

❖ Never leave both the hands at a time from the position held. When the position is changed then one hand should be moved to the next position without moving the other hand.

❖ Never playfully do the hand positions, as they are spiritual in nature and should be respected in such way only.

Beginning the process of Hands on self-healing

❖ Sit comfortably on a chair. Keep the feet apart and the hands on the knees with the palms facing the sky. The ankles should never be locked. Close your eyes and raise both the hands upto the level of your chest. The palms should be in a cupped form. Now say the attitude of gratitude with full dedication and purity in the heart, if you are not able to remember the Attitude of gratitude given in this book, you can also do the prayer that you are accustomed to.

❖ Stay in the position for a while and when you will feel a tingling sensation, warmth etc. in the palms. In the beginning it is possible that you will not be able to judge the sensation or the warmth for getting the sensational experiences. But after 21 days of dedicated practice you will be able to judge the sensation or vibration in the palms.

❖ The cup of the palms should be on the position described. As the fingertips contain the energy points and the centre of palm has the minor chakra.

Important: Disrespect and irresponsible behaviour are not part of the healing process as it is a spiritual experience.

The healing involves the whole body the front as well as the back of the body. We will start with the frontal part then proceed to the back of the body.

Hands positions on the front part of the body:

POSITION -1 : EYE

Other areas covered by this position are : Nose, mouth, forehead, eyes, eyebrows.

This is the spiritual point of starting the exercise. This position covers the Third eye chakra (ajna chakra), two minor chakra located on either side of the cheeks and the two important nadis located behind the eyeballs. Many Reiki channels have felt their tension being released when they are using this position and some have even felt a vibrant energy force passing through this chakra.

POSITION -2 : TEMPLES

This position helps in relieving the tension from the body. Both the Ida and the Pingala nadis which control over the conscious brain are balanced with this hand position.

Other areas covered by this position are : eyebrows, ears.

POSITION -3 : EARS

Other areas covered by this position are: Temples, sides of the neck, sides of the brain, jawbone.

The benefit derived from this position is very similar to the benefits derived from the second position. Many people have felt the sound 'Aum' when using this hand position.

Spiritual Energy of Reiki

POSITION -4 : FOREHEAD AND BACK OF THE HEAD

The benefit is similar to the benefit derived in the first position. The added benefit is that the third eye chakra is balanced from the front as well as the back of the head. This position also helps in balancing the left and the right of the brain.

Other areas covered by this position are: forehead, eyes, eyebrows, back of the head, cranium.

POSITION -5 : BACK OF THE HEAD

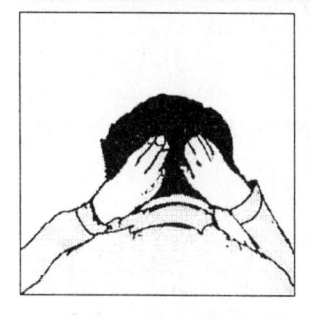

Back of the head position helps in understanding the concept of life. This position releases the past life traumas. The alternate method of doing this position is to put one hand over the other in horizontal position. This position covers the third eye chakra, vishuddhi chakra, Ida and pingala nadis. Other areas covered by this position are: back of the head & neck, cranium.

POSITION -6 : THROAT FRONT & BACK

This is an important position as it covers the vishuddhi chakra/ throat chakra. When this chakra is healed or balanced then the channel will be in control of the vayu tatva and the ap (water tatva).

Other areas covered by this position are: lower back of the head, upper wind pipe area.

POSITION -7 : THYMUS & THYROID GLANDS

This position covers the minor chakras located near the collarbone and the nadis flowing behind it.

Other areas covered by this position are: lower wind pipe area, rib cages, and upper part of the lungs.

POSITION -8 : HEART REGION

This is another vital hand position as it covers the heart chakra. This chakra is the source of love and emotion. This position balances and harmonises the flow of the life force i.e. the blood.

Other areas covered by this position are: chest, rib cage and lungs.

POSITION -9 : SOLAR PLEXUS

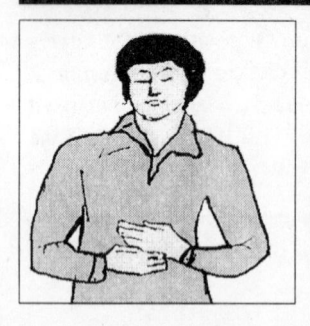

This is another vital position in our body, which according to many, is the source of assimilation and dissimulation of the sun energy.

Other areas covered by this position are: lower part of the rib cage, lower part of heart, part of the upper stomach.

Spiritual Energy of Reiki

POSITION -10 : LIVER

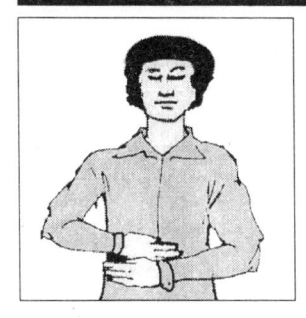

This position allows healing and harmonising the minor chakra located near the liver. This body part is also very vital for our physical and spiritual development.

Other areas covered by this position are part of the stomach, intestines.

POSITION -11 : PANCREAS AND SPLEEN

This position helps in healing and harmonising the flow of the minor chakra located near the pancreas.

Other areas covered by this position are part of the stomach, intestines.

POSITION -12 : SHOULDER TIPS

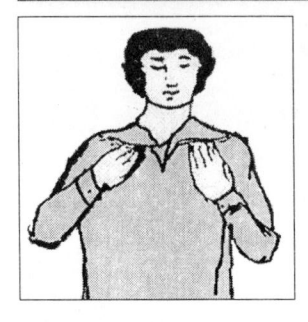

This position helps in healing and harmonising the two minor chakras located at the shoulder tips.

Other areas covered by this position are: rib cage, part of the chest region.

POSITION - 13 : HARA

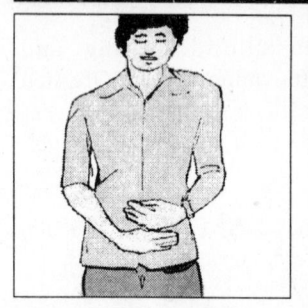

This position helps in harmonising and healing the major chakra and two minor chakras associated with it. This position also helps us to be earthed.

POSITION -14(A) : SPERMATIC CHORD (FOR GENTS)

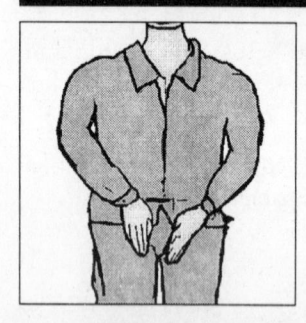

This position covers the base chakra or the Mooladhara chakra. This position helps in getting the person detached from the earthly desires. This is the first position for the transformation of a man from animal.

POSITION -14(B) : OVARIES (FOR WOMEN)

Same as position 14(a)

Spiritual Energy of Reiki

POSITION - 15 : THIGHS

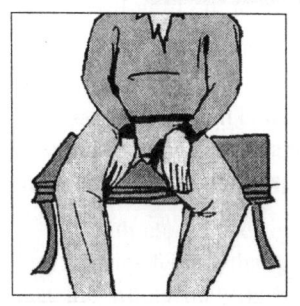

This position helps in channeling the flow of the energy towards the earth, so that there is no blockages in the reverse flow of it.

POSITION - 16 : KNEES

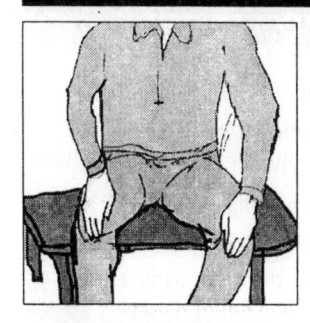

This position covers the two minor chakra located on the knee points.

POSITION - 17 : CALF MUSCLES

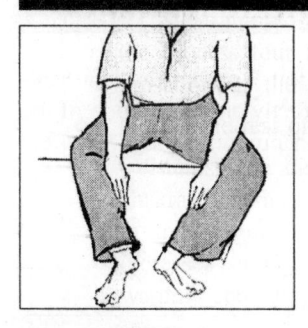

Like the position of Thighs, this position also helps in smooth transmission of energy flow.

POSITION - 18 : ANKLE AND FOOT SOLES

This is final stage in the front part of the body, which helps in earthing of the flow of the energy.

In this diagram, only one foot is shown as being healed, the channel should heal the other feet also. This is important as in the centre of the foot there is a minor chakra and the tips of toes is the place of giving the energy.

Hands positions on the back part of the body :-

POSITION -19 : BACK OF THE SHOULDER

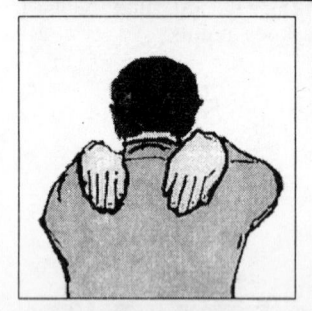

Same as position 11. The only difference is that the healing is done directly on the location of the chakras, i.e. in proximity of the spine.

POSITION -20 : THYMUS AND THYROID GLANDS

Same as position 7 except that the healing is done directly on the location of the chakras, i.e. in proximity of the spine.

Spiritual Energy of Reiki

POSITION - 21 : HEART

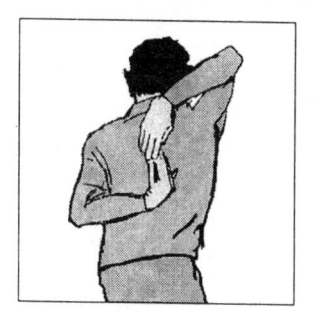

Same as position 8 except that the healing is done directly on the location of the chakras, i.e. in proximity of the spine.

POSITION - 22 : SOLAR PLEXUS

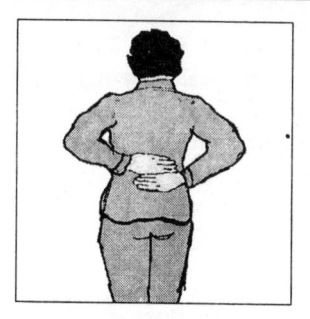

Same as position nine. The only difference is, the healing is done directly on the location of the chakras, i.e. in proximity of the spine.

POSITION - 23 : KIDNEYS

This position helps in harmonising and healing the two minor chakras located on the either of spine near the kidneys. These minor chakras control the required energy by the kidneys.

POSITION - 24 : HARA

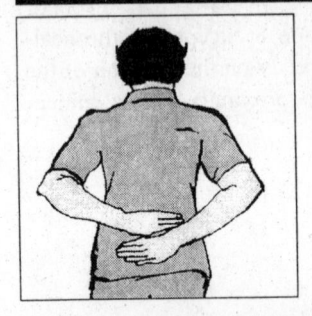

Same as position 13. The only difference is that the healing is done directly on the location of the chakras, i.e. in proximity of the spine.

POSITION - 25 : BASE OF THE SPINE

Same as position 14 (a) or (b). The only difference is that the healing is done directly on the location of the chakras, i.e. in proximity of the spine.

After the student has done the 25 hand positions, he should bring the hands in front as he had done in the beginning and say the attitude of gratitude. Bow the head down a little in reverence and complete the healing by saying

Full body healing of me is completed, I am healed,
May the fire of Reiki burn in me
and heal the body physically, emotionally
and mentally. thank you

Now open the eyes and the healing process is complete.

The details of the minor and major chakra can be had from the Kundalini section of this book.

After you have practiced the 25 positions for 21 days, you will be in a position to understand your body more subtly and closely. For checking your development you can also do the week 11 & 12 AURIC ENERGY exercise of the *WATCHING THE INNER SELF.*

DOING HEALING WITH OTHERS

a. One on one healing : This process is done when one person does hands on healing to another person. This method will be same as self-healing process. 25 positions are to be covered using 3 minutes each. Thus, a full body healing to another person will take around 75 minutes.

b. Many on one healing : When many people do the full body healing to a person then, it is called a **Team healing session (THS)/ Many on one healing (MH)**. Some important things to be remembered while doing THS/ MH:

i. Every healer should take a part of the body, which is to be healed. For example, if four persons are doing full body healing to a person, then one person can take the position from head upto the neck, second can take the positions from the thymus to liver, third can take the positions from the liver to the spermatic chord and the fourth can take positions from the upper thighs to the soles. The same distribution can be done with the front as well as the back of body.

ii. All the healers should have pure interest and dedication. This will increase harmonisation process of the pooling of the energy.

GENERAL INSTRUCTION FOR HEALING OTHERS:

i. The place to be used for healing should be open, spacious for you to move freely. Strong perfume smells should be avoided. If desirous, one can use incense sticks and light instrumental music; this will create an ambient environment.

ii. It is important that the hands are to be washed before and after doing the healing session.

iii. Tell the person to be healed what you are going to do and if possible show the positions and the body areas, which will be covered. After you have told everything, ask the person to lie down with closed eyes, feet apart and hands on the sides with the palms facing the sky.

iv. Make the person relax first before starting any hand positions.

v. Never touch the body parts of the person to be healed if he does not feel comfortable with the idea. You can also do the healing by keeping your hands one to two inches away from the body.

vi. Never exert force while doing the hand positions on the eyes, throat, ears and other sensitive parts.

vii. Before you begin, ask the person to pray in heart, that he receive the energies send by the healer.

viii. Begin the session by saying the attitude of gratitude given in the book or created by you. Never forget to thank the person you are healing, as he is the one who has given you a chance for healing him.

ix. After the attitude of gratitude, start with the positions for the front part of the body.

x. Have continuous conversation with the person while the healing is being done. Do not worry this will not cut you away from the universal soul or reduce the healing power's.

This conversation will help you to find out how the person is feeling, while he is being healed.

xi. After completing the front part of the body stand near the chest of the person. Spread both your hands in front of you, pray again :

> *I thank thee O universal soul*
> *I thank thee O great Reiki masters*
> *I thank thee O the soul in (person name)*
> *For allowing me to use this universal energy*
> *On the front body parts of person's name*
> *Bless me that I may be able to do the healing*
> *On the back body parts of person's name*

Place the left hand on your heart chakra, with the right hand draw clockwise spirals from the tip of right hand of the person to the right shoulder tips and from there to the right toe of the leg. Chant the following mantra while moving with each of the spirals.

> *I heal thee, You be healed*

Now do the clockwise spiraling from the tip of the left hand of the person to the left shoulder tips and from there to the left toe of the leg.

After completing the spiraling, spread both the hands in front of you and say 'You are healed, all chakras and nadis are balanced'.

Important: While doing the spiraling on the person's body, it is important that the left hand is place on your heart chakra and not removed.

xii. Place your right hand under the head of the person and slowly whisper in his ear, 'Frontal healing is over, please turn over so that the healing on the back is also done'. You can also help the person to turn over.

xiii. Start with the back positions. Continue to do the healing in the same way as done on the frontal part.

xiv. After reaching the last hand position i.e. Back of the Spine, remove both the hands from the body of the person.

xv. Stand near the chest of the person. Place the first finger (ego finger) and the middle finger on the lower part of the neck (back). With force and speed, pull the fingers down from the lower part of the neck to the base of the spine as if drawing a line, simultaneously chant the following mantra:

> **I bow to thee, O universal force,**
> **Heal this person, <u>person's name</u>**
> **Let the chakra get harmonised**
> **Let the nadis get balanced**
> **Peace, Peace, Peace**

Do this for three times.

This process will smoothen out the energy flow between the chakras.

xvi. Again, stand near the chest of the person with the hands spread in front of you. Move the right hand towards the head of the person and the left hand to the feet of the person. The height of the hands from the body should be around 2 to 3 inches.

Slowly sway the right hand over the body towards the heart chakra, simultaneously sway the left hand from the feet towards the heart chakra.

After reaching the heart chakra, sway the right hand again, back to the head and the left hand towards the feet.

Do this for four or five times. This will balance the auric energy around the body.

Join the hands together in the position of namaskar, say the attitude of gratitude, bow down to the soul of the person with full reverence and whisper in the ears of the person that the full body healing is over.

xvii. Never claim to be a healer to an unknown person, as he would not be able to comprehend what you are saying. Even though Reiki has been accepted by many people and is understood to be a very good system of healing without medicines, many people still eye it with suspicion.

xviii. Never diagnose and prescribe medicines unless you are a medical practitioner.

xix. Never do the healing under force, obligation or due to guilt.

You are not a healer but a channel, the energy is received from the universe and through the blessings of the master.

Reiki passes through anything and can work if done in the auric level also. This can include plasters, bandages, walls, doors etc.

STOP, LOOK AND WALK

Walking is a routine affair for us. There are many styles of walking, the true spiritual way of walking can be Stop, look and walk. It is a simple affair yet very difficult to achieve. The method is to

- take the first step, stop
- look what the air is saying, the soles of the shoes are saying, the earth is saying, feel the smooth caress of the air touching you, hear the chirping sounds of birds, crumpled dry leaves under your soles.
- take another step and repeat the process.

You will get more closer to the nature all around which you have ignored for so long.

REIKI II – THE KNOWLEDGE OF TIME AND SPACE

A stage comes when the channel becomes totally aware of his body and the flow of the energy. In Reiki I the channel is provided with a glimpse of the spiritual power of the Reiki. In advanced course the channel is exposed to the energy tapping methods, which could enhance the healing and spiritual practice of the person. This is the stage of self-awareness, the awareness of the energy residing in us the energy of the nature.

From the ancient time, the initiation process was held in secrecy, the major reason was the misuse of the energy. As told earlier each mantra has an effect on the body, soul and the atmosphere, if these symbols are received by some unscrupulous person then the power could be misused. So the great sages created a method of initiation, by which only the initiated person could use the mantra.

In the same manner after getting initiated to Reiki I, the channel has to complete the 21-day cycle before the master could call him up for initiation to the second stage of Reiki or Reiki II. Before initiating the channel from Reiki I to the second stage, the channel is scanned (will be discussed later) and only after finding the channel has progressed upto a certain level the master should initiate the person.

THE SYMBOLS

Reiki symbols like many mystic symbols are sacred and should be revered. These symbols are nothing but simple Kanji script, and for a lay man it does not mean anything more. However, for a person initiated into the second degree, these symbols possess unlimited powers.

Like the correct usage of the mantras gives mystic powers to the user, in the same manner if the channel use the symbols in correct manner then he is sure to get the unlimited power of healing from the super consciousness.

Spiritual Energy of Reiki

HOW THE SYMBOLS WORK

In Reiki II the student is told about three powerful symbols. There are other symbols, which are also taught to the student with their uses. The first three symbols given to the student are part of the Usui method of Reiki teaching, while the others have been drawn from various other religious sources.

When a person is initiated into the second degree of Reiki, he is also told about the method of using these symbols. These symbols should not be used as a casual thing but used in a spiritual and pious manner.

During the attunement, the symbols are imbibed in the subconscious mind as well as with the God consciousness. The symbols become a part of your life and works when called upon. The flow of the energy also varies as per the requirement after the symbols have been used.

In Hindu tradition, the uses of symbols are common for invoking the Gods and asking for boons. In the same manner these symbols act as a key to the opening of the mystic door towards the supra consciousness.

The symbols must be drawn and used correctly to activate them. Reiki channels can meditate on these symbols and receive guidance on how to use them directly and to achieve siddhi over them. Some methods of achieving siddhi from the symbols are given in the meditational section at the end. Thus if concentration is done on the symbols, the channel may be guided with new ways of using the symbols.

How the symbols are to drawn and used.

Three symbols are taught in Reiki-II, they are
(a) Hon Sha Ze Sho Nen
(b) Sei Hei Ki
(c) Cho Ku Rei

Method of drawing the Symbols and the way of using them:
- ❖ Sit in a comfortable position and say the attitude of gratitude.
- ❖ Use first finger with the middle finger or the whole hand to draw the symbols.

Never use the ego/ first finger to draw the symbol. This will attract negative energy.

- ❖ The symbols should be drawn in the following order :
  * Hon Sha Ze Sho Nen
  * Sei Hei Ki
  * Cho Ku Rei

Each time the symbol is drawn the name of the symbol should be repeated three times.

- ❖ The symbols should be practiced in the following methods
  * Start by drawing the symbols with the hands.
  * After getting proficiency in drawing the symbols with hands, practice drawing the symbol with the tongue.
  * After getting proficiency in the above two methods, draw the symbols above your head through the thought process.
  * Now visualise the whole symbol above the head and let it enter through the Sahasrar chakra and let it pass through the Ajna chakra, Vishuddhi chakra and finally settle in the Anahat chakra. From the Anahat chakra let the energy pass to the whole body, especially the finger tips.

- ❖ When you have proficiency in drawing all the three symbols, only do the last stage of practice as given above.

- ❖ After all the symbols are drawn, start with the hands on healing. On every hand positions visualise the three symbols and repeat the name of the symbol thrice. This will help in energising your healing many folds. Each of the symbols can also be used separately or in conjunction with one another.

Spiritual Energy of Reiki

HON SHA ZE SHO NEN

Hon – lines 1-5, Sha- lines 6-7, Ze- 8-14 Sho- 15-16, Nen- 17-21

This is first symbol used by the Reiki channel to be connected with the universal soul. Hon Sha Ze Sho Nen means No Past, No Present and No Future. As per the book of P.G. O'Neill, 'Essential Kanji', Hon Sha Ze Sho Nen means

Hon : unit for counting, origin

Sha : person

Ze : right or just

Sho: correct, exactly, certainly

Nen: idea, wish, thought

All this can be summarised as the origin of the light that flows in the right direction for the benefit and right purpose of the person.

This light is the universal energy, which we are connected to, in short we can say "The God in me greets the God in you". As the soul is existing in all the beings and this soul is nothing but the representation of the God.

The method of drawing this symbol has been shown in the second diagram. Draw the symbol once and repeat the name thrice.

The pronunciation of the symbol is **Hohn Shah Zey Show Nain**, the method of repeating the name of the symbol should be in the heart.

After continuous, meditation on the symbol gave me the realisation as to the actual meaning of the symbol. The whole symbol represents the Kundalini awakening cycle, Hon symbol represents the Sahasrar chakra, Ajna chakra and the Vishuddhi chakra. Sha represents the Anahat chakra, Ze represents the Manipura chakra and the Nen represents the Swadhisthana chakra, Mooladhara chakra.

This symbol is used for:

- ❖ To do distant healing by Reiki healing energy.
- ❖ This symbol can be used to send energy in the past or future for healing past traumas and experiences.
- ❖ You can send this symbol for healing even the dead people for releasing their traumas.

Spiritual Energy of Reiki

SEI HEI KI

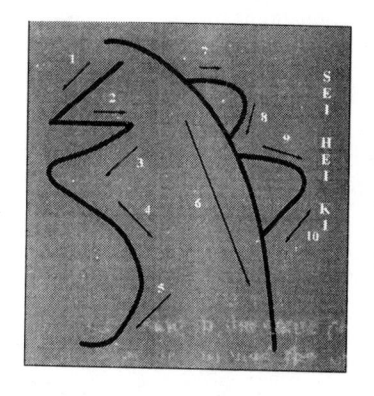

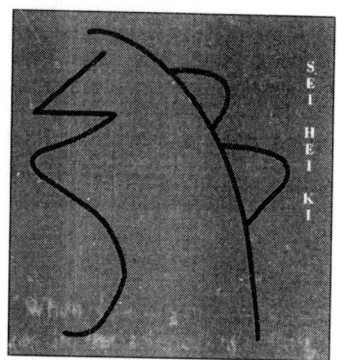

This is second symbol used by the Reiki channel. Sei Hei Ki is the symbol used for emotional and mental healing.

Sei : state of embryo, correct form

Hei : shine, light

Ki : Spirit, unseen force

Sei Hei Ki means Man's is Brahma. In Indian scriptures, also there are references to the sloka 'Aham Brahma Asmi' meaning 'I am Brahma'. One can become Brahma only when he is emotionally in love with the supreme power. If you see the Sufi dancing to the songs of the Supreme Being, you will be astonished by the aura and energy developed by them.

If you meditate on the symbol, you will realise that the line 6 represents the spinal column and the curved lines 7-8 and 9-10 correlate with the Anahat chakra and the Manipura chakra. The other lines represent the front part of the body with the aura circles. The best time for meditating on this symbol is in the early morning.

This symbol is used for:

- ❖ For emotional and mental healing
- ❖ For balancing the left and right brain, bringing in peace and harmony.
- ❖ For improving memory
- ❖ For enhancing the use of the affirmations, healing unwanted habits and also for improving relationships.
- ❖ This symbol is very useful for pregnant mothers, psycho-somatic patients and neurological problems.

Spiritual Energy of Reiki

CHO KU REI

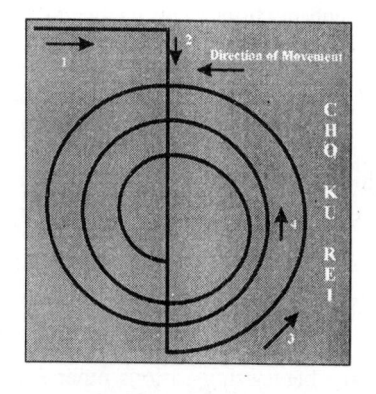

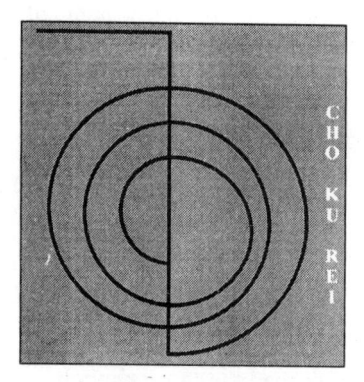

Cho : curved sword

Ku : shine, light

Rei : ghost or soul

To summarise we can say Cho Ku Rei means 'To bring the power here'. In the above both the diagrams the symbol is drawn in anti-clockwise direction, the symbol can be drawn in the clockwise direction also. The clockwise drawn symbol helps in removing the bad karma and the anti-clockwise drawn symbol helps in removing the obstacles and also helps in energising the other symbols.

When I meditated on this symbol, I realised that the symbol showed the awakening of the Kundalini. The three and half coils representing the Kundalini energy sleeping in the three and half coil and the central line represents the spinal column, which is the path for it to raise. The horizontal line 1 represents the Ajna chakra.

This symbol is used for:

- ❖ For increasing the power of other symbols.
- ❖ To stop the leaking of the energy flow between the healer and the client.
- ❖ To manifest the desire and wants in conjunction with other symbols.
- ❖ It removes the negativity in the room and protects the healer from attracting the negative energy while healing the client.
- ❖ When Cho Ku Rei symbol is drawn with both the hands, it is called the **double Cho Ku Rei**. This doubles the power of the symbol.

Other than the three symbols, we have been using various other symbols for spiritual development and healing purposes. These symbols have been drawn from various religious sources and have been used in rituals for ages. Most ancient traditions had their own symbols for worshipping like ancient Egyptians, Sumerians, Indus valley civilizations, Mesopotamian civilization worshipped the Sun God. The symbols varied from places to places and the method of drawing these symbols also changed from time to time. Many of the ancient symbols have been lost in the mysterious realm of time.

If some readers would like to know more about the symbols and their methodology, they should contact the author in person. Many of these symbols can be used only after being initiated into the process.

Meditational Techniques with Reiki 1 & 2

❖ **SANDWICH ENERGY**

* This is a very powerful technique for healing a person and also to achieve any goals set by you. This technique should be used only after getting full practice in all the individual symbols. When one symbol is drawn between two symbols then we release powerful energy, which is useful. Some combinations can be

    ◆ Hon Sha Ze Sho Nen + Sei Hei Ki + Cho Ku Rei

    ◆ Cho Ku Rei + Sei Hei Ki + Cho Ku Rei

    ◆ Cho Ku Rei + Hon Sha Ze Sho Nen+ Cho Ku Rei

* The methods of drawing these symbols are one after the other. Visualise the symbols flowing from your third eye chakra to the person to be healed repeating the names of the symbols thrice.

* Depending on the requirement of the person the symbols are sandwiched for example

    ◆ For treating people who are having psychosomatic problems, it is important to energise the emotional symbol. The combination which can be used is by first drawing the Hon Sha Ze Sho Nen + Cho Ku Rei + Sei Hei Ki + Cho Ku Rei, and let the symbols be send to the heart chakra and the third eye chakra of the person. This will help the heart chakra to be healed and will balance the chakra between the heart chakra and third eye chakra. This method is also good for curing people with tension, depression etc.

    ◆ For treating people with sexual disorders, the three major chakras are to be balanced (Mooladhara chakra, Swadhisthana chakra, and Vishuddhi chakra). Visualise the symbols in the following sequence for the respective chakras.

- ◆ Mooladhara Chakra : Cho Ku Rei + Sei Hei Ki + Cho Ku Rei
- ◆ Swadhisthana Chakra : Hon Sha Ze Sho Nen + Cho Ku Rei + Hon Sha Ze Sho Nen
- ◆ Vishuddhi Chakra : Sei Hei Ki + Hon Sha Ze Sho Nen + Sei Hei Ki

* Let these symbols from your heart chakra to the three chakras of the affected person and you will see that there is quite a improvement in the problem.

❖ **MIRROR ENERGY :**

* There are two method of doing this methodology

- ◆ Sit in front of the mirror with feet on a rug. Draw required symbols with both the hands. While drawing, the symbols remember to use both the hands in a synchronised manner and repeat the names of the symbols thrice. This will increase your healing power multifold.

- ◆ The second method is to draw the symbols with both the hands, thus the symbols drawn will be exactly mirror opposite.

- ◆ The process of sending this energy is simple either visualise that the concerned person is being bathed in the energy or spread your hands in front (palms cupped position) and let the energy travel from your hand in the sky to reach the person. If you want to use this energy for yourself just cup your hands and let the energy flow towards the heart.

Tip: Drawing of the symbols while moving the hands front and back helps to energise the aura and removes the obstacles in the flow of the energy.

Use of Symbols for healing other people:

❖ HANDS ON HEALING WITH SYMBOLS

* After the client has been made comfortable, draw the symbols as per the instructions given in '**Method of drawing the Symbols and the way of using them**'.

* The method for healing is similar to the one that has been explained in the Reiki I section.

* For every hand position, draw the symbol once repeat the name thrice.

❖ DISTANT HEALING

* This is a powerful medium of healing people who are at a distance, the steps for healing are :

* Transformation

♦ Sit in a comfortable position with closed eyes. Breathe deeply, until totally relaxed.

♦ Visualise the person who is to be healed. Each feature of the person should be clearly visible. Now let the body of the person become you. Your body becomes the body of the person to be healed.

♦ Say the attitude of gratitude replacing your name with the person to be healed.

♦ Start the hands on healing exercises as has been given in Reiki I section but with the symbols.

* Photograph

♦ Place the photograph in front of you and start the healing as you would be doing while doing hands on healing with other person.

♦ Instructions on the type of photograph to be used are given in the section on '**Healing the Dead**'.

* **Dummy**
  - Take a pillow or a toy and visualise that the toy/ pillow is the whole body of the person to be healed.
  - Start the hands on healing exercises as has been given in Reiki I section but with the symbols.

* **Timed Healing**
  - Ask the person to be healed to lie down on the bed at a specific time with eyes closed, legs and hands apart. At the instructed time, visualise the person on the bed with the position as specified by you.
  - Start with the attitude of gratitude.
  - Draw the symbols Hon Sha Ze Sho Nen, Sei Hei Ki and Cho Ku Rei, in the order mentioned. Send the symbols in the sky and visualise that the person concerned is receiving the symbols. Go on sending the energy symbols and mentally do the hands on healing to the person.

❖ **PROGRAMMING THE ENERGY**
  * This method is useful in cases where the client requires healing session throughout the day. The procedure for doing this type of healing is:
  * Sit in a comfortable position in a meditative mood.
  * After saying the attitude of gratitude, visualise fully the person requiring the continuous healing session.
  * Visualise the clock with the current time and date, merge the image with the image of the person. Start your healing session, as you would normally do. At the start of every position visualise the current time and date, when you finish the position visualise the time and date till which you want the healing to continue automatically. Continue this process for all the body positions. I have personally done this method and had very good success in it.

❖ HEALING THE DEAD

* This method is very helpful in treating the karmic deeds of the dead person. This certainly does not mean that all the bad karma done by the dead person will be resolved but it will certainly reduce the effects of it.

* There are two ways of healing the dead person, we will do both the methods of healing the karma's. The first method involves the usage of a photograph of the deceased person and in the second method, there is usage of the visualisation technique.

❖ First Method

◆ The photograph to be used for the healing should be

* Full length with all the features visible

* If full-length photograph is not available then the following procedure can used for making it a full photograph.

* Suppose the photograph is covering portion upto the waist, then place your left hand on your heart and the right hand on the waist portion of the photograph and close your eyes. Slowly lower your right hand from the photograph visualising that the portion you are moving your hand is being converted into the limbs and legs. Chant the following mantra while moving the hands:

'Oh universal light help me to transform the photograph of (deceased persons name) into the being he was, fill him with the full features all the limbs and parts of the body'.

When you feel that the whole photograph is complete remove the left hand from the heart and place both the hands on the photograph and say: *'Thank you, Oh universal light for helping me in doing what, I required. Let the energy keep flowing in the photograph till, I may be able to complete the healing'*.

- Sit in a comfortable position with closed eyes. Place the photograph in the centre of a piece of cloth (preferably maroon/ red/ violet/ orange in colour).

- Start with the attitude of gratitude as given below

  I thank myself (name............) for being here

  thank the cosmic that is Reiki for being here

  I thank my parents (names............) for being in my Life

  I thank my Guru (name............) for being in my life

  I thank my God (name............) for always being in my life

  I thank my all the Reiki masters for their loved blessing

  I thank (deceased person's name) for allowing me to heal his karmic deeds.

- Visualise a pyramid around the place you and the photograph is kept. The pyramid should be orange/maroon in colour. You should be able to visualise that you are sitting inside the pyramid and the pyramid is absorbing the energy emitting from the universe.

- Place both your hands on the photograph. Open your eyes and concentrate on the third eye of the person in photograph. Continuously draw Hon Sha Ze Sho Nen, Sei Hei Ki and Cho Ku Rei mentally and let it float inside the pyramid. After a certain period, you will feel vibrations flowing from your fingertips. Now first draw Cho Ku Rei, Sei Hei Ki and lastly Hon Sho Ze Sho Nen and send the energy symbols to the third eye of the deceased persons photograph. Chant the following mantra "Oh universal lord, Let all the traumas of (deceased person's name) be released and absorbed by the energy pyramid. Sealing all the negativity with it.... Thank You".

- ◆ Go on sending the energy symbols, until you feel coolness spreading in the pyramid you are sitting in. The coolness has been experienced by many Reiki channels as white light filling the pyramid. Remove both your hands from the photograph.

- ◆ The healing for the deceased is complete. Say the attitude of gratitude and sit down with closed eyes. Spread your hands (palms facing the sky) in the air as if expelling the force around you and say :

- ◆ "Thank you for the help given to me for healing the traumas of the deceased person (persons name). I am also thankful to the energy-pyramid for absorbing the traumas of the deceased person and also for protecting me from the negative forces." Bow down with reverence and join the hands in the namaskar posture.

- ◆ Open your eyes and relax.

REIKI BOX

❖ This is a unique method of manifesting the needs. These needs can be materialistic, spiritualistic or achieving the goals set by you. These needs are miraculously satisfied within the specific period.

❖ For doing this method you would require

* a air tight container, the container should be clean & dry.

* a piece of writing paper

* a pencil (preferably with a orange/ maroon lead)

❖ The method of creating a Reiki box :

* Light some incense sticks and let the perfume spread in the room.

* Sit comfortably in a position. On the piece of paper, write down the needs or requirement or an affirmation.

* Say the Attitude of gratitude and add the following line of gratitude :

I thank the desire (affirmation/needs written on the paper) for allowing me heal

* Fold the paper and keep the paper tightly between both the hands. Mentally draw Hon Sha Se Sho Nen, Sei Hei Ki and Cho Ku Rei and send the energy symbols to the hands and pray for the fulfillment of the desire written by you.

* Keeping the affirmation paper in one hand, take the airtight container on the other hand in such a way that the centre of the container is in the palm. Mentally draw

Spiritual Energy of Reiki

Hon Sha Se Sho Nen, Sei Hei Ki and Cho Ku Rei and send the energy symbols to the hands and pray for the fulfillment of the desire written by you.

* Go on sending the energy symbols to the hands, put the paper in the container and close the lid. Hold the container in the both the hands and repeat the process of sending the Hon Sha Se Sho Nen, Sei Hei Ki and Cho Ku Rei to the box.

* The Reiki box is ready. Give the energy to it once or twice to in a day. You can also programme the energy sending.

❖ **Tips for Reiki Box :**

* Before writing the affirmation/ needs on the piece of the paper, say the attitude of gratitude. Draw the symbol Hon Sha Ze Sho Nen on the top of the paper, Sei Hei Ki on the left side of the paper and Cho Ku Rei on the right side of the paper. In the centre of the paper write the affirmation/ need.

* Crystals can also be put in the container with the affirmation/needs as crystals have the potency to absorb any energy send to it. More of crystals will be discussed in later section on crystals.

Remember! Only one affirmation should be kept in one Reiki box. Multiple Reiki boxes can be created and combined healing can be given to it.

GROUP HEALING

Group healing is a very important and useful technique available to the Reiki channel after being attuned for Reiki II.

Before group healing is done, the following details of the people to be treated are to be known:

Name of the person

Date of Birth

Male/Female

Diseases for which the cure is required

Number of years suffering the diseases

Time of the day when the person is free

If the above details are received in the person's own handwriting the better, will be the process for healing.

Sit in a comfortable place and place all the details of the people to be healed in front of you and say the attitude of gratitude in the following way:

I thank for Reiki being here
I thank all the gurus and masters of Reiki
I thank myself for being here
I thank (person's name, sex, and age) for allowing me heal him

(Repeat the last line of Attitude of gratitude for every individual)

I thank all the people for allowing me heal them

Place both the hands on the requests for distant healing and mentally visualise a universal white light entering the room, in which you are sitting and covering you to form a cocoon. Mentally send Hon Sha Se Sho Nen, Sei Hei Ki and Cho Ku Rei in the sequence one after the other in the space repeating the name of the symbols thrice.

In a hush tone repeat the time mentioned in the request form with the name of the person and in the end visualise all the different time mentioned merging into the time of your healing session. Even during the process of mentioning the time and the name of the person to be healed, visualise the symbols being sent to the request forms.

If the healer knows the person then the healing will be strong if the person is visualised.

Visualise the symbols one by one entering the crown chakra and passing through the third eye chakra, throat chakra to reach the heart chakra. Visualise the energy symbols flowing from the heart chakra to reach the heart chakras of the persons to be healed. Let the energy so sent travel to the diseased area and heal the portion. Go on sending the energy till you feel a coolness surrounding you.

When the coolness surrounds you then you know the healing has been received. After this say the attitude of gratitude and bow in reverence to the people for allowing you the opportunity to heal them.

The more distant healing is done the better will be the sensation received. The hands and the heart chakra tell the response of your healing sessions. The feelings and sensations vary from person to person and thus it cannot be described.

What if all the details of the person to be healed are not known then the following process can be used.

While saying the attitude of gratitude, say the following stanzas:

Oh lord, help me to heal the person concerned,

I donot know much of the person to be healed,

Let the universal energy direct me to it,

Thank you Oh lord, Oh lord.

Let the healing flow through the time and space to heal the person, state, country, world and the universe

REIKI IIIA & IIIB – MASTERSHIP

No knowledge is complete without the knowledge of spreading.

During any process of learning there are three stages of development for the student

- First stage is the process of gaining the knowledge in which the student is more or less the recipient of knowledge. In this stage, the student accepts whatever is told to him without questioning much.

- Second stage is the process of expansion of the knowledge received. In this stage, the student expands the knowledge base through a process of question answer session. This stage has twin benefits :

    * Student is motivated to ask more and more questions, so that he is able to get satisfaction from the knowledge received by him.

    * The guru is able to determine the development and initiative of the student for considering the next level of teaching and initiation.

- Third stage is when the guru accepts in his heart that the student has developed to a level where he can be taught the secrets of initiation and happily hands over the reins of the knowledge to his disciple for spreading the knowledge so attained.

In the same way the Reiki Channel is in the first stage when he is taught the Reiki I and in the second stage when he is attuned for Reiki II. When the Master feels that the Reiki channel has progressed to a level where he is eligible for the knowledge of the Reiki III, the channel reaches the third stage.

Soul Searchers The Art of Breathing

Like a tree laden with fruits stoops down so does a sadhaka with true knowledge

- Aghoree Pinardika

Traditionally the knowledge was passed on to the student through two ways: one was a process of oral learning which began at a very early age and when the teacher finds the student suitable for higher learning, he was given the shaktipata and many new things were subconsciously included into the students mind.

In ancient times when a pupil went for learning this spiritual science, he had to study for years before he was able to consider himself a healer. They used to practice this science for hours together to gain the power to heal a person without even blinking their eyes. During that, time the number of people who were taught this science were few in numbers and this science was kept a secret not to be revealed to an unworthy one.

It was only after the rediscovery of this lost science that it was taught to every person who requested for it. Every endeavour is being made to make this science known to every man on this earth, so that we have a big family of healers and channels in this world.

In the mastership stage, one more symbol is taught to the student other than the three symbols already taught to the students in the second stage of Reiki.

Eight Fold paths as told by Gautam the Buddha :-

1. Right understanding
2. Right aspiration
3. Right speech
4. Right conduct
5. Right vocation
6. Right effort
7. Right alertness
8. Right concentration

Spiritual Energy of Reiki

DAI KO MYO

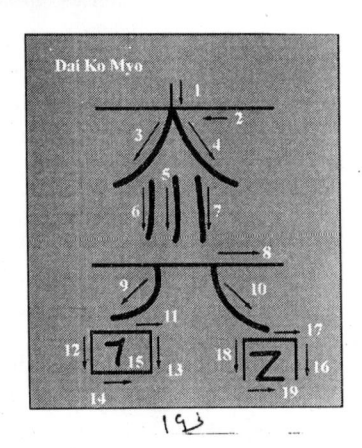

Dai Ko Myo can be simply said as the great universal light of energy. This energy can be translated as the light of true knowledge, the knowledge of enlightenment.

When a bud blossoms into a flower, it becomes responsible for spreading the fragrance that has been in its fold. A flower that does not spread its fragrance is like a dead flower. In the same way a person who wants to do the mastership should take the responsibility upon himself for the spreading the knowledge without falling into the trap of business profitability. This spiritual science should spread a fragrance and not spread the hatred. The knowledge should be given to the person who deserves and should not be distributed for gaining monetary benefits.

When a person has been trained for the mastership, he gains the knowledge for transmission of this science to others.

Any person who has been trained in Reiki I, II, III A & B (Mastership) can give attunements for Reiki I, Reiki II and Mastership.

205

PRE-REQUISITES FOR TRAINING IN THE ABOVE STAGES

- Before a person is attuned for Reiki I
  * The person should be checked for the ability to sustain the attunement process. If a person is not strong enough to withstand the attunement process, he should be started with the hands on healing process till such period of time that he is able to sustain the attunement process.
  * The unevenness of the aura should be balanced before the attunement process.
  * The body should be scanned for finding out the method of attunement to be used for the person.
- After the Reiki I the channel must practice continuously for the first 21 days and after that he should also start healing others.
- Before a channel is attuned for Reiki II, the following things are important to check
  * The Reiki I channel is able to sense the subtle energies flowing around his body.
  * The Reiki I channel is able to sense the subtle energies flowing around the person he is healing.
  * The Reiki I channel is able to understand the inflow and out flow of the energies.
- After a channel is attuned for Reiki II
  * He should practice for another 21 days with the symbols provided to him so that he is able to feel the flow of the energies inside the body
  * He should also practice the symbols while doing hands on healing for others and should try to sense the flow of the energies inside the body of the healee.
  * He should practice distant healing with the symbols for as many people as possible.

Spiritual Energy of Reiki

❖ Before a channel is attuned for Reiki III A & B (Mastership)

* The channel should be well versed in the hands on healing as well as the distant healing.

* The channel should be able to scan and find out the diseases of the person with ease.

* He should be able to visualise the symbols without the breaks.

* His auric energy should be balanced to a great extend.

* He should be able to take upon the responsibility which the mastership grants.

Attunement process

Attunement process for Reiki I, II, IIIA & III B (Mastership)

ॐ

Attunement process is a spiritual experience, which can only be felt and not expressed in words. For attunement process, it is important that both the master and the pupil should be in peace and harmony.

The master can achieve success in his endeavour for passing on the knowledge to the pupil only when he has cleansed himself of the tamo guna. Master should practice the techniques regularly for gaining optimum energy and also, to get in smooth flow of energy.

Before the attunement process of a new person, it is important that the master has done the aura scanning of the person and also decide the method of energy transmission.

On the day of the attunement, it is important that the master should get up early morning (preferably during the Brahma muhurata), sit facing north direction, and do meditation. After that, he should visualise all the persons who are to be attuned and seek the blessings of the lord, guru, and parents.

Items required for the attunement process:
- Room with ventilation and enough space for moving about.
- One chair
- A rug / carpet preferably a cotton/ wool one
- Some incense sticks and a incense holder

Desirable items
- A small idol of the lord.
- Photographs of the guru, Reiki masters.
- A lighted til (Sesame seed) oil lamp made of clay.
- A light instrumental music

PRIMER FOR THE ATTUNEMENT PROCESS

❖ Some Do's and Don'ts

* Never do the attunement for the purpose of materialistic gains only.

* Never start the workshop without cleansing the room of the negative energies (process has been given later in this section)

* Close your eyes and pray for few minutes for success in the process of training the people in the spiritual art of Reiki.

* If possible place the idol of the lord with the photographs of the guru and the Reiki masters on a table and light the lamp with 'til' (sesame seed) oil. Light some incense sticks and place it near the idol of the lord. Bow in reverence before the idol and photographs and seek their blessings.

* For Reiki I class explain the students about the History of Reiki, Original Masters of Reiki and all the other information given in the Reiki I section. People should be made to practice all the hand positions, so that they become conversant with the positions (both self and healing others).

* For Reiki II class, explain the students about the process of distant healing, group healing technique, symbols, and other details as explained in the Reiki II section.

* For the mastership, explain the third symbol and the method of attunement for the Reiki I, Reiki II and Mastership.

* Never start the attunement process without first explaining the parts of the body that will be touched and telling the person of the various experiences he might feel while the attunement is being done.

* Never do the attunement before calming the minds of the people so that they become receptive and the process of attunement is successful.

* While doing the attunement it is important to follow the following instructions :
  - ◆ For every person say the **Attitude of Gratitude** and take deep breaths before starting the attunement.
  - ◆ During the whole process of attunement, the breath should be held and the tip of the tongue should touch the palate.
  - ◆ The mind should only be filled with the spiritual thoughts during the attunement process. The moment any other thoughts enter the mind the process of attunement should be restarted after asking for the forgiveness of the spiritual energies and sealing yourself.
  - ◆ Complete the process of attunement for one person before proceeding to the next person.

A person who controls the breath controls the mind,

A person who controls the mind controls the world

A person who controls the world controls the heart

METHOD OF ATTUNEMENT

The attunement process used by me is a combination of the Usui and the special Tibetan technique. Reiki originated in Tibet, therefore, the use of the Tibetan technique and symbols create a stronger connection with the origins of Reiki. I did the addition of the Tibetan attunement technique to the Usui system, this has greatly improved the attunement process, and the benefits are manifold.

<u>IMPORTANT</u>: *<u>No person should try to do attunement process given in this section without getting proper training in the tantric rituals as it will give both physical and mental trauma to the person.</u>*

- ❖ After calming the mind of the person who has to be attuned and the person is asked to sit on the chair with closed eyes.
  - ✻ I make sure that the person does not cross his legs while sitting as it cancels the flow of the energy.
  - ✻ If a cotton rug is available, place the rug under the feet of the person to be attuned.
- ❖ After the person is comfortable, ask the person to sit with hands in namaskar position and pray.
  - ✻ The prayer should be done in heart to the universal soul for helping in receiving the attunement in a proper manner. Donot start the attunement process unless and until the person is deeply engrossed in prayer.
- ❖ When the person is in prayer position, I close my eyes, spread my hands towards the sky, and pray for the successful completion of the attunement and cleanse the room of the negativity.

Spiritual Energy of Reiki

* After lighting the incense sticks, the following attitude of gratitude is said in heart :

O lord, help me to attune them with your energy
O lord, I thank you for giving me this science
I thank myself (name...) for being here
I thank the cosmic that is Reiki for being here
I thank my parents (names....) for being in my Life
I thank my Guru (name....) for being in my life
I thank my God (name...) for always being in my life
I thank my all the Reiki masters for there loved blessing
I thank (name of the person to be attuned) for being here.

* After saying the attitude of gratitude, I bow down to the idol of the lord, bow down to the person to be attuned. After bowing down, I go around the person thrice in anti-clockwise direction sealing the person from any negativity in the room.

* From the four corners of the room, I create a pyramid covering the person to be attuned with myself. At this moment, I visualise that the white universal light is entering the room and covering the room with its cool and rejuvenating energy.

* After this process I touch the third eye of the person with the first and middle finger and invoke the blessing of Goddess saying the following mantra

A' Aah' E' Eeh' Oo' Ooh' Shr' Shr' Lrih' Aey' Aaey' O' Ouh' Am' Amh' K' Kh' G' Gha' Dm' Ch' Cha' Ja' Jha' Tr' Ta' Tha' Da' Dha' Na' T' Th' D' Dhha' Na Pa Fa Ba' Bha' Ma Ya Ra' La' Va' S' Sha' Sa' Ha' La' Sh' hum phat

I let the fingers slide down the face, chest, abdomen, thighs, knees, ankles, feet and touch the fingers on the earth.

Note :

1. The right hand fingers should be used for touching the third eye of the person.
2. The left hand during the whole process should be on the heart and the tongue should touch the palate while reciting the mantra.
3. Breathing should be held for reciting the mantra for the first seven times.
4. While sliding the fingers down the body of the person, only the aura of the person should be touched and not the physical part of the body.

❖ While keeping the fingers on the earth, I repeat the same mantra 21 times.

 * The breathing should be held for the first seven times and in the second set of repetition breathing should be done very slowly. In the last set of recitation the breathing should be heavy and fast.
 * After finishing the 21 rounds of mantra, I go around the person three more times in anti-clockwise direction and bow down to the person.
 * While still keeping the tongue on the palate I recite the following mantra

   Om Ah Hum Om Ah Hum Om Ah Hum

   and blow out the breath from the mouth with full force on the heart chakra of the person to be attuned.
 * Spread my hands in prayer position in front with the palms facing the sky.

The above used techniques are common for all the three levels i.e. Reiki I, Reiki II and Mastership.

Shining of the jewel only occurs after polishing and cutting, In the same manner polishing of the inner self brings forth the true beauty of the nature.

Spiritual Energy of Reiki

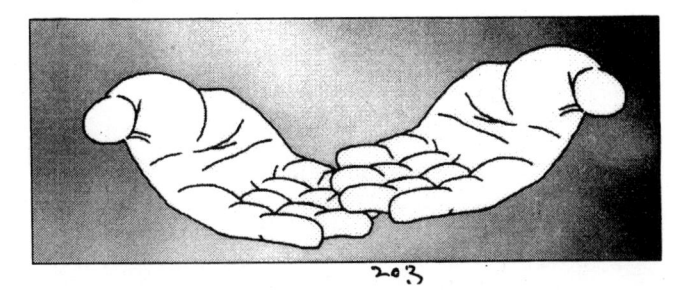

PROCESS FOR REIKI I ATTUNEMENT

I) After saying the prayer for invocation of the goddesses of Kundalini, I bow down again.

II) I move behind the person in the anti-clockwise direction.

III) After placing the right hand over the head of the person at a distance of about two to three inches, the following symbols are drawn in sequence

Dai Ko Myo
Cho Ku Rei
Hon Sha Ze Sho Nen
Sei Hei Ki

While drawing the symbols, the names of the symbols are repeated 3 times mentally.

IV) Moving in front of the person and both the palms of the person are cupped and the names of the person are chanted in the following order.

Dai Ko Myo
Cho Ku Rei
Hon Sha Ze Sho Nen
Sei Hei Ki

V) While still cupping the palms of the person, both the hands are raised in such a manner that the thumbs of the palms are eight inches in front of the third eye chakra.

VI) Now the breath is inhaled from the mouth as if drawing the energy from the universe itself. The breath so inhaled is deep and the following mantra is mentally recited for seven times

Om Ah Hum

With the energy of the prana blow on the heart chakra by saying Cho

VII) Repeat the step (VI) and blow on the third eye chakra by saying Ku.

VIII) Repeat the step (VI) and blow from the heart chakra to the third eye chakra saying Rei.

IX) The hands of the person are put back in the namaskar position, thumbs touching the heart chakra.

X) In the same position the fingers are cupped again, Cho Ku Rei is drawn mentally, and the same name is repeated thrice. Right hand is used for cupping the fingers while the left hand is used to hold the wrist.

XI) After this round I thank the person and pray with closed eyes. After this stage, I allow the person to stay in the bliss for a period of two to three minutes.

2nd round

XII) After two or three minutes, I again say the attitude of gratitude and go behind the person in the anti-clockwise direction. I pray again with the hands spread out in front. The right hand is placed on the persons head at a distance of about two to three inches and the left hand is held up in sky.

XIII) Mentally visualise that the energy is flowing from the left hand and the same is being passed on the right hand draw

Dai Ko Myo
Hon Sha Ze Sho Nen
Sei Hei Ki
Cho Ku Rei

While drawing the symbols, the names of the symbols are repeated 3 times mentally.

XIV) After the symbols are drawn press the forehead and the back of the head slightly and repeat the names of the symbols in the sequence drawn.

XV) After doing this process, I again repeat the spiritual mantra

Om Ah Hum

seven times and move in front of the person in anti-clockwise direction.

3rd round

XVI) Make the person sit namaskar position

XVII) I again say the attitude of gratitude and go behind the person in the anti-clockwise direction. I pray again with the hands spread out in front. The right hand is placed on the persons head at a distance of about two to three inches and the left hand is held up in sky.

XVIII) Mentally visualise that the energy is flowing from the left hand and the same is being passed on the right hand draw

Dai Ko Myo
Cho Ku Rei

While drawing the symbols, the names of the symbols are repeated 3 times mentally.

XIX) After the symbols are drawn the temple of the person is pressed with both hands and the names of the symbols are repeated in the sequence drawn.

XX) After coming in front of the person, inhale deeply from the mouth as if drawing the energy from the universe itself. The breath so inhaled is deep and the following mantra is mentally recited for seven times

Om Ah Hum

With the energy of the prana blow on the heart chakra by saying Cho

XXI) Repeat the step (XX) and blow on the third eye chakra by saying Ku.

XXII) Repeat the step (XX) and blow from the heart chakra to the third eye chakra saying Rei.

XXIII) Touch the third eye chakra with the first finger and the middle finger and again repeat the names of symbols Dai Ko Myo, Cho Ko Rei, Hon Sha Ze Sho Nen and Sei Hei Ki three times.

XXIV) After this round I thank the person and pray with closed eyes. After this stage, I allow the person to stay in the bliss for a period of two to three minutes.

4th round

XXV) Make the person sit namaskar position

XXVI) I again say the attitude of gratitude and go behind the person in the anti-clockwise direction. I pray again with the hands spread out in front. The right hand is placed on the persons head at a distance of about two to three inches and the left hand is held up in sky.

Mentally visualise that the energy is flowing from the left hand and the same is being passed on the right hand draw

Dai Ko Myo
Cho Ku Rei

While drawing the symbols, the names of the symbols are repeated 3 times mentally.

After the symbols are drawn come to the right side of the person and place your right hand over the third eye chakra and the left hand over the back of the head in such a manner so that the fingers of the left hand overlaps the right hand.

XXVII) Chant the names of the symbols

Dai Ko Myo
Cho Ku Rei
Hon Sha Ze Sho Nen
Sei Hei Ki

And visualise the symbols flowing from you to the third eye chakra and crown chakra of the person.

XXVIII) Again coming to the back of the person circling the person in the anti-clockwise direction. Place the right hand over the head of the person at a distance of two to three inches and draw the following symbols

Dai Ko Myo
Cho Ku Rei
Hon Sha Ze Sho Nen
Sei Hei Ki

Repeat the names of the symbols as you draw them.

XXIX) After coming in front of the person, inhale deeply from the mouth as if drawing the energy from the universe itself. The breath so inhaled is deep and the following mantra is mentally recited for seven times

Om Ah Hum

With the energy of the prana blow on the heart chakra by saying Cho

XXX) Repeat the step (XXIX) and blow on the third eye chakra by saying Ku.

XXXI) Repeat the step (XXIX) and blow from the heart chakra to the third eye chakra saying Rei.

XXXII) Touch the third eye chakra with the first finger and the middle finger and again repeat the names of symbols Dai Ko Myo, Cho Ko Rei, Hon Sha Ze Sho Nen and Sei Hei Ki three times.

XXXIII) After this round I thank the person and pray with closed eyes. After this stage, I allow the person to stay in the bliss for a period of two to three minutes.

XXXIV) I open the arms of the person and cross them in such a way to form a cross.

XXXV) After the attunement process is complete, I bow down and say the attitude of gratitude again.

Reiki I attunement has the more steps compared to Reiki II as it is important to open up the basic chakras of the person in the Reiki I level, in Reiki II the minor chakras with the upper three major chakras are opened up.

ATTUNEMENT PROCESS FOR REIKI II

I) After saying the prayer for invocation of the goddesses of Kundalini, I bow down again.

II) I move behind the person in the anti-clockwise direction.

III) After placing the right hand over the head of the person at a distance of about two to three inches, the following symbols are drawn in sequence

Dai Ko Myo
Cho Ku Rei
Hon Sha Ze Sho Nen
Sei Hei Ki

While drawing the symbols, the names of the symbols are repeated 3 times mentally.

IV) After drawing the symbols I move to the front of the person in anti-clockwise direction.

V) Spread both the arms of the person to the height of your heart and hold the palms face up holding them by the wrists. Close the eyes and chant the following mantra

Om Svabhava Shuddhah Sarva Dharmah Svabhava Shuddho Ham Om Rudraye Phat Om Rudraye Phat Om Rudraye Phat

The tongue should touch the palate with breath held, while chanting the mantra. Breathing should be done only after chanting of the mantra. After the mantra has been chanted for seven times blow the on both the palms.

VI) Place the left palm of the person on his heart chakra and hold the right palm with the left hand and draw the symbol Hon Sha Ze Sho Nen with the first and middle finger and tap the palm three times repeating the names of the symbol.

VII) Holding the right hand, draw the symbol Sei Hei Ki and the tap the palm three times repeating the names of the symbols.

VIII) Holding the right hand, draw the symbol Cho Ku Rei and the tap the palm three times repeating the names of the symbols.

IX) Place the right palm on the heart chakra and hold the left palm with the right hand and draw the symbol Hon Sha Ze Sho Nen with the first and middle finger and tap the palm three times repeating the names of the symbol.

X) Holding the left hand, draw the symbol Sei Hei Ki and the tap the palm three times repeating the names of the symbols.

XI) Holding the left hand, draw the symbol Cho Ku Rei and the tap the palm three times repeating the names of the symbols.

XII) Place both the hands back in namaskar position, cup the hands and draw the Cho Ku Rei, Hon Sha Ze Sho Nen, Sei Hei Kei symbols on the finger tips.

XIII) Chant the names of the four symbols in the order Dai Ko Myo, Cho Ku Rei, Hon Sha Ze Sho Nen, Sei Hei Ki. While still cupping the palms of the person, both the hands are raised in such a manner that the thumbs of the palms are eight inches in front of the third eye chakra.

XIV) Now the breath is inhaled from the mouth as if drawing the energy from the universe itself. The breath so inhaled is deep and the following mantra is mentally recited for seven times

Om Ah Hum

XV) With the energy of the prana blow on the heart chakra by saying Cho

XVI) Repeat the step (XIV) and blow on the third eye chakra by saying Ku.

XVII) Repeat the step (XIV) and blow from the heart chakra to the third eye chakra saying Rei.

XVIII) After this round I thank the person and pray with closed eyes. After this stage, I allow the person to stay in the bliss for a period of two to three minutes.

XIX) I open the arms of the person and cross them in such a way to form a cross.

XX) After the attunement process is complete, I bow down and say the attitude of gratitude again.

Attunement process for Reiki III A and B

I) After saying the prayer for invocation of the goddesses of Kundalini, I bow down again.

II) I move behind the person in the anti-clockwise direction.

III) Spread my hands in front, palms facing the sky chant the following mantra

Om Vajraye Phat
Om Agni Phat
Om Bhur Phat
Om Bhuva Phat
Om Apa Phat

After reciting the mantra for 7 times with tongue touching the palate and the breath being held, inhale the breath through the mouth in such way produce a hissing sound (Shitli Kriya). Hold the breath and mentally visualise the symbols

Dai Ko Myo
Cho Ku Rei
Hon Sha Ze Sho Nen
Sei Hei Ki

And let the symbols get connected to the third eye chakra.

IV) Visualise the symbols again and let them enter from the crown chakra and flow through the third eye chakra, throat chakra to reach heart chakra. When done with full concentration and dedication you will definitely feel a tingling sensation in the base chakra. Feel yourself filled with the universal energy, let this flow from the heart chakra to the palms.

V) When you feel that the hands has been filled with energy place right hand on the back of the head and the left hand over the heart chakra. Visualise that the third eye is sending the energy from it to the person on the throat chakra.

VI) Blow forcefully from the third eye chakra to the heart chakra.

VII) Repeat the step (III) and (IV).

VIII) When the energy is felt in the hands place the left hand on the base chakra and right hand over the heart chakra. Visualise that the third eye sending the energy from it to the person on the Swadhisthana chakra.

Soul Searchers The Art of Breathing

IX) Blow forcefully from the base chakra to the heart chakra.

X) Stand in namaskar position and thank the person. I repeat the step (III) with the left hand over my heart chakra and the right hand on the sky and visualising the thunderbolt between the first finger and the middle finger.

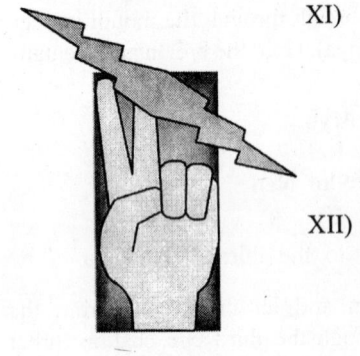

XI) Draw Cho Ku Rei on the third eye, Vishuddhi chakra, Heart chakra, Solar plexus chakra, and Root chakra in one breath. Mentally repeat the name of the Cho Ku Rei three times for every time the symbol is drawn.

XII) Draw Sei Hei Ki on the third eye, Vishuddhi chakra, Heart chakra, Solar plexus chakra, and Root chakra in one breath. Mentally repeat the name of the Sei Hei Ki three times for every time the symbol is drawn.

XIII) Draw Hon Sha Ze Sho Nen on the third eye, Vishuddhi chakra, Heart chakra, Solar plexus chakra, and Root chakra in one breath. Mentally repeat the name of the Hon Sha Ze Sho Nen three times for every time drawn.

XIV) Draw Dai Ko Myo on the third eye, Vishuddhi chakra, Heart chakra, Solar plexus chakra, and Root chakra in one breath. Mentally repeat the name of the Dai Ko Myo three times for every time drawn.

XV) Move to the right side of the person draw the symbol Cho Ku Rei from the third eye chakra to the base chakra.

XVI) Move to the front of the person draw the symbol Cho Ku Rei from the third eye chakra to the base chakra.

XVII) Move to the left side of the person draw the symbol Cho Ku Rei from the third eye chakra to the base chakra.

XVIII) Move to the backside of the person draw the symbol Cho Ku Rei from the third eye chakra to the base chakra.

XIX) Still holding the breath, I concentrate on the third eye and visually draw Dai Ko Myo, Hon Sha Ze Sho Nen, Cho Ku Rei, Sei He Ki above my head and let it flow from the Crown chakra to the third eye chakra.

XX) As the breath is released both the hands are placed on the crown chakra the thumbs of the hand touching. The left palm is slipped approximately half a inch to the left of the crown chakra and the symbol Cho Ko Rei is drawn with the right hand. After the symbol is drawn, the area is tapped three times repeating the names of the symbols on each tap.

XXI) Symbols Sei Hei Ki, Hon Sha Ze Sho Nen and Dai Ko Myo are also drawn and after drawing each symbol the area is tapped three times repeating the names of the symbol on each tap.

XXII) After coming in the front, both the hands of the person are spread in front the palms facing you. Hold the right hand of the person with your left hand and draw the symbol Cho Ku Rei on it, repeating the name of the symbol thrice.

XXIII) Let the right palm touch the heart chakra of the person and place the left hand on the right palm.

XXIV) Kneel down in such a way that the right knee of yours touches the floor. Hold the right leg of the person with your left hand. Breathe in deeply with the tongue on the palate and hold. On the base of the leg, draw Cho Ku Rei repeating the name of the symbol thrice with the right hand of yours.

XXV) Place the feet back on the ground.

XXVI) Now stand straight in front of the person, extend your hands in front with the palms facing the sky, breath is inhaled from the mouth as if drawing the energy from the universe itself. The breath so inhaled is deep and the following mantra is mentally recited for twenty one times

Om Ah Hum

XXVII) Blow on the Third eye chakra, with full force and repeat the step (XXVI).

XXVIII) Repeat the step (XXVI) and blow with full force on the Throat chakra.

XXIX) Repeat the step (XXVI) and blow with full force on the Heart chakra.

XXX) Encircle the person in the anti-clockwise direction to reach the back of the person.

2nd stage

I) Thank the person and mentally visualise the symbols Dai Ko Myo, Hon Sha Ze Sho Nen, Cho Ku Rei, and Sei Hei Ki. Breathe in deeply and withheld breath draw the symbol Cho Ku Rei on the third eye chakra, throat chakra, heart chakra, Swadhisthana chakra, and Mooladhara chakra. Repeat the name of the symbol thrice.

II) Breathe in deeply and hold the breath draw the symbol Sei Hei Ki on the third eye chakra, throat chakra, heart chakra, Swadhisthana chakra, and Mooladhara chakra. Repeat the name of the symbol thrice.

III) Breathe in deeply and hold the breath draw the symbol Hon Sha Ze Sho Nen on the third eye chakra, throat chakra, heart chakra, Swadhisthana chakra, and Mooladhara chakra. Repeat the name of the symbol thrice

IV) Breathe in deeply and hold the breath and draw the symbol Dai Ko Myo on the third eye chakra, throat chakra, heart chakra, Swadhisthana chakra, and Mooladhara chakra. Repeat the name of the symbol thrice.

V) Move to the right side of the person and draw the symbol Cho Ku Rei repeating the name of the symbol thrice. On the front side of the person, also draw the symbol Cho Ku

Rei while repeating the name of the symbol thrice. Move to the left side of the person, draw the symbol Cho Ku Rei, and repeat the name of the symbol thrice. On reaching the back of the person again draw the symbol Cho Ku Rei while repeating the name of the symbol thrice.

VI) Both the hands are placed on the crown chakra the thumbs of the hand touching. The left palm is slipped approximately half a inch to the left of the crown chakra and the symbol Cho Ko Rei is drawn with the right hand. After the symbol is drawn, the area is tapped three times repeating the names of the symbols on each tap.

VII) Symbols Sei Hei Ki, Hon Sha Ze Sho Nen and Dai Ko Myo are also drawn and after drawing each symbol the area is tapped three repeating the names of the symbol on each tap.

VIII) After coming in the front, both the hands of the person are spread in front the palms facing you. Hold the left hand of the person with the left hand and draw the symbol Sei Hei Ki on it, repeating the name of the symbol thrice.

IX) Let the left palm touch the heart chakra of the person and place the right hand on the left palm.

X) Kneel down in such a way that the left knee of yours touches the floor. Hold the left leg of the person with your left hand. Breathe in deeply with the tongue on the palate and hold. On the base of the leg, draw Sei Hei Ki repeating the name of the symbol thrice with the right hand

XI) Place the feet back on the ground.

XII) Now stand straight in front of the person, extend your hands in front with the palms facing the sky, breath is inhaled from the mouth as if drawing the energy from the universe itself. The breath so inhaled is deep and the following mantra is mentally recited for twenty one times

Om Ah Hum

XIII) Blow on the Third eye chakra, with full force and repeat the step (XII).

XIV) Repeat the step (XII) and blow with full force on the Throat chakra.

XV) Repeat the step (XII) and blow with full force on the Heart chakra.

XVI) Encircle the person in the anti-clockwise direction to reach the back of the person.

3rd round

I) Thank the person and mentally visualise the symbols Dai Ko Myo, Hon Sha Ze Sho Nen, Cho Ku Rei, and Sei Hei Ki. Breathe in deeply and withheld breath draw the symbol Cho Ku Rei on the third eye chakra, throat chakra, heart chakra, Swadhisthana chakra, and Mooladhara chakra. Repeat the name of the symbol thrice.

II) Breathe in deeply and hold the breath draw the symbol Sei Hei Ki on the third eye chakra, throat chakra, heart chakra, Swadhisthana chakra, and Mooladhara chakra. Repeat the name of the symbol thrice.

III) Breathe in deeply and hold the breath draw the symbol Hon Sha Ze Sho Nen on the third eye chakra, throat chakra, heart chakra, Swadhisthana chakra, and Mooladhara chakra. Repeat the name of the symbol thrice

IV) Breathe in deeply and hold the breath and draw the symbol Dai Ko Myo on the third eye chakra, throat chakra, heart chakra, Swadhisthana chakra, and Mooladhara chakra. Repeat the name of the symbol thrice.

V) Move to the right side of the person and draw the symbol Cho Ku Rei repeating the name of the symbol thrice. On the front side of the person, also draw the symbol Cho Ku

Spiritual Energy of Reiki

Rei while repeating the name of the symbol thrice. Move to the left side of the person, draw the symbol Cho Ku Rei, and repeat the name of the symbol thrice. On reaching the back of the person again draw the symbol Cho Ku Rei while repeating the name of the symbol thrice.

VI) Both the hands are placed on the crown chakra the thumbs of the hand touching. The left palm is slipped approximately half a inch to the left of the crown chakra and the symbol Cho Ko Rei is drawn with the right hand. After the symbol is drawn, the area is tapped three times repeating the names of the symbols on each tap.

VII) **Symbols Sei Hei Ki, Hon Sha Ze Sho Nen and Dai Ko Myo are also drawn and after drawing each symbol the area is tapped three times repeating the names of the symbol on each tap.**

VIII) After coming in the front, both the hands of the person are spread in front the palms facing you. Hold the right hand of the person with the left hand and draw the symbol Hon Sha Ze Sho Nen on it, repeating the name of the symbol thrice.

IX) Let the right palm touch the heart chakra of the person and place the left hand on the right palm.

X) Kneel down in such a way that the left knee of yours touches the floor. Hold the right leg of the person with your left hand. Breathe in deeply with the tongue on the palate and hold. On the base of the leg, draw Hon Sha Ze Sho Nen repeating the name of the symbol thrice with the right hand

XI) Place the feet back on the ground.

XII) Now stand straight in front of the person, extend your hands in front with the palms facing the sky, breath is inhaled from the mouth as if drawing the energy from the universe itself. The breath so inhaled is deep and the following mantra is mentally recited for twenty one times

Om Ah Hum

XIII) Blow on the Third eye chakra, with full force and repeat the step (XII).

XIV) Repeat the step (XII) and blow with full force on the Throat chakra.

XV) Repeat the step (XII) and blow with full force on the Heart chakra.

XVI) Encircle the person in the anti-clockwise direction to reach the back of the person.

XVII) Repeat the process from (VII).

XVIII) After coming in the front, both the hands of the person are spread in front the palms facing you. Hold the left hand of the person with the left hand and draw the symbol Hon Sha Ze Sho Nen on it, repeating the name of the symbol thrice.

XIX) Let the left palm touch the heart chakra of the person and place the right hand on the left palm.

XX) Kneel down in such a way that the right knee of yours touches the floor. Hold the left leg of the person with your left hand. Breathe in deeply with the tongue on the palate and hold. On the base of the leg, draw Hon Sha Ze Sho Nen repeating the name of the symbol thrice with the right hand

XXI) Place the feet back on the ground.

XXII) Now stand up straight and breathe in deeply. Place the hands of the person in the cross position in such a way that the finger tips of the right hands touch the left collar bone and the left hands finger tips should touch the right collar bone.

XXIII) Now stand atleast one feet away from the person. Close your eyes and spread your hands out towards the sky. Visualise a universal white light entering your crown chakra let it pass through your body in such a way that the light totally engulfs you.

XXIV) Touch both the collarbones of the person and let the energy merge. Stay in the position till you feel numbness in the palms of the hand.

XXV) Move away from the person and bow down in reverence to the person. Say the attitude of gratitude and pray for forgiveness for any unknowing fault of yours.

XXVI) Let the person stay in the blissful position till he wishes.

CLEANSING TECHNIQUES

- ❖ Lighting of the incense sticks, Dhoop in the room can ward of negative energies.
- ❖ Lighting of the Til (sesame seed) oil can cleanse the negative energy in the room.
- ❖ Group meditation, Satsangs and Jaagrans can cleanse the environment.
- ❖ Crystals can also absorb the negative energies in the room.

CERTIFICATION FOR THE DEGREES

Certification for the various levels of Reiki is western concept. Certification only shows the stage of attunement the person has achieved and not the level of perfection he has achieved in the stage.

Reiki is a spiritual energy and it is not possible for a person to acquire the qualities of a Reiki channel in a day of attunement. In ancient times when a student used to complete a particular level he had to pass the examination given by the master only then he could be verified by the master of becoming a competent student. Even today, the actual method of practice of Reiki done in Tibet, Japan is very arduous and very few people are taught higher levels without first practicing the techniques provided in a particular level. For example a Reiki I channel is asked to practice for a period of atleast a year atleast doing hands on healing for self and others, after testing the person for his ability in the Reiki I only does the Master agree for teaching Reiki II. For the Mastership, it is not the student but the Master who decides if the student is fit or not for acquiring the knowledge of Mastership.

Some of the conditions for reaching higher levels have been given in the **Pre-requisites for training in the above stages** section.

MEDITATION IS COMPLETE...

In Zen monastery there is unique concept of meditation. In the monastery students come with their own rug for sitting and meditating. When they complete their meditation they fold their rug and go out of the monastery without thanking the master as they believe that they have to thank nobody but the universal lord . This is Zen meditation.

If a student thanks the master then he is told to continue the meditation, as his meditation is not yet complete. He has not achieved the perfection of merging with the nature's flow of life.

DEVELOPMENT OF ENERGY (CH'I)

For teaching and passing on the attunements the Reiki master should be able to withhold the energy for the transmission. If a person is to attune several people in a day, then he should be able to have much energy saved in his body for the transmission. Although, the Reiki master only acts as a medium for the attunement process, he is also passing on the attitudes that are carried by him.

A plant growth depends upon the earth it has been planted upon, so does a student growth depending upon the master

The Reiki masters attunement processes require both physical and spiritual energies. In the following section, the reader can find some useful meditational exercises that can increase their energy. These meditational exercises can also be done non-Reiki channels.

Some important instructions for doing the following meditational exercises:

- ❖ Purify yourself before doing these exercises. By purification we donot mean only the cleansing of the physical body but also cleansing of the inner thoughts and self.

- ❖ Never do these exercises on full stomach. Atleast 3-5 hours should elapse after the intake of food before doing Hum Technique & Carry load Technique.

- ❖ Asthmatic and heart patients should consult a doctor before doing the above said exercises.

- ❖ Never do the exercises when the body is hot especially during the noon.

- ❖ Doing breathing exercises before doing the meditation is very helpful in gaining the concentration.

Development of the Chi Energy

SPOT ENERGY TECHNIQUE

This exercise is very good in strengthening the heart and lungs. The method of doing this exercise is:

Stand on a mat with hands on the waist. The spine should be kept straight, the feet should be slightly parted.

STAGE # 1

Start walking on the same spot slowly. When a step is taken the knee should reach the level of the waist. When the knee reaches the waist level, the breath should be taken in and when the knee is lowered, the breath should be exhaled.

Do this process for 5 minutes. After that stand again with the feet apart and hands on the waist.

STAGE # 2

This stage controls the breath flow in a person. Inhale deeply retain for a minute and exhale with full force. Repeat this process for 5 minutes.

Important : Never inhale or exhale with the mouth

STAGE # 3

Move your right hand over the navel area while keeping the left hand over the waist. Start massaging the navel area slowly in clockwise for males and anti clockwise for females. While massaging the navel area continue to breathe slowly. This process should be done for two minutes.

This stage helps in balancing the navel chakra.

Soul Searchers The Art of Breathing

CANNOT HEAR ANYTHING

On the first night of their marriage, Mrs. Gupta found her husband listening to something by putting his ears on the wall. This surprised her a lot, what was more surprising was that this same ritual was performed by her husband every night.

One night, Mr. Gupta found Mrs. Gupta trying to listen something by putting her ears on the wall. On seeing this Mr. Gupta asked her what she is doing. Mrs. Gupta said 'What do you listen, I have been trying to hear something for last 20 minutes but I am not able to hear anything'

'Darling, for the last 20 years, I am putting my efforts. And till now I am not able to find success, how can you imagine to achieve success within a short span of 20 minutes' Mr. Gupta said laughingly.

Putting efforts without tiredness helps in achieving success one day.

HUM TECHNIQUE

This is important technique for building the confidence and also to re-energise the heart and stabilise the aura.

Stand on a mat with hands on the sides. The spine should be kept straight, the feet should be slightly parted.

STEP #1

Close your eyes and breathe in deeply. Fill the lungs and release the air with full force. Continue to do this for a minute.

STEP #2

Breathe in deeply. Inhale and chant HUMMMMMMM. The process of chanting is to chant inhale and rapidly chant HUM. When the exhalation is done chant SAAAAA in the same manner. Continue the process for five minutes.

STEP #3

Breathe in a very slow manner, like the soft touching breeze of the seas of the morning. On every inhalation chant HUMSA and on every exhalation chant HUMMMMMMM the length of the chanting should not exceed the length of the inhalation or exhalation. Continue this process for five minutes.

STEP #4

Sit on the spot with the siddhasana. Spread your hands in front and tense the muscles in the arm. Visualise a wall appearing in front of you. And put the hands against the wall. Push the hands against the wall with full force. Do this for two to three minutes.

STEP #5

Lie down on the place and let all the muscles relax in the body. Visualise that every part of the body is getting rejuvenated by the universal energy.

CARRY LOAD TECHNIQUE

This exercise helps in energising the base chakra, navel chakra. The process of doing this technique is

Stand on a mat with hands in front of you at a height of the shoulders. The spine should be kept straight, the feet should be slightly parted.

STAGE # 1

Lower the left-hand in front of the base chakra and lift the right hand at the height of the third eye chakra. Move the hands up and down as if pushing and pulling a pulley.

Do this process for 5 minutes. After that stand again with the feet apart and hands in front of you at a height of the shoulder.

STAGE # 2

Again lower the left-hand in front of the base chakra and lift the right hand at the height of the third eye chakra. Spread out your feet with a feet's between them. Turn both hands into fist.

STAGE # 3

Close your eyes and visualise that you are near a well and your hands are holding the ropes of the bucket filled with water. The well is very deep filled with the nectar of energy. The bucket with the nectar of energy weights more than 30 kilos. You have to pull the filled bucket up to drink the nectar of energy. Start pulling the bucket up with both the hands. The weight of the bucket goes on increasing with every pull of yours. Do this process till you pull the bucket out of the well. Put the bucket on the wall of the well and relinquish your thirst of energy by the nectar.

Every time you do this process feel the nectar of energy increasing your energy manifold times.

TIP :

1. If you have a very good visualisation power then this process works wonders for the development of the energy.
2. Increase the weight of the bucket every time you do this exercise as this will help to build the energy levels.
3. Tensing of the muscles while pulling the bucket will also help in building the physical energy.

HEALING THE PAST
ADVANCE TECHNIQUES FOR REIKI CHANNELS

Past is very important event in the life of a human being, be it the recent past or the events that occurred in the past life, both continue to haunt the current life to a great extent. This exercise is developed for those people who have been exposed to the symbols of Reiki healing process.

Many phobias and traumas that we carry in day to day life may be due to the karmic deeds of our in the past life. These phobias and traumas hamper the growth of our mental and spiritual levels.

This dhyana is to be done only after reviewing the risk factors which are involved like :
- [i] *during this dhyana it is quite possible that you might see some incidents events related with your past life, which may be very distressing and release the traumas in the form of outbursts, uncontrollable weeping, bursts of anger etc..*
- [ii] *this exercise should be done only after getting sufficient practice of the symbols.*

PROCESS OF DOING THIS DHYANA

Stage 1   Connecting with one self

The best position for this meditation is to sit on a chair comfortably, close your eyes and place your hands on the knees, palms facing the sky. It is important that the feet are kept apart and are placed on a wollen rug. Inhale and exhale deeply and with each inhale feel the fresh air coming into your body and releasing the tensions in the muscles. Go on breathing deeply till you find every part of your body is relaxed. After relaxing every part of the body bring the concentration to the heart. Synchronise the heart beat with the breathing pattern, i.e. to say you exhale when there is a beat and inhale when there is gap.

This synchronising will help in connecting to the brain cells responsible for the storage of the past life information.

Spiritual Energy of Reiki

Stage 2 Reiki connectivity

In the same posture and breath say the attitude of gratitude in the following manner

I thank Reiki for being here
I thank the Universal energy being here
I thank the Reiki Guru and Channels for being here
I thank   myself   (name) being here
I thank the life's before me for being here
Slightly bow down your head in reverence.

Mentally draw Hon Sha Ze Sho Nen over the head and let the symbol convert into pure energy and enter the Crown chakra, Ajna chakra, Vishuddhi chakra, to reach the Anahat chakra. Repeat the same procedure for Sei Hei Ki and Cho Ku Rei.

Mentally draw Hon Sha Ze Sho Nen near the feet and let the symbol convert into pure energy and enter the Mooladhara chakra, Swadhisthana chakra, Manipura chakra, to reach the Anahat chakra. Repeat the same procedure for Sei Hei Ki and Cho Ku Rei.

Let the combined energy accumulated on the Anahat chakra flow to the hands and onto the palms.

Place your left palm on the Anahat chakra and the right palm on the Ajna chakra.

Step 3 Getting Connected to the Past Life

Pray mentally in the following manner

O Universal Lord help me to Reconnect
to the life Lived by me
To be able to heal the Bad Deeds
As aptly as had been done
May the Healings be Done when I Wake
Let all bygones be dealt with in a manner subtle
to the nature and Let it not effect me
in the life led by me now Thank you. O lord.

Visualise a cosmic white light engulfing you. Let the cosmic energy form a cocoon around you tightening its hold on your body. The more the cocoon tightens the more comfortable and relaxed you will feel.

Visualise Hon Sha Ze Sho Nen, Cho Ku Rei and Sei Hei Ki symbols and let it start flowing into a cosmic path. Visualise yourself stepping on the path and walking towards the direction of the flow of the energy. This energy path will take you to the concerned area where the healing is required.

When you reach the spot you will see that the cosmic path has stopped for a particular distance and after that has again started flowing. The area where there is gap is the area that requires healing.

Visualise the following symbols in the order

Cho Ku Rei
Sei Hei Ki
Hon Sha Ze Sho Nen
Cho Ku Rei

Repeat the names of each symbol thrice.

Let the symbols flow from the Sahasrar chakra to the Ajna Chakra, Vishuddhi Chakra to reach the Anahat Chakra.

Mentally pray

O Lord help me to heal the breaks
in the Karmic cycle
let all the energy of the symbols
combine to heal and resurrect
the karmic energies
Let all the bad karma's be healed
And the flow of the good karma's begin

and let all the energy of the symbols stored in the Anahat chakra be released through the palms to the area where there is gap.

Spiritual Energy of Reiki

Continue to do this process till you find that the cosmic path has changed the colour to golden and sparkling rays are being emitted from it.

Step 4 Releasing from the Past

When the cosmic path has started releasing cosmic rays, the healing for that area of karmic deeds has been done. Now start walking back from the path in the same manner as you had done while stepping on the path. After getting down from the path say the Attitude of Gratitude. Bow down in reverence.

Visualise that the cosmic path is contracting to form a huge palm radiating cosmic energy. Feel that the palm is blessing you and disappearing.

Benefits of this meditational process :

a. All hidden trauma and other psychological problems will burn away

b. Regular healing session will help in sorting out the various problems you are facing in this birth

ENERGISING THE AURA

ADVANCE TECHNIQUES FOR REIKI CHANNELS

This is a important exercise for strengthening and energising the Aura.

Sit in a comfortable place with close eyes. Visualise the symbols on the third eye chakra

Hon Sha Ze Sho Nen
Sei Hei Ki
Cho Ku Rei

Repeat the name of each symbol thrice.

Let this energy flow from the third eye chakra in the form of energy ball. Repeat the process till you feel that your whole body is being covered with the energy ball.

Visualise that this energy ball is forming a cocoon around you emitting spiritual fire from the edges of the cocoon.

Feel the cosmic fire burning away all the negativity from your body and entering your body for healing the blockages in the flow of the chi.

During the whole process repeatedly draw the symbols and chant the names of the symbol thrice.

The cosmic fire will heal every flaw in the aura and balance the energy flowing in the body.

Benefits of this exercise

- ❖ this exercise will balance the auric flaws
- ❖ Continuous practice of this exercise will energise the aura and sensitise your psychic energy.

PRACTICE IN PARTNERSHIP

ADVANCE TECHNIQUES FOR REIKI CHANNELS

In this meditational process, the healing is done between partners.

Sit facing each other at the distance of a hand.

Hold each other's hands in such a manner that each finger of one person touches the others.

Close your eyes, say the Attitude of Gratitude, and do hands on healing with one another as done in Hands on healing or as done in Distance Healing.

Benefits of this exercise

- The energy developed through this exercise is double than done individually
- Regular practice of this exercise also gives insights into the breaks in the aura
- The healing is faster as compared to individual healing session.
- Energy sensitisation happens when this exercise is done regularly.

Asanas (Postures)

Art of sitting is the most important
part of the
Meditational Proacess
Like the roots of the sapling
piercing the
Mother Earth
So does the Asana pierce
the Physical realm
of the Sadhaka
To reach the Spiritual Heights.

IMPORTANT INSTRUCTIONS FOR DOING THE ASANA

1. Always do the asana slowly till you reach a level of perfection.

2. Never do jerky movements for the asana or any of the exercise as it can damage more than helping the problem.

3. Continue with the Asana with which you feel comfortable with.

4. For those people who are suffering from any joint pains or diseases should consult a doctor before proceeding with the exercise. For the benefit of the sadhaks who are facing the above said problems in doing the asana few asanas have been given in the end of this section.

5. These asanas should be done with great reverence as they help you to get connected with your spiritual soul.

6. Before you do the asana you make sure that body is at normal temperature.

7. Before you begin any exercise or asana join both your palms together in the Namaskar posture and pray to the universal soul for helping you in achieving your spiritual goals.

8. Except the Vajrasana no other asana should be done after having a meal. The gap between the meals and the asana should not be less than four to six hours.

9. Select a asana with which you feel comfortable.

SAVA ASANA

(POSTURE OF THE DEAD)

For doing this asana, place a rug on the centre of the room and lie on it. The legs should be streched out and the hands should be loosely placed on the sides.

The legs should be slightly apart. Close your eyes and slowly inhale and exhale.

Strech out the feet and tense the hands by tightly clenching in a fist.

Release the tension and relax all the muscles in the body.

Visualise yourself as a dead body with no movement in the body.

BENEFITS :

1. Relaxes all the muscles in the body.
2. This asana helps in controlling Blood pressure.

SUKHASANA

(EASY POSTURE)

Sit on the floor with stretched out feet. Bend the left feet and place the foot under the right thigh.

Now bend the right feet and place the foot under the left thigh.

Keep your spine straight and make sure that both the heels of the legs are touching the ground. Place both your hands on the knees (you can bent your hands if keeping them straight is not comfortable) and sit in the Gyan mudra or Chin mudra.

This is Sukhasana because it is very easy to sit on this posture and also a beginner should start with this posture as it helps him to sit in other advanced stages of asana.

WARNING : persons with stiff legs and knees should not do this exercise without consulting a doctor.

BENEFITS :
1. Gives a firm base to the sadhak to meditate.
2. This asana gives stress on the Anahat chakra and stimulates the chakra.

VAJRASANA

(THUNDERBOLT POSTURE)

For this asana first stand straight on the floor and then bend your knees slowly and kneel down on the floor. Bring the toes of the feet together and spread the heels to form a cave. Sit down on the spread heels with the buttocks placed between them. The heels should touch the hips and now place both the hands on the knee, the palms facing downwards.

WARNING : persons with stiff legs and knees should not do this exercise without consulting a doctor.

BENEFITS :

1. Gives a firm base to the sadhak to meditate.

2. This asana gives stress on the Manipura chakra and helps in the digestion process. This asana also helps the pancreas, liver and kidney.

3. This asana can be done after having meals also.

SIDDHASANA

(POSTURE OF THE SIDDHA)

Sit on the floor with stretched out feet. Bend the left feet and place the left sole of the foot against the inner right thigh. Adjust the left foot in such a way that the pressure is felt in the pubic area. When you feel comfortable in the position, bend the right feet over the left feet, in such a way that the right ankle is directly above the left ankle. Push the sole of the right foot in the left calf. Keep the spine erect and shoulders should also be kept broad.

In the beginning do not put high pressure on the pubic area as this will reduce the blood supply in the region and continuous high pressure can hamper the veins in the region. The pressure should be such that you may feel the toes in the cleft between the genitals and the inner thighs.

Place the palms on the knee facing upwards in the gyana mudra over the knee. You can bend the elbow if you feel comfortable.

Siddhasana is one of the prominent asana which a sadhaka should practice to achieve greater heights in the meditational process. This is the most important exercise for the practice of the Pranayama and also activating Kundalini.

WARNING : persons with stiff legs and knees should not do this exercise without consulting a doctor.

BENEFITS :

1. Gives a firm base to the sadhak to meditate.
2. This asana gives stress on the Mooladhara and Swadhisthana chakras. This asana helps in activating the Mooladhara as well as Swadhisthana Chakra.

PADMASANA

(LOTUS POSTURE)

Sit on the floor with stretched out feet. Bend the left feet and place the left ankle over the right thigh (sole facing upwards). Now fold the right feet over the left thigh, in such a way that the sole faces upward. Make sure that the sole are as close to the hip joints as possible. Place both the hands on the knee and assume the posture of gyana mudra with the palms facing upwards. Keep the spine erect and shoulders wide.

This posture is called as padma asana because when a person sits in this posture he looks as if he is sitting on a lotus.

WARNING : persons with stiff legs and knees should not do this exercise without consulting a doctor.

BENEFITS :
1. Gives a firm base to the sadhak to meditate.
2. This asana gives stress on the Vishuddhi and Ajna Chakra.

CROSS BOW ASANA

Sit on the floor with stretched out feet. Bend the left leg under the right leg in such a way that it is touching the right buttock. Now bend the right leg in such a way that it crosses the left leg and the heels of the right leg touches the left buttock. Adjust the legs till you are comfortable. Now place the left palm over the right knee facing downwards and over that place the right palm. Keep the spine erect and shoulders wide.

This asana is called Cross bow asana because the person who is in this asana looks like a Cross Bow.

WARNING : persons with stiff legs and knees should not do this exercise without consulting a doctor.

BENEFITS :
1. Gives a firm base to the sadhak to meditate.
2. This asana gives stress on the Mooladhara and Swadhisthana chakras. This asana helps in activating the Mooladhara as well as Swadhisthana Chakra.

SARVA SUKHA ASANA

ASANAS FOR THOSE WITH JOINT PAINS

(Total Relaxing Posture)

Sit on the chair with the back erect and place the hands on the knee facing downwards. While sitting on the chair remember to keep the shoulder wide and close your eyes.

Note : While sitting on the chair do not cross the legs and neither place the feet on the plain floor. Make sure that there is a mat on the floor which will safeguard your energy from getting earthed.

BENEFITS :
1. This asana does not put undue stress on the knee thereby giving you the benefit of sitting in an easy manner
2. This asana is also good for the people with arthritis problems.

TRATAK - THE WAY OF YOGI

This exercise is best when done in the night or before the sunrise. For this exercise it is important for the person to sit in a upright position on the floor, with erected spine and is better if done in Padma asana/ Siddha asana. At a distance of around two feet place a lighted candle on a table in such a manner that the light of the candle is in right angle to the centre of the eyes or the bhu madhya.

STEP - 1

Tratak is the first step in controlling the mind according to one's wishes and also to transform the energy thus stored in creative usage. The method of doing this kriya is to first glance at the tip of the flame of the candle light for a minute without blinking your eyes. For starters it is better to do for 30 seconds to 1 minute and gradually increase the duration of the gazing. When you feel that it is not possible to gaze anymore without blinking, rub your both hands together until you feel heat in both of your palms, then place your palms on the eyes and relax. After few seconds do this process again. This exercise should be done till you are able to gaze at the candle light for more than a minute then follow the instructions for the next step.

STEP - 2

For the next step the steps are to be followed in the same manner till the time you feel tiredness in your eyes and then close your eyes and move your eye balls to the bhu madhya or the point of the joining of the eyebrows and visualise the flame of the candle light burning brightly at the centre of the eyebrow, see the flame, feel the heat of the flame on the eye brow. Visualise this flame for a period of one minute and open your eyes and gaze at the flame again and do the process again. When you feel tired close your eyes and rub your palms vigorously till you feel heat is generated and then place your palms on both eyes. Do this for two or three times.

STEP - 3

This step involves concentrating on an unlit candle thread and visualising that there is a flame on the thread. Concentrate and visualise the exercise of seeing the flame on the thread as if it was actually lit. for a period of 30 seconds to 1 minute and when you feel tired rub both your palms till you feel they are hot and place them on the eyes and relax.

The purpose of doing this exercise is to get control over the senses i.e. when you feel that your eyes are about to blink ,it is nothing but the conscious mind trying to regain control over the body and mind.

BENEFIT OF DOING TRATAK

[a] Improving the concentration

[b] Improving the eyesight

[c] Removing black circles around the eyes.

CAUTION : *If your eyesight is weak then do not put strain on the eyes as this exercise will work against you rather than helping you. Also consult your doctor before this exercise.*

Pranayama

(The Art of Breathing)

Breath is the most vital necessity for a human being which controls all the life forces of the person and the sadhak who achieves control over it is said to be master of the siddhis

From the time of inception till the point of death human lives on the breath. This breath is the most important part of the existence of a human being without it a person cannot survive. In our scriptures also it is said that a man can live without water for a week, without food for a month, without air for not more than few seconds. This breath is the prana, the cosmic divine energy which flows through the veins of the living beings. This energy has a tendency to flow downwards from the universe to the human body. Under normal circumstances this energy flows through the body without any voluntary action. The importance of the prana had been understood by our great rishis and sages through in-depth research into this field. The basis of Patanjali's Yoga sutra can be said to be the mastery of the prana. A sadhak who can control the flow of the breath can be the master of great siddhis.

This section has been prepared in such a way that even a novice with no experience in pranayama can easily and quickly grasp the art of breathing in a very short period of time. No traditional names have been given to these exercises but have been arranged in a format of stages which will be easy for the sadhak to follow.

The sadhak should start with the Alpha level and should try to achieve proficiency in the processes before starting with the exercises explained in this section.

IMPORTANT INSTRUCTIONS FOR THE PRANAYAMA

1. Do the breathing exercises on empty stomach or there should be atleast 6 hours gap between the time of the food intake and the exercise.

2. Never do the breathing exercises when the body is hot.

3. Never do the breathing exercises in the afternoon except when the climate is cold.

4. Breathing exercises are recommended during the early morning or after the sunset.

5. Except where mentioned the breathing should be done only through the nostrils.
6. People suffering from heart disease, bowel problems, asthmatic problems should consult a doctor before doing the exercise.
7. People suffering from cold and stuffy nose should not put undue pressure on the breathing exercise.
8. People who are suffering from fever should not do these exercises until they have fully recovered.
9. Wear loose cotton clothes for doing the breathing exercises.
10. For doing the breathing exercises it is recommended that the eyes are closed.
11. Each stage of the exercises mentioned in this section should be practiced till you are confident of the stage.

INNER INVOCATION

Sit in Siddhasana with the back erect. Close your eyes and take deep breaths. Each breath should be taken slowly with the feeling of the flow of the breath inside the body.

- ❖ Every breath you inhale feel the flow of the universal energy going inside the body and lighting up all your body system with the whiteness of the cosmic energy.

- ❖ Every breath you exhale feel the outflow of the negative thoughts and tensions from your body and going into oblivion.

Place your palms facing upwards in the gyan mudra.

Keeping your back erect lower your head in such a way that the chin touches the joint of the neck. Press the head against the joint and go on taking deep breathes following the same pattern as has been mentioned. This exercise is good for the invocation of the energy between the heart chakra and the ajna chakra.

ADVANCED METHOD

The steps for this method are as follows :

- ❖ Inhale deeply as has been done in the beginning and then retain the breath for a count of I and visualise that all the energy is seeping into every part of the body.

- ❖ Exhale also in the same manner as has been done in the earlieer stage

PRECAUTIONS FOR THIS EXERCISE

1. People suffering cervical spondilytis or having neck injuries should consult doctor before doing this exercise.

2. Never give jerk to the head while tilting the head forward or backward. Slowly tilt the head and should be tilted only to the extend you feel comfortable with.

CALLING TO THE UNIVERSAL SOUL

Sit in Siddhasana with the back erect. Close your eyes and take deep breaths. Each breath should be taken slowly with the feeling of the flow of the breath inside the body.

- ❖ Every breath you inhale feel the flow of the universal energy going inside the body and lighting up all your body system with the whiteness of the cosmic energy.
- ❖ Every breath you exhale feel the outflow of the negative thoughts and tensions from your body and gong into oblivion.

Place your palms facing upwards in the gyana mudra.

Keeping your back erect tilt your head in towards the back in a way that the lower back of the head touches the back of the neck joint. Press the head against the joint and go on taking deep breathes following the same pattern as has been mentioned. This exercise is good for the invocation of the energy between the Vishuddhi chakra and the Ajna chakra.

ADVANCED METHOD
The steps for this method are as follows :

- ❖ Inhale deeply as has been done in the beginning and then retain the breath for a count of 2 and visualise that all the energy is seeping into every part of the body.
- ❖ Exhale also in the same manner as has been done in the earlier stage.
- ❖ Visualise that from the Ajna chakra a white crimson light is emerging and forming a cocoon aaround your body in such a way as to engulf your whole body.
- ❖ Stay in this cocoon and follow the breathing as has been mentioned.

PRECAUTIONS FOR THIS EXERCISE
1. People suffering cervical spondilytis or having neck injuries should consult doctor before doing this exercise.
2. Never give jerk to the head while tilting the head forward or backward. Slowly tilt the head and should be tilted only to the extend you feel comfortable with.

ART OF BREATHING

BEGINNERS POSE

Sit in Siddhasana with the back erect. Close your eyes and take deep breaths. Each breath should be taken slowly with the feeling of the flow of the breath inside the body.

Place your palms facing upwards in the gyana mudra.

STAGE - 1

The breathing should be done in such a way as a cat walks on the floor to catch a mouse. No noise should emit from you but the breath taken in should be deep which fills the lungs from bottom to top with the cosmic energy.

Start the method with deep inhalation and deep exhalation without any retention. Feel the heat generated in body.

STAGE - 2

In this stage the breath should be such as the stage of the cat readying itself for the jump on to the mouse. After every deep inhalation stop the breath for a second or to a count of one and feel the air inhaled seeping through every part of the body. And now exhale in such a way like The breathing should be done in such a way as a cat walks on the floor to catch a mouse. No noise should emit from you but the breath taken in should be deep which fills the lungs from bottom to top with the cosmic energy.

Start the method with deep inhalation and deep exhalation without any retention. Feel the heat generated in body.

STAGE - 3

In this stage after every deep inhalation stop the breath for a count of two and feel the air inhaled seeping through every part of the body. And now exhale in such a way like the time taken for the exhalation should also be upto the count of two.

STAGE - 4

Follow the stage 3 but after each exhalation retain the empty lung for a count of two before inhaling again.

THE ART OF BREATHING FOR ADVANCED STUDENTS

These exercise should be performed only after the sadhaka has achieved confidence in the Beginners pose. The sadhak should sit in Siddhasana with the back erect and palms facing upwards with gyana mudra.

STAGE - 1

In this stage inhale for a count of one retain for a count of two and exhale for a count of two and follow the pattern again but the inhalation or exhalation should be done in a very slow manner and not in a haphazard or hasty manner.

STAGE - 2

In this stage inhale for a count of one retain for a count of four and exhale for a count of two and follow the pattern again. If the sadhaka feels drained after this round then he is still not ready for this round and should go back to the stage 1.

STAGE - 3

The sadhaka should practice this exercise only after getting full confidence in the stage 2.

In this stage inhale for a count of two retain for a count of eight and exhale for a count of two and follow the pattern again.

STAGE - 4

In this stage visualise your chest to be like a inverted balloon and start inhaling slowly and as you inhale feel that the lungs are filling from the bottom in such a way that the lungs fill from bottom to top.

Do not try to inflate the stomach

As you have filled the lungs from bottom to top, so release the air from top to bottom in a very slow manner. The speed of drawing in and releasing of the air should be like that of a toddler trying to stand up. Never too fast and never too slow.

INNER VOICE

Man gets distracted with the voices around while doing any japa or dhyana. This distraction is dual in the sense that there are external distractions like noises etc. and internal like the flow of the mind. External distractions boosts the mind to flow in the direction of the distraction and thus there is lack of concentration.

While doing the dhyana or japa if you feel discouraged due to the distractions, this exercise will help in controlling the mind by shutting out the external distractions.

For this exercise, sit in siddhasana with the back erect and palms facing upwards in gyana mudra. Close your eyes while doing this exercise.

- ❖ Every breath you inhale feel the flow of the cosmic energy going inside the body and lighting up all your body system with the whiteness of the cosmic energy.

- ❖ Every breath you exhale feel the outflow of the negative thoughts and tensions from your body and going into oblivion.

Now take a deep breath through both the nostrils and after retaining the breath, lift your right hand from the knee and place the thumb tip in the right ear, forefinger and the middle finger on the right eye, ring finger on the right nostril and the little finger on the right side of the lips.

After you have placed the right hand in comfortable position, now place the left hand also in the same position as that on the left side of the face.

After you have placed all the fingers on the face your both the ears, eyes, nostrils and the lips will be closed. The pressure should be exerted on all the ten points to such a extent you feel comfortable with. In the beginning you may be able to listen to the sound of buzzing, Om chant.

Place your fingers on the pressure points till you feel comfortable with.

BENEFITS :-

This exercise will help in

1. the process of concentration and dhyana.
2. reducing the stress and fatigue in the body and mind.
3. opening of the ajna chakra in the Antarmukh or the inner view.

ENERGY BURST

This is an important breathing exercise and allows you to gain control over the breath and also over the flow of the energy through the chest and the stomach.

The following things should be kept in mind while doing this exercise :

1. Do this exercise only on empty stomach.
2. Never do this exercise when the body is tired and needs rest.
3. The best preferred time for doing this exercise is before the sun rise and before the sun set.
4. It helps in increasing the body temperature and thus is very good in the cold regions. It is said that one who does the energy burst for 10 minutes gets as much benefit as a person running for 2 kilometres.

Sit in a comfortable posture and breath normally. Hands should be placed on the knees in the chin mudra. Eyes should be closed as it can reduce the distractions. When you feel completely at ease start with the exercise. Breath out with full force and take a small breath in and again breath out with full force. The duration of the inhalation and exhalation will be short and the force will be exerted on the stomach (as it will tucked in with full force) while breathing out.

Do this exercise till you feel tiredness creeping through you and then stop and lie down in Posture of Calmness (Shavasana).

BENEFITS :-

This exercise will help in

1. The process of concentration and dhyana.
2. Reducing the stress and fatigue in the body and mind.
3. Opening of the ajna chakra, Vishuddhi Chakra, Swadhisthana Chakra in the Antarmukh or the inner view.

Aura

Energy of the Universe is no where

except inside us, Flowing through our body,

invisible to the naked eye, Those born

in contact with nature are aware of it,

They flow with the energy to be one with them

Breathe is not just a flow of air in and out

It is the pure energy of the nature itself.

From the time immemorial, our great rishies and sages could judge the nature of the man at the first sight. They were no magicians or spies, but had the ability to judge a person depending upon on the energy emitting from the person coming to them.

They could sense and understand the energy flows from the animals and other objects in the nature. Understanding of this energy was kept secret to a few. This knowledge was passed to a student in the last phase of learning with the shaktipata for awakening the Kundalini. Many people also have said that they have the capabilities of knowing a person by seeing them.

What is the energy they see in a person to know and judge about the person. This energy has been given many names like Shaktipunj, Shakti abah, Aura etc.

AURA

Aura can be simply defined as a circle of energy engulfing a living or a non-living object.

In the diagram, it is easy to see the silvery white oval circle engulfing the body of a person.

The visibility and reach of the aura is dependent upon the health of a person. Health does not mean just the physical health, but both spiritual and mental health also.

YOU HAVE NOT DRESSED HIM PROPERLY...

Sant Soordas, was blind from birth, he was a devotee of Lord Krishna. He used to sing in the Lord Krishna temple. The songs were so engrossing and descriptive of the lord that some people used think that the saint was able to see. To test his spiritual sight, some devotees of the lord asked the priest not to decorate the lord with all the ornaments. In the evening when Soordas came to the temple and sat at his usual place, he cried out "Pujari, Why have you have not dressed the Lord as he should be...?" and fell to the feet of the idol of the lord. Hearing this the priest and the other devotees apologised to the saint. Saint Soordas could not see, but he could feel the energy flow from the idol.

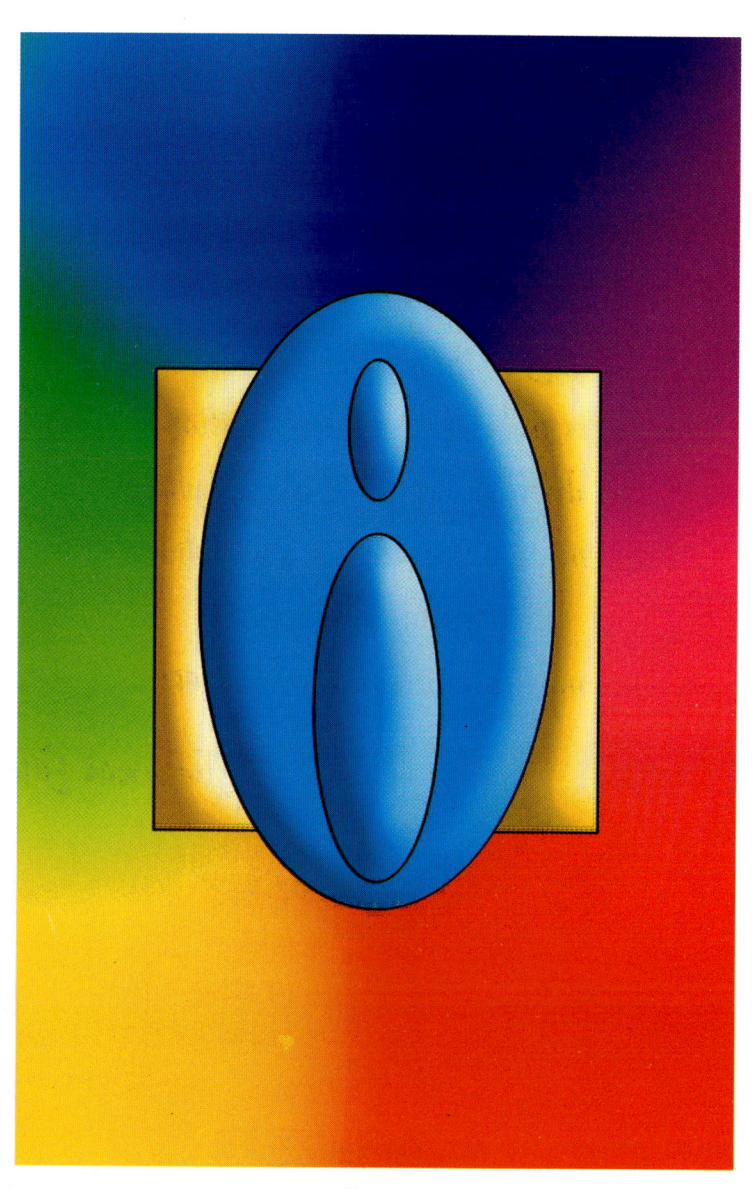

Aura

For those whose mind is unbridled, self-realization is difficult work. But he whose mind is controlled and who strives by appropriate means is assured of success

Bhagawat Gita

Aura

In the pictures of Gods and Goddesses, saints and rishies, we can see a circle of mysterious energy behind the head. This mysterious light is called the **Halo**. This energy depicts the high level spiritual development.

When a saint or a rishi reaches a high level of spiritual attainment, the energy emits from the three-chakra Vishuddhi, Ajna, and Sahasrar chakra. This energy is so high that it attracts the people around it. This is evident from the crowds of people that flock to listen to the saints. The more the auric range, the stronger will be the pull. The range of aura can be from few millimeters to many miles in range.

When a person who has weaker aura gets in contact with the person having high and strong aura, his aura is repaired and energised. This happens due to the exchange of the energy levels.

DOES THE ENERGY TRANSFER OCCUR ALL THE TIME?

Energy transfer occurs all the time as every one has unique and different energy levels and the frequencies of two energies do not match. Energy flows in all the bodies of the nature. When a child is born, he is born with the spiritual energy and the energy surrounding him is called aura. The idiom that 'Child is the true face of the god himself', is true as the aura of a child is golden in colour.

As the child grows in contact with the societal norms and rules, the auric energies changes and the colour of the aura also changes accordingly.

> Flowing with the flow everyone does, one who flows against the flow is the one who achieves the success.

The more materialistic a person becomes, the more energy depletes. In the above diagram, you can see two persons, one on the right side and the other on the left side.

The auric energy of the person on the left side is golden in colour, with clear auric circle. The person on the right side has light energy levels, with the light auric circle. When such a person with weak auric energy gets in contact with a person with strong energy levels, the auric damage is automatically reconstructed and give a balance between the energies. This is reason why it is said that people should attend Satsangs, religious rituals etc., as these places are filled with the energies of the sattvic nature and help in reconstructing the depleting auric energies of a person. If on the other hand the person who has strong aura of negative energy, he can siphon off the sattvic energy of a person with weak energy. The above discussion may not be clear at this moment as whole concept of aura will become clear from the next topic of discussion.

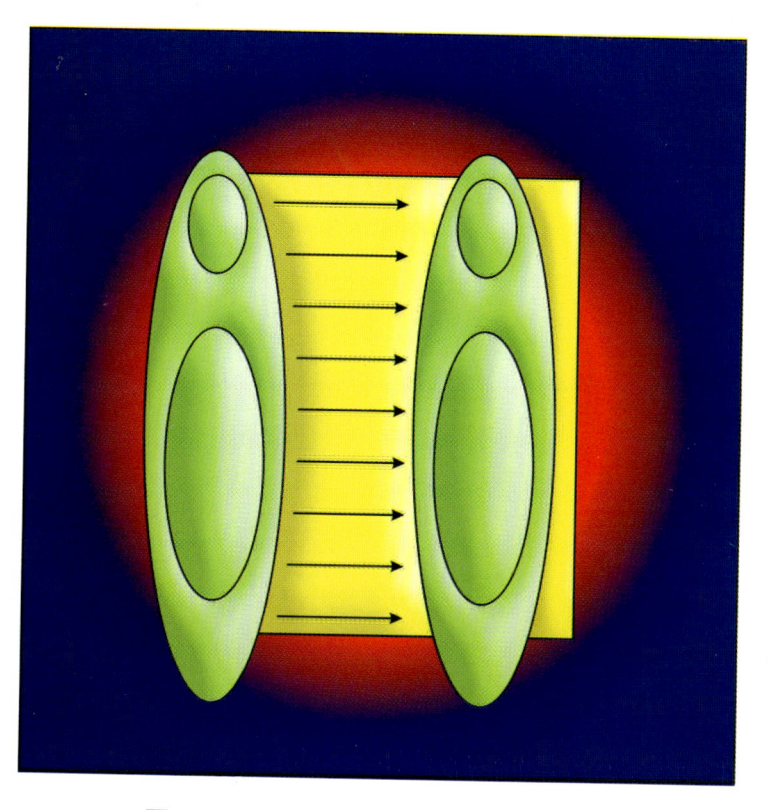

Energy transfer of Aura

God exists in nature according
to some, learned people
believe them to exist in
the heaven, the blind men
search them in stones
and Yogi's search
in themselves.

An Old saying of the Aghorees

S.No.	Development of Body	Age between (In years)
1	Physical body seen	0-7
2	Ethric body	7-14
3	Astral body	14-21
4	Mental body	21-28
5	Spiritual body	28-35
6	Cosmic body	35-42
7	Body nobody	42-49

When a child is born his sahasrar chakra is fully opened and this is the reason why the child is more inquisitive until the age of seven. Until the age of seven years the **physical body** of the child develops, this is the time when his limbs and other internal organs develop. After the age of seven there is only growth in terms of size and not in term of natural growth. After the age of seven, there is growth of intelligence in the child. This intelligence leads to two things; one the child is detached from the nature and the other he gets his basic knowledge from the material world. This also leads to knowledge about his sexual organs and the desire for opposite sex. This stage develops the **ethric body,** the body of knowledge.

The above two stages are important, the reasons being

❖ Even when the child is in the womb of the mother the subconscious mind of the child is active. Whatever activities the parents do the same are imbibed in the mind of the child. This memory decides the basic nature of the child.

  ✳ If there are frequent fights between the parents, while the child is in the womb, the child is born with a depressive nature, sadistic tendency and can have neurological problems from birth.

* Smoking, drinking, drugs, medicinal drugs can have the side effects on the child. The child who is born can have asthmatic problems, paralytic problems, and psychosomatic problems.

* The child easily takes diseases of the parents.

* The problems are taken by the child due to a simple fact that the child in the womb fights for two things

* It cuts himself from the past life information. Although the information is stored in the brain, the connection has to be cut. Sometimes the connection to the past life is not cut, then the child suffers lot of mental traumas by means of dreams, physical and emotional stress etc.

* The child takes on whatever information it could gather from the womb. The child gets the information through the life connection and hearing. This knowledge was known even before the time of Mahabharata. An event in this epic says that when Abhimanyu was in the womb of his mother. Arjuna was telling about the Chakravyuha Rachna of Guru Dronacharya to his wife and Abhimanyu was listening attentively. But Abhimanyu could only listen to the point of breaking in the Chakravyuha Rachna, but before he could listen to the breaking out of the rachna, his mother fell asleep. This knowledge was utilised by him in the epic battle of Mahabharata.

❖ After the child takes the first breath on delivery, he accumulates the information from all the five senses. At this moment, the child is very receptive, and even a slight level of vibration is recorded in the brain. The level of receptiveness can be judged from the fact that the child can easily judge the mother by variation of body temperature and odour.

❖ Till the child reaches the age of seven, he is very inquisitive of the surroundings. He uses all the physical senses for finding out more information from those things.

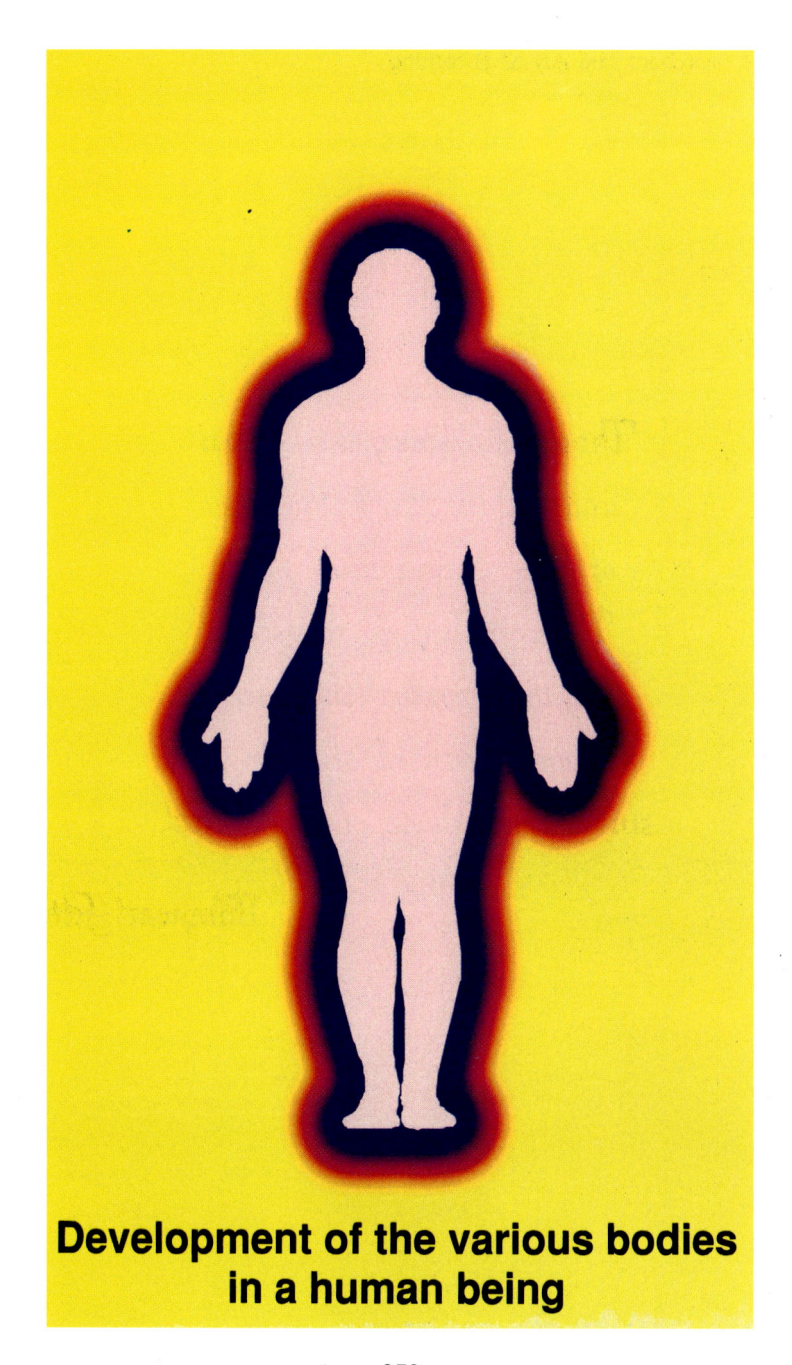

Development of the various bodies in a human being

Those who study the Vedas and imbibe the knowledge of Rg, Sama and Yajur Veda in life ae respected in the society. They are born cleansed of their sins in the abode of the Lord.

— Bhagwat Gita

❖ Until the age of fourteen whatever guidance is given to the child, the same information is stored in subconscious mind of the child. The more information he gathers the more he is detached from his childhood memory. Although the memory of the childhood is inside his brain but he rarely utilises them. These memories become a part of life and every step he takes is nothing but an extension of the characteristics imbibed in him.

From the birth to the age of fourteen can be equated with the **period of emerald**, the amount of knowledge for the development of whole life is stored during this period. If this period is wasted then it is like wasting a whole life.

From the age of fourteen to twenty-one, he attains knowledge for the atman or soul. This knowledge develops his **astral body**. Thus, we can say the age between 14-21 years is the ripe period for a person to develop physically and mentally. The information which a person can store upto the age of 21 is maximum after which the storage capacity decreases. This is the **golden period of development**.

After the period of golden age, the person grows spiritually from inside. This is the age between 21 to 28 years. A person earns for the truth, the knowledge of the nature. The knowledge, acquired in the childhood, is expanded in the form of development of the spiritual experience. This experience can be in the form of a transfer of the spiritual knowledge in the form of shaktipata from a guru or from the process atman gyana (soul searching). This period of development of the **mental body** gives person knowledge of parkayapravesh, telepathy, telekinesis etc. The body loses its human colour and acquired the luster of knowledge, the parma-gyana or ultimate knowledge. The period until the age of 28 is the time for getting the riddhis and siddhis and allows the person to reach the stage of sadhaka.

After attaining the riddhis and the siddhis, the sadhaka turns into a yogi and he is ready for the kundalini awakening. Like a snake, which removes its skin to adorn a new skin, a yogi discards the material body to reach the level of the spiritual bliss. This is time when he develops the **spiritual body** and moves to the path of enlightenment. A yogi at this level is called the Brahma gyani or Brahmana (one who knows the Brahma the creator)

Development of the spiritual body gives the yogi the atman gyana or the path of enlightenment. The **cosmic body** develops and the aura of the yogi becomes so powerful that the sight of such a yogi could transforms any person. At this stage the yogi stays in his physical body yet has no body, eats but does not eat, sleeps but does not sleep. This is the stage of **Body- No Body**. This means that the yogi lives in the physical form with the strength of the cosmic energy.

AURA COLOUR CHART

There are many colours of aura and the colours depend upon the development of the person mentally, physically and spiritually. In this section, we will discuss the various colours that can be seen and their true meanings.

GOLDEN COLOUR

Golden colour reflects high level of spiritual energy. The more the colour of the gold is bright the higher would be the development and the light shades of golden colour reflects the process of development towards the spiritual growth. When a person reaches the golden auric colour, then we can sense the smell of sandal emitting such people.

VIOLET COLOUR

This colour reflects, soothes, and calms people around them. Yogis who have reached this level are able to attract large number of followers and they are able to transform them to the path of spirituality. This stage balances the root chakra with the heart chakra and the heart chakra with the third eye chakra. When a sadhaka reaches this level his third eye chakra opens to show him the path of final bliss.

INDIGO COLOUR

This stage reflects the process of transformation from the withdrawal stage to the stage of spiritual upliftment of others. They begin to see the universal energy everywhere in every human being, trees, animals, animate, and inanimate objects they are in supreme bliss.

BLUE COLOUR

Blue is colour of coolness. When the earthly desires of a person subsides down, he becomes like a slow and smooth flowing river with no overtones. This level of auric development provides the sadhaka the ability to good intuitive power and telekinetic abilities. This level also brings the sadhaka more closer to his natural thoughts, thereby taking him away from the material world. Such people love to sit alone and contemplate on the thoughts rather than going for a social gathering. In the material sense, such people look as if they are facing lot of depressive problems like forgetfulness, blank thoughts etc.

When nonprofessionals face such kind of problems then those are liseases for which consulting a good healer or doctor is necessary.

GREEN COLOUR

Green is the colour of nature, which gives freshness, coolness, and calmness. Like nature does not require anything in return for the things provided by it in the same way, people reaching this level loose their greediness and the concept of 'mine' and they become 'one with the nature'. This is the second stage of spiritual development.

YELLOW COLOUR

This is the most visible colour of aura. This colour is like the freshness of the sunshine and reflects the energy transformation from the material world to the world of oneness. This is the colour of aura, which a lay man can also see, in a spiritual person, it reflects like the rays of the sun.

ORANGE COLOUR

This colour is the colour of fire. In India, one can find sadhus and other spiritual people wearing dress of this colour. This colour reflects the fire of purity, warmth and creativity.

Mostly this aura colour occurs after the stage of yellow aura, except in cases of people who are born spiritual we can easily detect the orange colour.

RED COLOUR

Red is a volatile hot colour signifying high level of bodily or earthy desires (high sexual needs). This colour reflects the short-temper, anger, excitement, aggressive attitude, high ambitions, motivating qualities and high levels of creative ability. This is colour of the Mooladhara chakra or the Root chakra. Any sadhaka who is on the path of enlightenment faces lot of problems to overcome the traumas while breaking free of the earthy desires.

GREY COLOUR (AND ITS VARIANTS)

This is colour of sensuousness, eagerness, sympathy and love. This colour has a metallic nature to it with a touch of calmness. This is a phase of turbulence and secretiveness. The best way to define this phase is by using the idiom, "Woman looks more mysterious with clothes on than without it"; during this phase, the sadhaka becomes very secretive and introvert hiding everything learned by him.

WHITE COLOUR

White colour is the colour of purity and this colour has the energy of all the seven colours. This colour is mostly visible during the period of change of the person from the life of student to the life of a sadhaka or a yogi.

SILVER COLOUR

This colour signifies the creation of life; growing plants in particular have this colour. The more new leaves appeared the brighter the silver colour became. This colour has the smell of boiling milk/ sour milk. The colour is mostly seen in pregnant women in the advanced stages.

SILVER GREY COLOUR

Silver Grey colour is the colour of surrender, love and sympathy. This colour varies in people with the stage of pregnancy. In normal cases, if a man has this aura then there is a chance that the person has fallen in love, lost his physical materials.

OCEANIC BLUE COLOUR

Oceanic blue colour is the colour of smoothness, energy, dedication and resources. People with high level of motivational abilities have this colour.

BLACK

Black colour is a very peculiar and mysterious colour in nature. This colour signifies two extreme things one death/ major problems and the second being the ability of absorption. Death / major problems occur in cases when the colour black is seen, this aura would be mostly seen on the third eye chakra or the heart chakra (black magic is used). This colour also helps in absorbing the negative energy and repels the positive energies. When any person is sealed from negative energies through a process of mantra initiation then this colour flows throughout the body in a spiraling form, accepts the positive energy, and repels the negative energy.

Aura

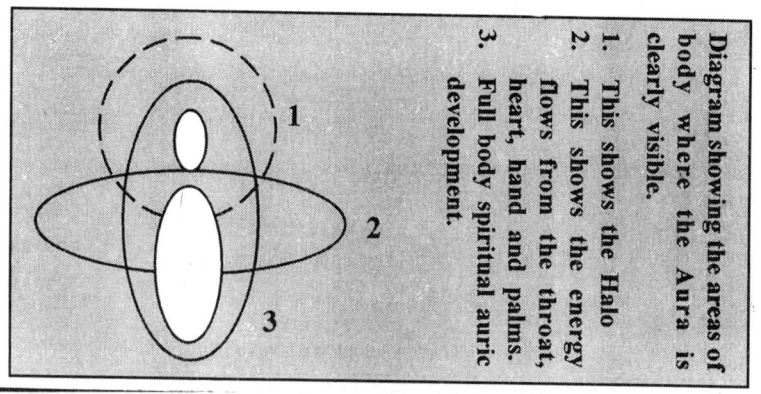

Diagram showing the areas of body where the Aura is clearly visible.
1. This shows the Halo
2. This shows the energy flows from the throat, heart, hand and palms.
3. Full body spiritual auric development.

The above diagram explains the major aura sites in the human body. Other than the auras given in the above diagram the aura can also be seen in the following parts of the body :

- Forehead
- Nasal regionTemple region
- Throat region
- Chest and stomach region
- Centre of the palms
- Finger tips
- Groin
- Ankles
- Base of the feet
- Toenails

The aura seen in the body parts given above shows the depletion or excess of the auric energy in those parts of the body. Depletion of the auric energy causes break in the auric circle in the body, which fore warns the occurrence of any disease. For example, a break or depletion in the auric levels in the throat region can cause cough, cold sneezing etc..

In the similar way, excess of the energy stored in a particular part of the body can cause imbalance in the flow of the energy in the body and interrupting the nadis, which in later years can cause damage to the major chakras.

Go Around the Guru
three times in anticlocwise
direction and touch the
Guru's feet with right hand.
Lie down with the hands
touching the lotus feet of
the Guru. A disciple who is
dedicated to his Guru can
only attain the
Siddhi others cannot.

Shiv Samhita

Exercises For Seeing Aura

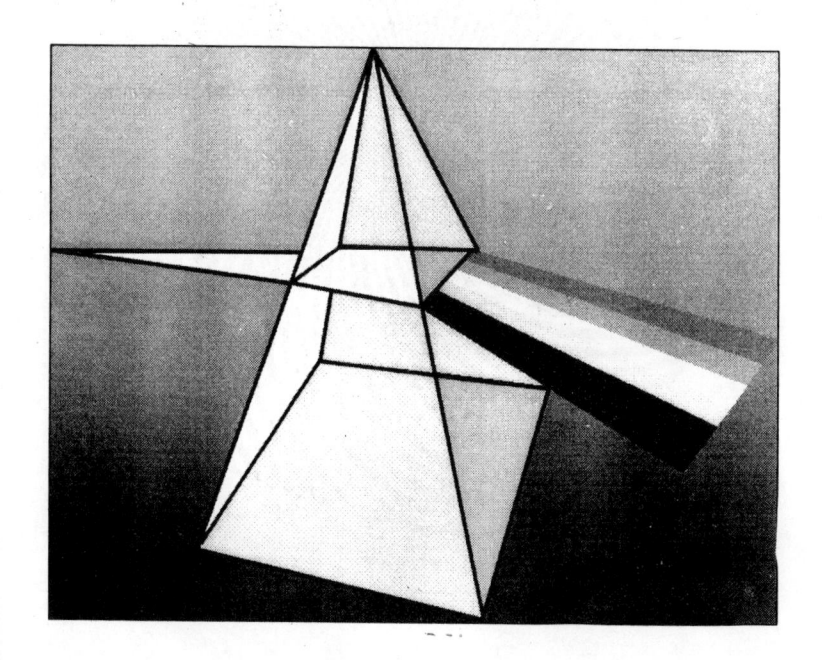

Soul Searchers The Art of Breathing

FLOW WITH ME

This is a important technique in creating a sense of flow in the eyes for sensing the auric activities in the body.

TECHNIQUE # 1

Place the above image in front of you, concentrate on the 'Om' in the centre of the spiral, and let the eye flow outward to the end of the spirals.

TECHNIQUE # 2

Place the above image in front of you, concentrate on the edge of the spiral and flow towards the 'Om' in the centre of the spiral.

Do both the exercises individually five times each.

Regular practice of the above exercises will enhance the receptive power of the eyes and will sensitise it to very subtle energy, which you had been missing for quite a long period.

CHECK ME OUT

Place the above image in front of you, concentrate on the central big circle, and let the eyes flow to the small circle on the bottom right. From there let the eyes flow the arrow directions shown in the second diagram. Repeat the same process with the first diagram.

Do this process for five times each on each diagram.

Regular practice of the above exercises will enhance the colour receptiveness power of the eyes and will sensitise it to very subtle energy, which you had been missing for quite a long period.

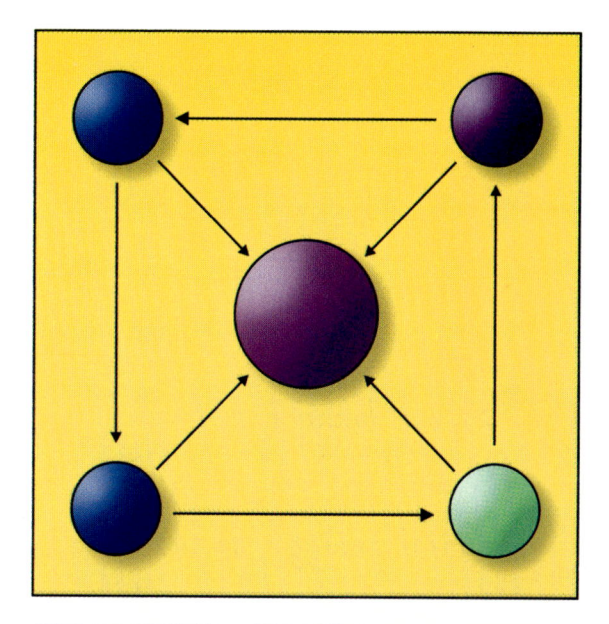

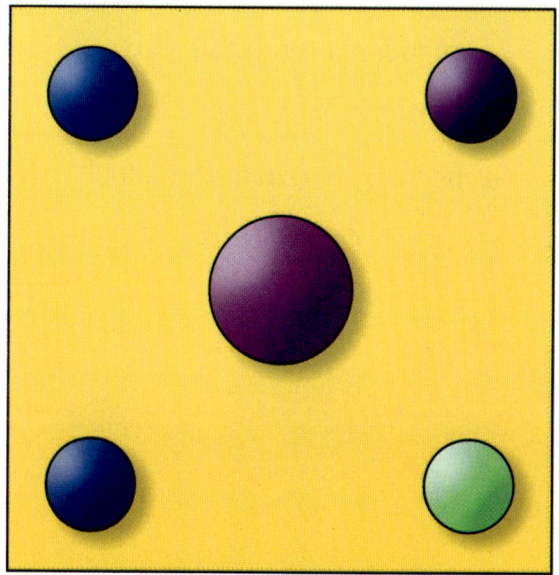

Check Me Out

Breath being a natural phenomenon which forms the vital energy (prana) in our body, if tapped and harnessed properly this energy can easily allow a person to reach the level of cosmic bliss.

CANDLE WATCH

Darken the room in which this meditation is to be done. Place a lighted candle at the height of eye level. Concentrate on the flame from the wick to the edge of the flame. Repeat the process from the edge of the flame to the wick of the candle in the beginning do this process for thirty seconds and slowly increase the time depending upon the practice.

INSTRUCTIONS FOR DOING THIS EXERCISE

- Donot blink while concentrating on the flame.
- The flames should be stable before this exercise begins.
- People suffering from eye problems should not do this exercise.

BENEFITS OF THIS EXERCISE

- This exercise will strengthen the colour distinguishing power of the eyes.

  Regular practice of this exercise will help in knowing the different layers of flame which normally, cannot be seen.

- Helps to concentrate more and develop the intuition powers.

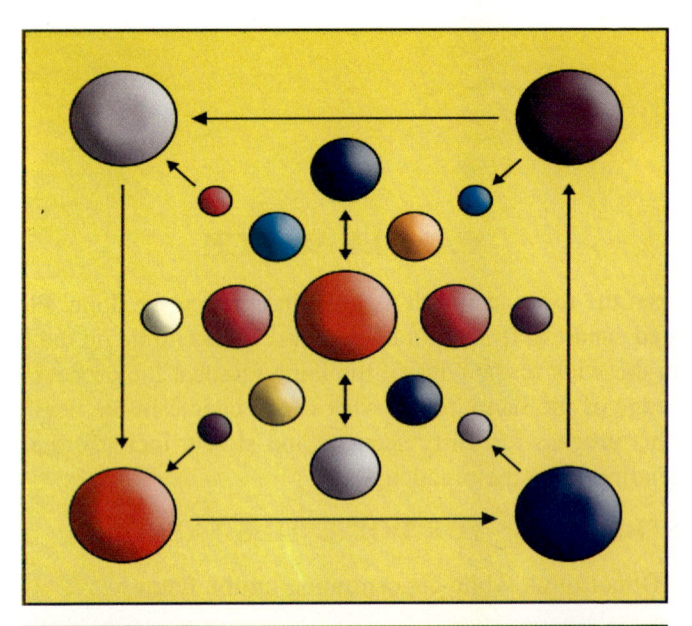

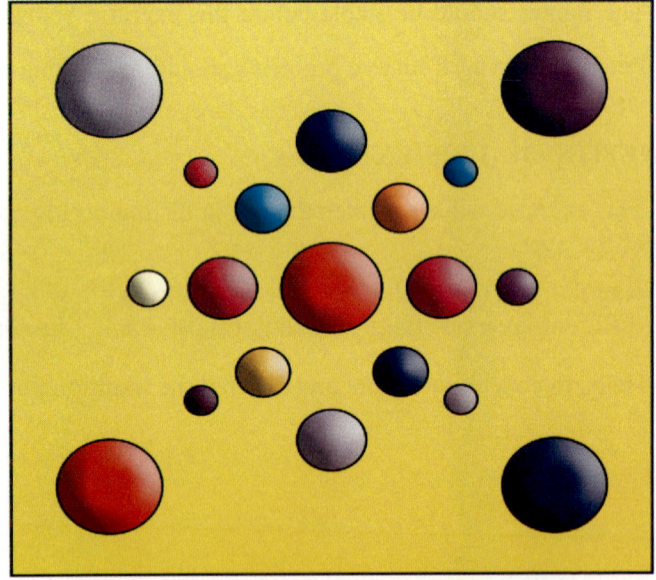

Advanced Check Me Out

ADVANCED CHECK ME OUT

Place the above image in front of you, concentrate on the central big circle, and let the eyes flow in the direction as shown through the arrows in the second diagram. Regular practice of this exercise will sensitise the eyes to the various colours and also help in merging the colours into one. Repeat the same process with the first diagram.

Do this process for five times each on each diagram.

WATCH ME

STEP - 1

Sit in a comfortable position near a table and place your palms on the table facing down.

Open eyes as wide as possible and concentrate on the palms. Study every minor detail of the palms from the fingertips to the wrist.

Once you have studied every feature of the palm, close your eyelids in half-open position and again repeat the process.

Repeat the process ten to fifteen times at a stretch.

STEP - 2

Partially close your eyes and repeat this exercise again for ten to fifteen times.

BENEFITS OF THIS EXERCISE

- ❖ Regular practice of this exercise will help you to see a small circle around the palms. This will be your first sighting of Aura energy.
- ❖ This method will also sensitise your palms for receiving and giving energy.
- ❖ If the room is darkened slightly for this exercise then the benefits will occur very fast.

It is important that the light should directly fall on the place where this exercise is being done as this will cover the auric energy of yours. Neon bulbs are best for this exercise.

Normally the above given exercises should be practiced for a period of one month or more for getting the eyes sensitive enough to see and feel the aura.

'No Supra Ego
No Super Ego No Ego'
is the line used
by the people with
only EGO.

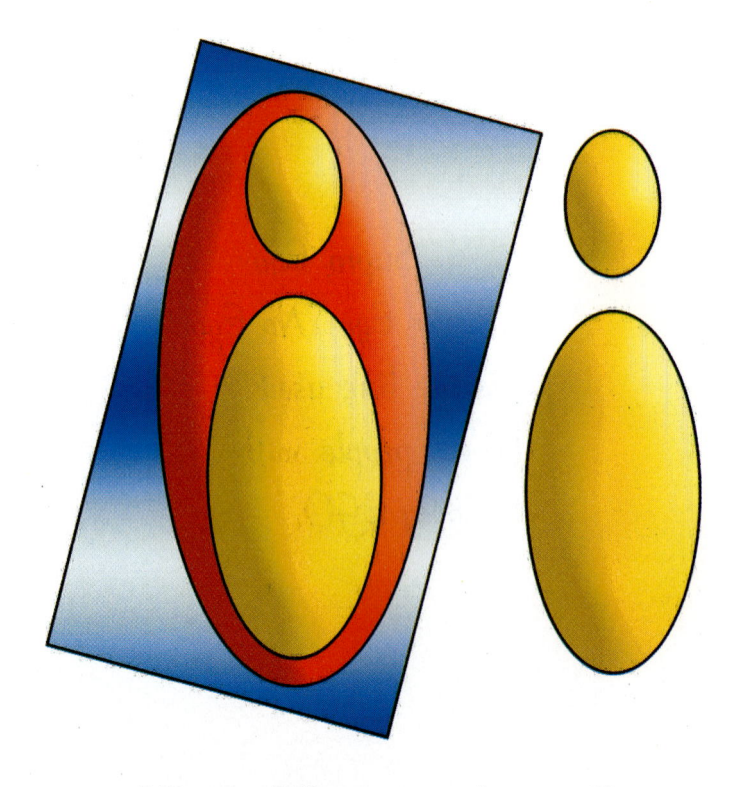

Mirror-Mirror on the wall

MIRROR - MIRROR ON THE WALL

For doing this exercise, you would require a full-length mirror and a chair.

Darken the room and light a night bulb. Place the chair at a distance of three-four feet in front of the mirror.

Sit in front of the mirror with closed eyes, palms resting on the knees and the feet's slightly apart.

Breathe in deeply and hold for ten to twenty seconds and then release. Repeat the breathing pattern five- six times.

Partially open your eyes and see your image on the mirror. Concentrate on the area, which are one to two inches above the head, neck, and shoulders.

If the concentration is good then, you may see a slight yellowish shadow around the region. This is the first sighting of the auric energy.

Once you are able to see the aura of the said regions move your concentration on the other parts of the body. Regular practice with full dedication will allow you to see the full auric circle around the body.

STEP - 2
Once you have mastered the art of seeing the aura with partial opened eyes, the sadhaka should repeat this exercise with eyes open wide.

STEP - 3
The room should be lighted normally and then this exercise should be repeated again with partial open eyes.

STEP - 4
The room should be lighted normally and then this exercise should be repeated again with open eyes.

STEP - 5
Repeat the **Step-1**. In place of the mirror, ask a person to stand in front of you. The background should be preferably white.

STEP - 6
Repeat the **Step-2** to **Step-5** with the person instead of the mirror.

IMPORTANT INSTRUCTIONS FOR DOING THIS EXERCISE

- ❖ Without getting mastery in a step, never jump to the next. This will not give the sadhaka proper control over the senses and he may see erratic things.

- ❖ The clothes worn should be preferably tight fitting. Never do this exercise with loads of woolen clothes, as it will hamper the beginner from seeing the aura.

BENEFITS OF THIS EXERCISE

- ❖ Regular practice of this exercise will allow the sadhaka insights into various colours of aura.

- ❖ This exercise will also help the sadhaka to see and understand the breaks in the Aura. The diseases which might be attached with it.

WATCHING THE INNER SELF

This is an important exercise for understanding the various levels of subtle energy flowing through your body. For this exercise the following things are necessary viz. :

1. The room should be well lit

2. A chair or a seat should be available for you to sit comfortably

3. A full length mirror is preferred (if the mirror is not available then you should have a full length photograph of yours one from the front and the other from the back).

WEEK - 1 & 2 - KNOWING MY BODY

Place the seat opposite to the mirror and keep your eyes wide open so that you are able to see the reflection of your body clearly. Breathe deeply but slowly. On each breath of yours feel the tension releasing from the mind. Place your palms on the knee and concentrate on the reflection of the body in the mirror. Begin from the feet first observe every feature of the feet, the toe area and the ankle. Observe even the minute spot or feature of the feet. After observing, the feet fully observe the ankle and calf area then the knee and thigh region. In the same manner move from the thigh region to the genital area, lower abdomen, abdomen, chest, shoulders, arms, neck, and then the face.

If you are using a photograph, start observing the photograph also in the same manner as you are doing with the mirror.

In the beginning, it is quite possible that you will discover new features about yourself that you were never aware of.

After you have observed every part of your body from the front part, start the same process but now you will have to sit with your body turned on one side and then on another side. Continue this exercise till a time when you are confident that you are fully aware of your body.

WEEK - 3 & 4 - THE INNER SELF

Do this exercise only after getting adequate confidence in the first part of the exercise.

Sit on the chair with the eyes closed. Inhale and exhale deeply. On each inhalation, believe that all the tension from the body will flow out with the exhalation. Visualise your body from the feet until the head in the same manner as you have done in the first two weeks but without the help of the mirror.

No part of the feature should be left out. Continue to do this exercise till you are able to visualise your whole body without any difficulty with no feature left out. You should be able to visualise your body from the front, back, and side ways fully.

WEEK - 5 & 6 - KNOWING THE SENSATION

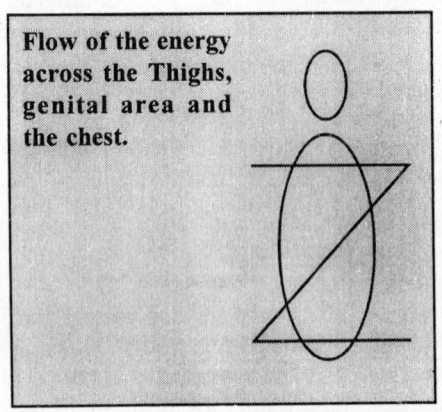

Flow of the energy across the Thighs, genital area and the chest.

After sitting down comfortably partly close your eyes and place your palms on your knee facing skywards. Place your feet 12 inches apart and make sure to use a cotton mat or a carpet to place your feet on. Now visualise that on the caved part of the feet there is a tingling sensation. Feel that the tingling sensation is so strong that you feel it spreading through the caved part of the foot to the entire feet. Let the entire tingling sensation spreading through the feet to the knee, thighs, abdominal area, chest, shoulders, neck, and face. Feel the sensation making your whole body shiver. Breathe in deeply and with every breath feel the sensation growing inside the body. The sensation has now grown so much that t is overflowing from the body and making the environment around you to shiver. The sensation in the environment condenses itself to form a cocoon around your physical self.

Sit in this environment till you feel that you are becoming blank and have become a part of the sensation.

WEEK # 7 & 8 - FEELING THE SPACE

Do the week 5 & 6, exercise first, and then start with the following steps.

After you have become a part of the sensation, feel that your body has become so light that it is floating in the cocoon created by it. Touch your tongue to the palette, lower your chin to touch the lower part of the neck and pull in the anus towards the lungs.

Feel the sensation flowing from the anus to the back of the neck. Let this sensation spread crisscross across the thighs, genital area, and the chest. The flow of the sensation has been shown in the diagram. After achieving this stage, feel that there is flow of energy from the genital area with an surge upwards.

As the energy flows from the Mooladhara chakra to the other chakra feel yourself becoming one with the cocoon.

After continuing with this stage you will achieve the following depending upon the practice :

1. you will feel so light that you may float to which ever area you want to go.
2. You will feel the emptiness growing inside you and transforming your nature from a volatile one to a sober and peaceful one.

WEEK # 9 & 10 - BODY NO BODY

This stage is the continuation of the exercise done in the week 7 & 8. Release the sensation from the body instantly and feel yourself getting lighter and lighter. Feel that the energy cocoon around is transforming into a glowing one with rays emitting outside and making your body cooler and cooler. Feel yourself so light and refreshed that you feel as if you are flying in the sky. Touch and sense the coolness of the clouds flowing by. See your physical body sitting in the room, see every feature of your body.

See the calmness on your face and the glow in the body spreading outward to the environment.

Spread out your ethric arms and swim through the ocean of fantasy. Enjoy this first time out of body experience for as long as possible.

WEEK # 11 & 12 - AURIC ENERGY

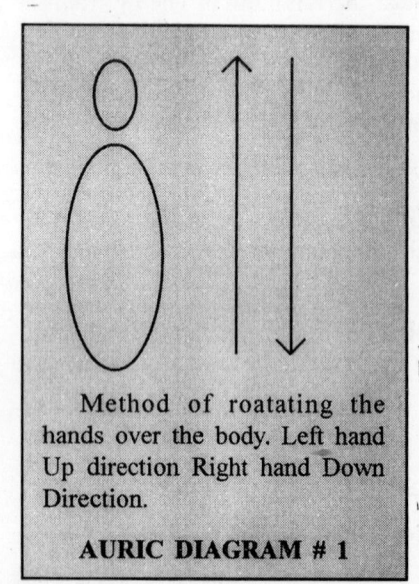

Method of roatating the hands over the body. Left hand Up direction Right hand Down Direction.

AURIC DIAGRAM # 1

This stage is the continuation of the exercise done in the week 9 & 10. Float near to the physical body and spread out your arms towards the body in such a way that your palms are around three to four inches away from your body. Now rotate your arms around the whole body in the method shown in the diagram.

The flow of the left hand should be from the lower part of the body to the upper part of the body and the flow of the right hand should be from the upper part of the body to the lower part of the body. The motion of the hands should be synchronous with the breath i.e. with each inhalation the left hand should move up the body and the right hand should flow down from the body and vice-versa. After you have done the exercise one till you have felt the tingling sensation in the hands move over to do the exercise given in the diagram # 2. Right hand should move towards the chest and the left hand should move towards the stomach. Both the hands should move in synchronous as has been done in the exercise # 1. After some time you will feel the energy vibration flowing through your body. This is the auric energy flowing through your body. It is an important exercise to get in contact with the spiritual energy flowing through your body.

Since this exercise is done through your ethric body, you will not feel tired.

Aura

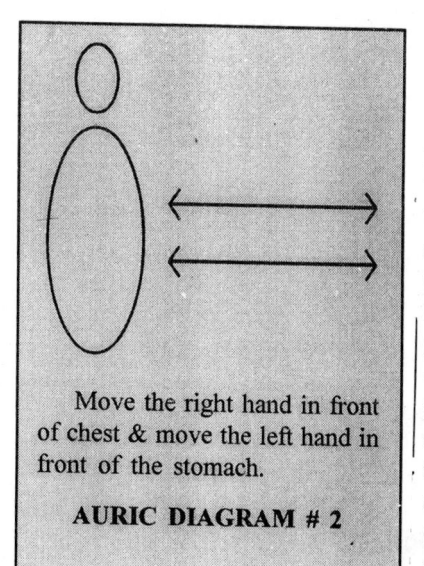

Move the right hand in front of chest & move the left hand in front of the stomach.

AURIC DIAGRAM # 2

Another methodology of doing this exercise:

it is necessary to have two people sitting in opposite direction. One person should sit with the eyes closed and the other should do the exercise one and two with the other person to know the auric energy of the person. Later the first person can do the exercise with the second person. The benefit of this second method is that it is possible to know the energy level of others also, but it should be done only after knowing your own energy levels.

This whole exercise is of 12-week duration, which can be increased as per the dedication of the Sadhaka but should not be decreased.

*Man's purpose is complete
freedom from unhappiness.
The moment he banishes
all pain beyond the possibility
of return, he achieves
the ultimate goal.*

Rg. Veda

Crystal

Humans became aware of the value and utility of the stones during the stone age which is evidenced during the excavation of the various sites. Village shamans and witchcraft practitioners had discovered the potential energies of the stones that were the reason of development of amulets for protection against the evil beings and spells.

Crystal is the most used stone for refraction, amplification, and storage for ages. While searching for the history of the use of crystals through time travel technique, I was surprised to find that the use of the crystals was extensively done during the Golden age of Atlantis. In Atlantis the crystals were used for multi faceted things
- For healing the sick
- For development of the spiritual energy
- For growing

Following small discussion of the advanced uses of crystals by the Atlantians can give insight to the power of crystal.

WHY WAS CRYSTAL ONLY USED?

Crystal has a unique ability to receive, store, and send energies. From the diagram, we can see that when a beam of light directed intensely and focused specifically on certain facets in a gem it will be amplified rather than diminished when exiting from the gem. This amplified energy can be used in many ways. Controlling of the energy is a technical process, some mantras are there, which, when used at the proper time can help in controlling the flow of the amplified energy. In ancient India, great rishies had stones, which could help in warding off the planetary effects on the humans. This science was developed to such an extent that depending on the birth stars gems and stones were provided to the people so that they could achieve more advancement in their materialistic life.

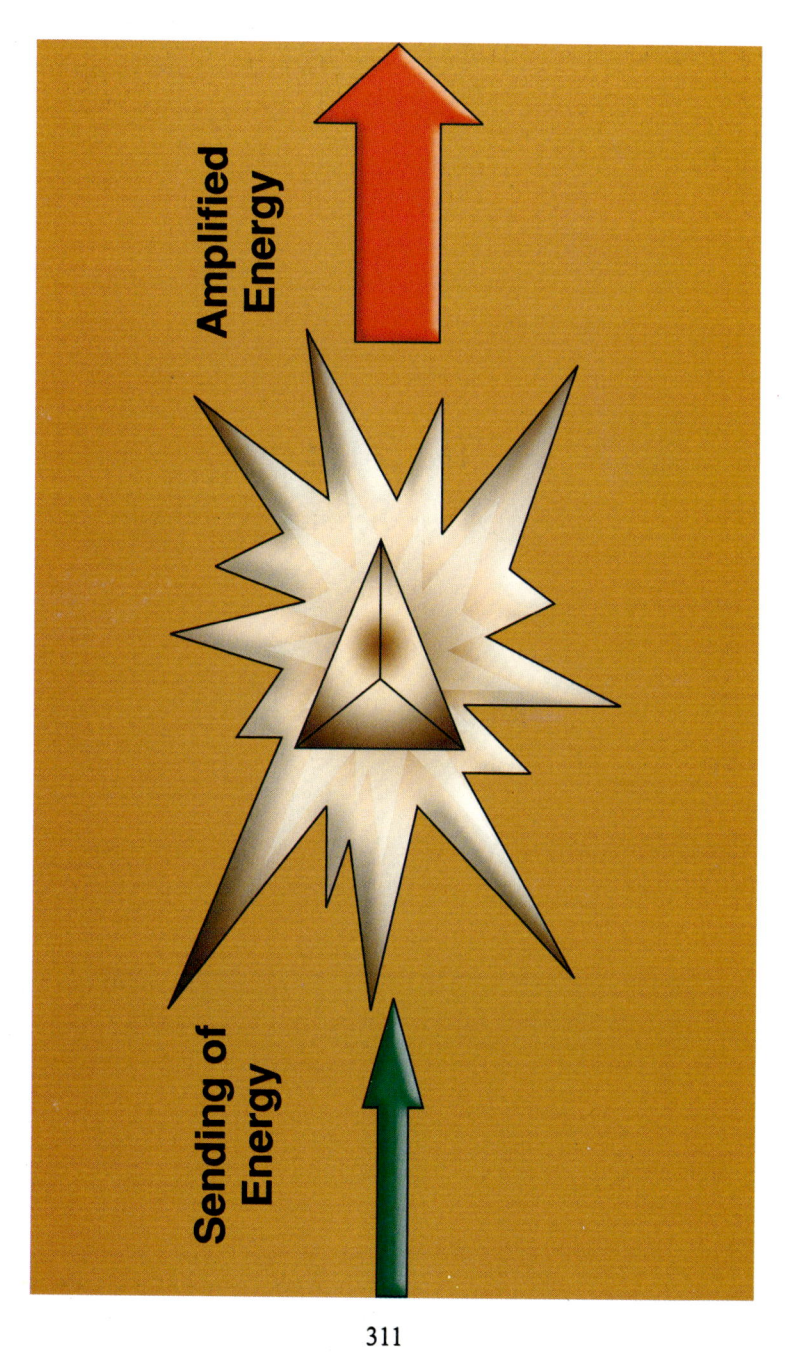

Amplified Energy

Sending of Energy

*The Most
Holy Science
is the
Science of
knowing one self.*

Birth star	Stones that can be used
Aries	Jasper, Ruby
Taurus	Rose Quartz, Lapis Lazuli, Carnelian, Sapphire
Gemini	Citrine, Rock Crystal, Tigers Eye, Agate, Rutile Quartz.
Cancer	Olivine, Emerald, Moonstone
Leo	Quartz Crystal, Diamond, Agate
Virgo	Carnelian, Agate, Jasper, Sapphire
Libra	Emerald, Aventurine, Jade, Sapphire
Scorpio	Garnet, Bloodstone, Ruby, Jasper, Beryl
Sagittarius	Topaz, Jacinth, Obsidian Snowflake
Capricorn	Smokey Quartz, Ruby, Onyx, Jet
Aquarius	Turquoise, Malachite, Aquamarine, Moonstone
Pisces	Amethyst, Opal, Moonstone

Crystals has the inherent ability to transfer, retain, and maintain the intensity of energy and to focus and transmit it and vice versa. Some particular shapes of crystals have more power to store and transmit the energy like crystal ball, pyramid, and energy pencils. In Atlantis, I have seen crystals that were of more than six feet in height with pointed tips. Crystals that were in shape of pyramids were used to harness and transmit the energy of the sun for the spiritual upliftment. Energy pencils were used for healing and psychic surgery. Crystal balls were used for harnessing the energy of the universe itself. The science that they used was simple in nature but the energy that was harnessed was even too much more for them to control.

Smaller crystals, were used for healing, meditation, spiritual development, psychic surgery and healing, development of the mental capacity, telepathic messaging and telekinetic powers were developed with them.

HEALING PROCESS USED BY ATLANTIANS WITH CRYSTALS

The base of the inverted crystal pyramids were used as psychic surgery table, the pyramid crystal was placed on earth after placing a white crystal ball underneath it. On the four corners of the base of the pyramid, four crystal balls were placed. Around the crystal balls, eight small pyramids were placed as shown in the diagram. Before the patient was treated he is asked to lie on the base of the inverted pyramid, healers stand around the pyramid and concentrated energy is sent to the grid of small pyramids in such a way that the energy travelled in anti-clockwise direction. Another group of healers sent the energy to the crystal balls that travelled in the clockwise direction. Both these energies fuse together to fully energise the inverted pyramid. When the inverted pyramid is energised it flows the energy outward to get connected with the crystal balls. At this stage, the patient was asked to lay on the pyramid table and concentrated healing energy was sent to the patient through the energised crystal pencils.

The patient was bathed in the energy of healing power, till he was healed from the cleansing energy. At a particular time, the patient was given only half-hour of treatment in a day. If the patient was having severe disease then the energy was passed on at a very subtle level and the potency was increased with every passing of the day.

A very important feature which was noticed was that when a patient had diseases in delicate parts of the body like brain, eyes, heart, lungs, liver, kidney and sexual organs; the base of the inverted pyramid was covered with golden colour and the patient was wrapped in golden or yellow colour clothing.

Atlantians also used to meditate with crystal grids; these used help in increasing the benefits of meditation. Continuous meditation in presence of crystals used to help Atlantians to sensitise their body parts for receiving and transmitting the energies.

Healing process used by Atlantians with crystals

315

*The Secret of Cosmic knowledge
should never be imparted to a
man who lacks penance,
devotion and attention.*

Bhagawat Gita

DREAM MEDITATION

- Keep a note book and a pencil near the bedside before going to sleep.

- Concentrate on anything that is of prime concern for five to ten minutes. Close your eyes and sleep.

- Whenever you wake up write down any dream you have seen (the sequence is not important).

- By the morning you will have your answer.

- Regular practice of writing about the dreams can help you to understand many of the mystical phenomenon.

318

The above diagram shows the manner in which the Atlantians used to energise their homes and surroundings. In the centre of the house, they used to keep a big crystal pyramid in a web of golden pentagon. Concentrated energy was regularly send to the pyramid sitting near the pentagon; this used to create an energy circle around the room.

This energisation of the pyramid crystal also helped the Atlantean to live for hundreds of years maintaining a youthful appearance.

The Atlantians had developed their science of crystal power to such an extend that they could use it to

- ❖ Propel even heavy ships to levitate and move in the direction so desired.
- ❖ Lifting of heavy objects for building purposes, many sun temples were built with it.
- ❖ Healing even the incurable diseases and rejuvenating skin
- ❖ Develop mind powers to use telepathic power for even conversing.
- ❖ Creating the climates as desired by them.

When the Atlantans became greedier for more power, they started using the crystals for destructive purposes like passing off the energies for making the volcanoes erupt, earthquakes etc., they even tried to shift the energy grid of the earth this led to their total destruction.

The transmission power of the crystals had become so powerful by now that even Atlantians were not able to sustain and control its power. The power of the crystals were so overwhelming that it caved into the oceans thereby drowning one of the most advanced civilisation under the covers of the sea.

321

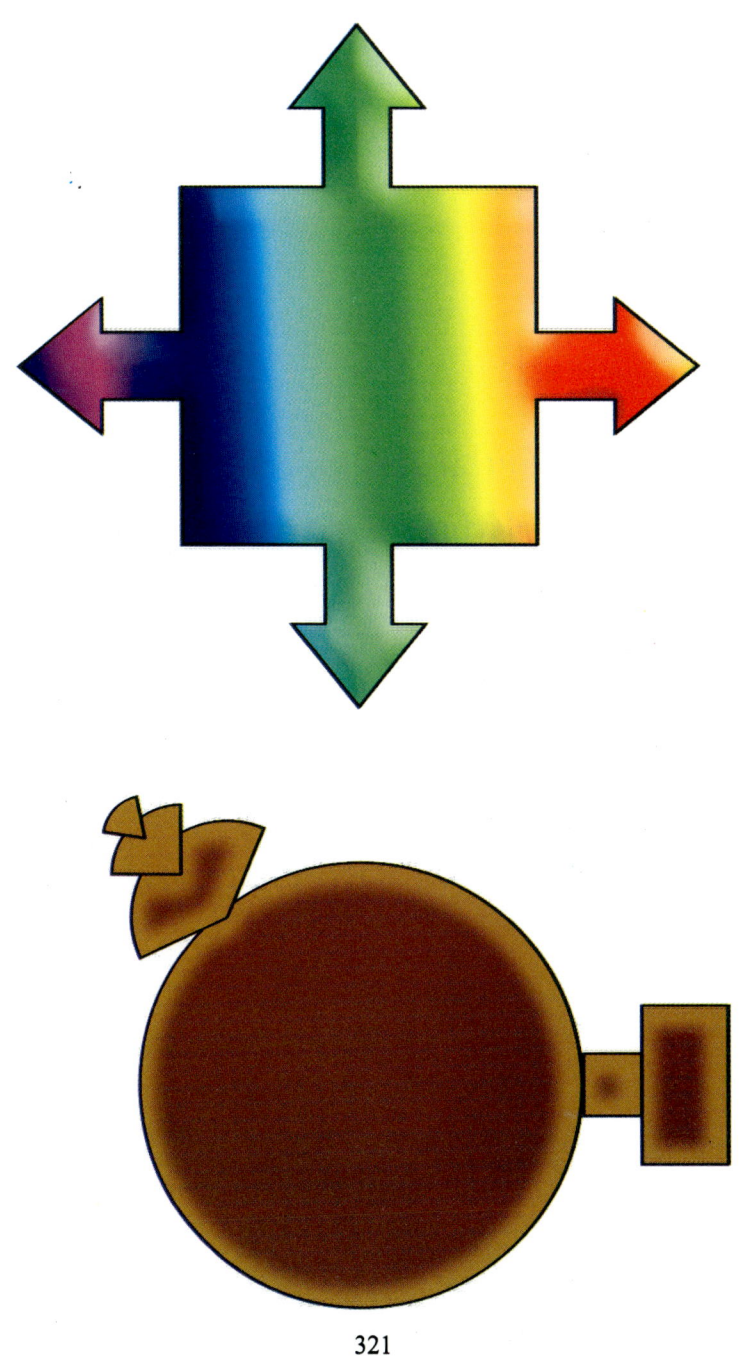

Man attains perfection by placing the petals of devotion through the process of his natural duties and is then considered to be the greatest devotee of the Lord.

Bhagawat Gita

Crystals can be programmed to emit energy for healing and other purposes. The following diagram shows some forms of crystals that have been energised for various purposes.

In the above diagram some different forms of energised crystals are being shown like

- *Two side pointed crystal pencil*
- *Single side pointed crystal pencil*

Both the above two types of crystals are used for healing purposes. One-sided crystal pencil is used for psychic surgery as well in the crystal grid.

- *Crystal six sided pyramid*
- *Crystal egg*

Both the above crystals are used in sending and receiving of the energy.

- *Crystal Sri-yantra (small inscribed)*

This crystal is used for worshipping the Goddess of wealth and prosperity. It also helps in warding off negative energies.

- *Crystal pendulum*

This is a very powerful utility for asking questions and receiving the answers for the same.

- *Crystal Nandi (bull) is used with the crystal box.*

CHOOSING CRYSTALS

Before any crystal is programmed it is necessary that the proper crystal is selected. As properly selected crystal would provide the most beneficial results to the sadhaka.

All crystals have their own individual frequency of vibration. Crystal that is liked at the first sight is the right crystal for us. Some useful methods, which can be used to select the crystal, liked by the individual.

- ❖ Stand opposite an array of crystals, close your eyes, and quietly meditate for a few moments with pure heart without touching any crystal. On opening your eyes, the first crystal or gem your eyes see is the crystal for you.

- ❖ Stand opposite an array of crystals, close your eyes, and move your right hand over the various crystals in a very smooth manner and after some time you will find one stone will be stuck to your palms. This is your stone, which is very similar to your auric energy.

- ❖ Stand opposite the array of crystals and move your gaze all the crystals in a very smooth manner and your eyes will be stuck on the crystal your body accepts.

- ❖ Stand opposite the array of crystals spread your right hand over the array of crystals (half to one inch above) without touching the stones. Move your hand back and forth over the crystals. At one place, your right hand will feel as if drawn toward the crystal like a magnet. This is the crystal for you.

- ❖ Stand opposite an array of crystals with a pendulum. Use the dowsing technique to find the most suitable stone for you.

CLEANSING YOUR CRYSTALS

After choosing your crystal, it is important to cleanse them. The main reasons for cleansing the crystals

- ❖ Crystals has the inherent quality of attracting all kinds of energies be it positive or negative. These energies if not cleansed properly can hamper your programming and using of the crystals

- ❖ Crystals can also accumulate energies when passing through various hands. These energies should be removed from the crystals.

Steps of the cleansing processes have been discussed below:-

- ❖ Hold the crystal with both the hands, close your eyes. Visualise a white light surrounding the room you are sitting in. Let the white light totally engulf you and the crystal. Now visualise a violet light entering your crown chakra. Let this violet light pass through the third eye chakra, throat chakra and heart chakra. From heart let the light flow to the hands holding the crystal. Let the violet light engulf the crystal. Pray in the following manner

> O Lord with your energy flowing through me
> I command that this crystal be cleaned
> of all the negative energies
> Let only the natural and
> pure energies remain
> The process of self-cleaning begin.

Feel that the negative energies are being dispersed from the crystal. Reiki channels can use the Reiki energy to cleanse the crystal. Reiki II initiate can use the following symbols in sequence to cleanse the crystal Cho Ku Rei, Hon Sha Ze Sho Nen, Sei Hei Ki, Cho Ku Rei.

- Hold the crystal under the running cold water from the tap. Waterfalls, free flowing rivers, lakes, sea are very powerful medium, if you find one then the same should be used for purifying the crystals. Visualize all the negative energies being washed away.

- After washing, keep the crystals under sunlight for a day.

- Take a bowl of sea water, if you cannot find seawater use a bowl of water with common salt (in one bowl of plain water, add half fistful of salt mix it very well). Put the crystals in the bowl for a day.

- After washing, keep the crystals under sunlight for a day.

- Locate a place in a garden, which has good quality sand without any stones or dirty material. If your house is in a flat then take a flowerpot made of clay fill it with fresh clean sand. Bury the crystal in the earth and let it say in it for a period of three days. If the crystals are buried in a pot, place the pot under a yellow bulb light for a period of five days.

- Take a bowl of sea water, if you cannot find seawater use a bowl of water with common salt (in one bowl of water, add half fistful of salt mix it very well). Put the crystals in the bowl for a day.

- After washing, the crystals keep the crystals under sunlight for a day.

- Now the crystal is cleansed of any negativity.

Satyug is the dawn,
Dwapar Yuga is the noon,
and Kalyuga is the night.

When a man is asleep
he represents Kalyuga
when he wakes it is Dwapar Yuga
and when he performes his
duties it is Satyuga

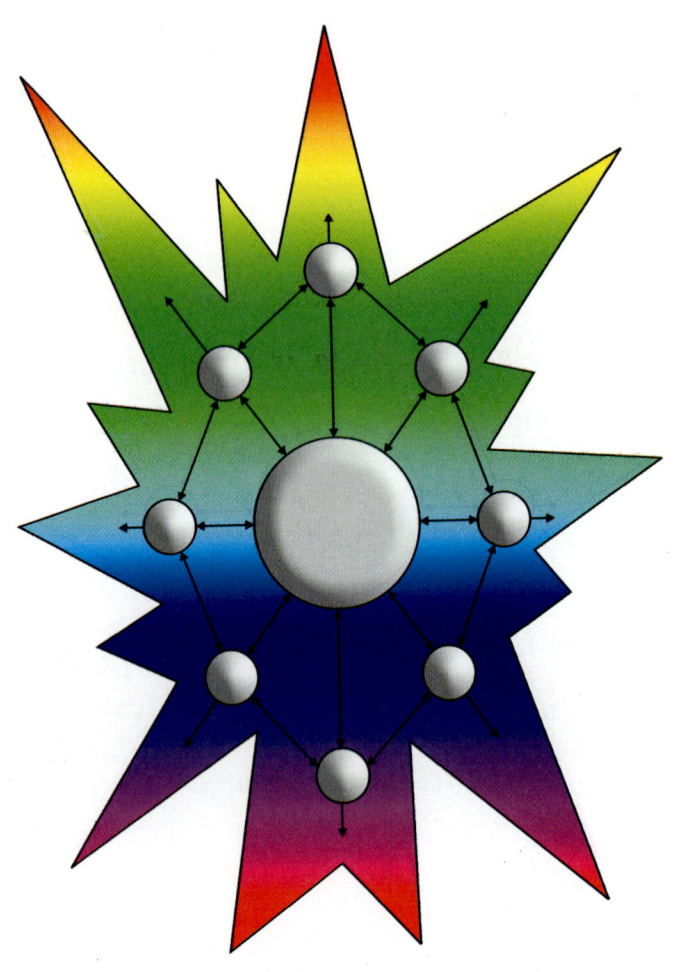

Programming your Crystals

PROGRAMMING YOUR CRYSTALS

The process of programming of the crystals is very simple and much effective. Some method of programming the crystals will be given in the following sections

Quartz crystals can be programmed in the following ways for the benefit of Studying, Meditation, Healing, and transmission of energy.

When meditation is done with the crystal touching the body or near the crystal, the energy development is fast. The subtle energies are absorbed by the crystals and as time passes by you will feel that you donot have to try hard to get into the state, as the energy of the crystal helps in transporting you to that state within minutes of sitting for dhyana. The more the crystals are used the more in-depth dhyana can be done by the sadhaka. It also helps in fast concentration and relaxing the tensed muscles. Many a times the crystals can provide the answers to problems faced by you during the process of dhyana.

If meditation is done in-group then the energy transmitted is very strong. If the group uses crystal while meditating then the energy so transmitted will be very high.

The group of crystals energises the crystal in centre and this energised crystal transmits the energy to the meditators. The central crystal acts as energy booster for the crystals used by the meditators.

If music is played while the meditation is done with the crystals then the energy stored up in the energy grid is far more than what can be achieved without the music. Caution should be taken that the music so played should be soothing to the mind. If the music is soothing then the crystal also reacts by change of colour or transmission of energy.

The energies of the crystals when used for healing can help in developing the healing energy manifold thereby allowing the person to be healed very fast. The following section will cover the various techniques to which crystal can be put to use for healing purposes.

CRYSTALS

Quartz Crystals have a cold tendency and this helps in maintaining the body temperature and keeping the blood pressure from going up.

If the sadhaka can wear crystal necklace then it is very good for him as

- ❖ It helps in maintaining the body temperature
- ❖ It helps in controlling the blood pressure
- ❖ Regular use of crystals also helps reducing the anger in the person
- ❖ The crystals eliminates the bad affects of the negativity will absorb most of the negativity surrounding the person.
- ❖ The crystals also absorb black magic and sorcery done by people.

Tamasic and Sattvic tatvas are two sides of one coin. Rajsic tatvas helps a person to reach from a tamasic activities to Satvic ones.

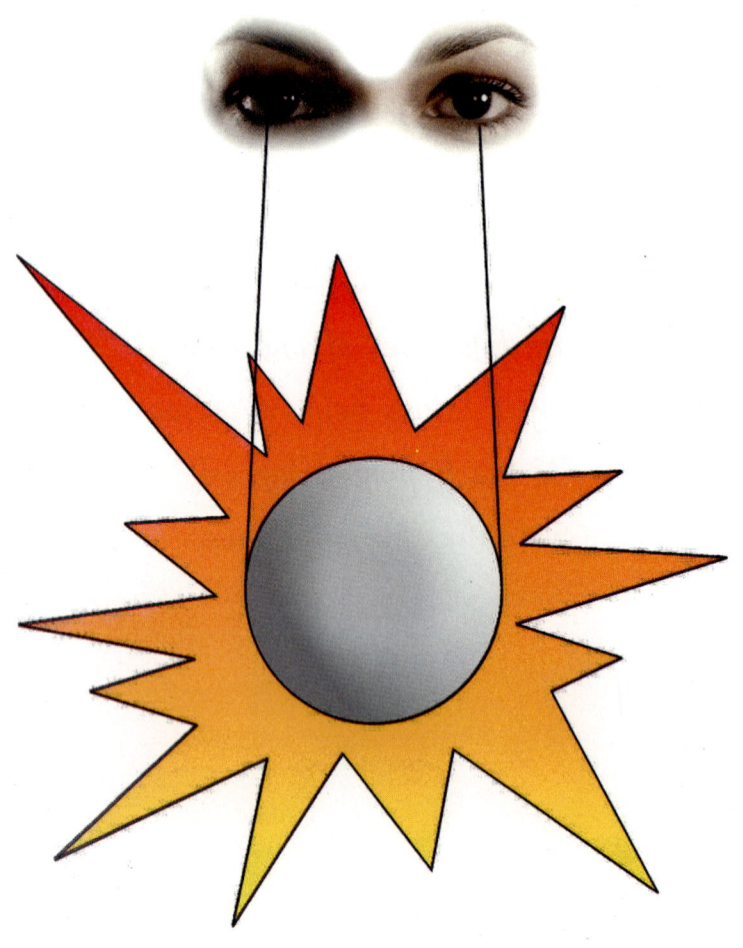

Crystal Meditation

CRYSTAL MEDITATION

Place the crystal in front of you. The crystal should be placed at the height of the eye level. Concentrate your gaze on the crystal feel that the energy is being passed from the third eye chakra to the crystal. Let the energy sent by you engulf the crystal.

Regular meditation on the crystal will give you insight into the true power of the crystal. This can be witnessed by closing the eyes opposite the crystal and spreading out your hands towards the crystal. The palms should face the crystal and move the hands in front and back of the crystal. After a particular period, you will feel the pulling sensation from the crystal. This energy from the crystal can be collected and transmitted to the desired place or location for healing and other purposes.

While concentrating on the crystal, if you have any mantra of your own then the same can be chanted while doing so. When meditation is done with mantra, then the crystal should be touched this will enhance the power of the crystal.

Reiki channels can use the following symbols for getting the maximum benefit from the crystal. Mentally

CRYSTAL BALL MEDITATION

Place a crystal ball in front of you on the table at the eye level.

Close your eyes and start breathing deeply from the stomach.

The breathing should be held on each inhalation and then released after a short time. This should be repeated for a period of five minutes.

Open your eyes and gaze on the crystal ball from the centre to the edges.

Visualise from the heart a ball of energy flowing out. Hold the ball of energy in the palm and direct the energy to the crystal ball.

When the energy ball hits the crystal ball feel that, the energy is released from the crystal engulfing you. Repeat the process till you feel the whole of the room you are sitting in is filled with the cosmic energy from your ethric body.

When the whole room is filled with the cosmic energy, visualise that the whole energy is converting in to a big ball of energy. Let this energy enter your body through the heart chakra.

If the energy is to be used for healing somebody then the huge ball of energy should be directed to the concerned person chanting the name of the person and praying for his speedy recovery.

Warning : When this energy is used for another person then it should be done only once in a day. If it is being for oneself then any number of times, it can be repeated.

BENEFITS OF THIS MEDITATION
- This meditation increases the energy levels of a person manifold.
- It helps in sealing the broken aura
- If the big energy ball is redirected to the crystal ball then the crystal is energised and regular meditation will enhance the energy of the crystal. This energy can be used later for redirecting the same for healing a person.
- Before beginning of any meditation, if this meditation is done then the depth of meditation will high.
- Reiki channels can also use symbols with this technique.

Crystal ball Meditation

Food should be eaten through the five senses each sense should be able to savour the taste of each particle of the food.

CRYSTAL GRID MEDITATION

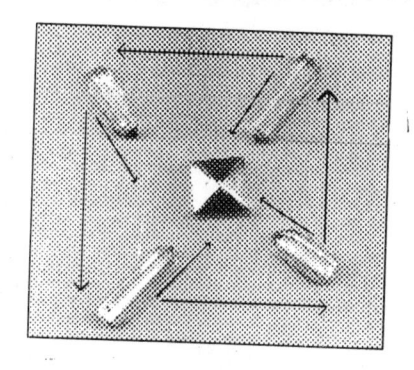

This is a very important technique of manifesting the energy. For the formation of the grid, you would require the following

One big crystal 4-8 one sided pencil crystals a piece of cloth or white paper. Place the big crystal on the white cloth in the centre and diagonally place the rest of the crystals around it as shown in the diagram.

Sit near the crystal and place the palms facing the crystal. Concentrate on the big crystal and feel the energy from the concentration travelling from the centre to the pencil crystal in the direction shown in the diagram.

Let the energy travel from the pencil crystal in the direction shown at the speed of thought. Siphon the energy in the form of pyramid from the crystal grid like water is drawn from the filled sponge.

This energy can also be left in the big crystal for later use.

This technique can also be used with the Reiki symbols.

PROCESS OF USING CRYSTALS FOR HEALING WITH REIKI ENERGY

Hold the crystal in the left hand close your eyes and say the attitude of gratitude and when the healing energies starts flowing cup the crystal with the right hand with only a part of the crystal showing and let energies flow into the crystal. When you feel ready release, the energy on the specific part of the body of the person Reiki II channels should draw the symbols in the following manner with the right hand using the first finger and middle finger

Cho Ku Rei
Hon Sha Ze Sho Nen
Sei Hei Ki

For healing session, crystals with one-sided tip are more useful.

The single-terminated end of crystal should point towards the person to be healed and gently move the crystal around the whole body in a clockwise direction. After every move, visualise the flow of the Reiki energy symbols in the same as above. This will strengthen the auric energy of the person.

The crystal should be then pointed towards the specific part of the person's body, which requires healing.

Mentally draw the symbols in the following order above your head

Cho Ku Rei
Hon Sha Ze Sho Nen
Sei Hei Ki

(names of the symbols should be repeated thrice)

Visualise that the symbols are converted into pure energy and entering the Sahasrar chakra, Ajna Chakra, Vishuddhi chakra and reaching the Anahat chakra. Let the energy from the Anahat chakra flow to the palms. This energy is redirected from the palms to the crystals that flow from the tip of crystal like the laser beam.

Crystal

This energy from the crystal is intensified with every passing second. This pure energy helps in healing the disease of the person.

The duration of crystal healing required can be understood when the flow of Reiki energy stops or when the heart intimates to stop the session.

The single-terminated end of crystal should again be pointed towards the person to be healed and gently move the crystal around the whole body in a clockwise direction. After every move, visualise the flow of the Reiki energy symbols in the same as above. This will strengthen the auric energy of the person.

Even when the disease of the person is not known, the crystal energy knows the place of the disease to be healed and reaches that spot and eradicates the disease before coming out like a war hero. The major reason for this is that every object in this world works on the concept of vibration, crystal and cosmic healing energies recognise this and flow in the direction of the need. This flow of energy helps in balancing the flaw in energy vibration. This explanation would look very simple this is so because for so many years we have been complicating normal things for no reason as such.

This technique can be used for healing one's own body also.

ENERGY MANIFESTATION WITH THE CRYSTALS

Hold the crystal in the right hand with the left hand supporting it. Concentrate on the centre of the crystal. Visualise that from the crystal a golden light is emerging and engulfing your hands.

Concentrate on the golden light covering your hands and let the energy flow from the crystal and changing the colour of the surrounding into rainbow colour.

Let the golden colour fill the room and the rainbow colour engulfs your hands.

Concentrate on the centre of the crystal and visualise the need for being etched on the centre of the crystal.

Visualise that the need etched on the crystal is already possessed by you. Visualise everything you would be doing when the need is fulfilled and let all the images are etched on the crystal. Let the energy from the third eye chakra energise the crystal so that the needs are manifested.

Repeat the whole everyday twice till the need is fulfilled.

IMPORTANT :

    a. Never use the crystal used for manifesting of needs for any other purposes.

    b. Never visualise more than one need at a time. If there are more needs then different, crystals can be used. As a advice it is proper to use only one crystal and one need at one time as multiple needs and multiple crystals can disintegrate the flow of the energy.

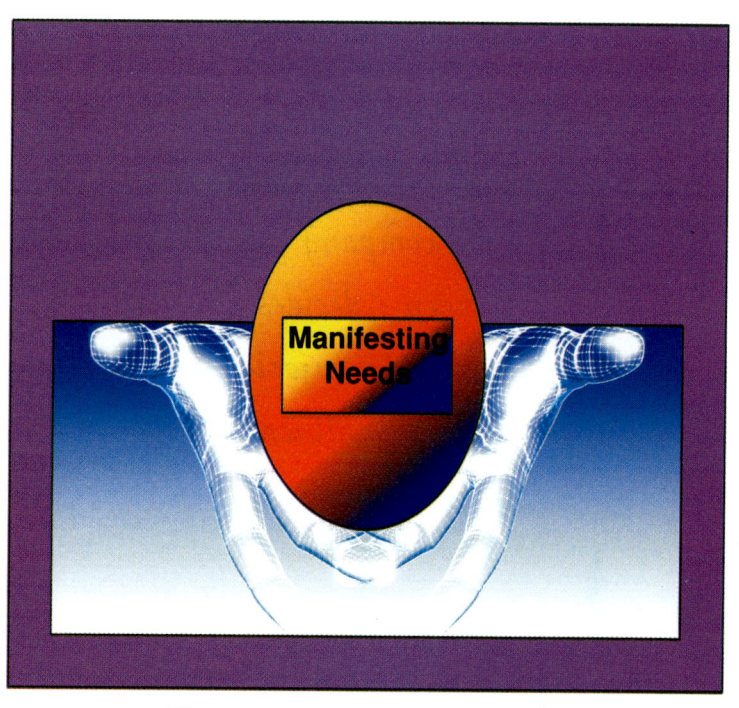

**Energy Manifestation
with the Crystals**

The places you frequent,
the company you
keep - decides
the **sattvic**, **rajasic** or
tamasic influences
on your mind.

Charak Samhita

Marma Gyana and Mudra

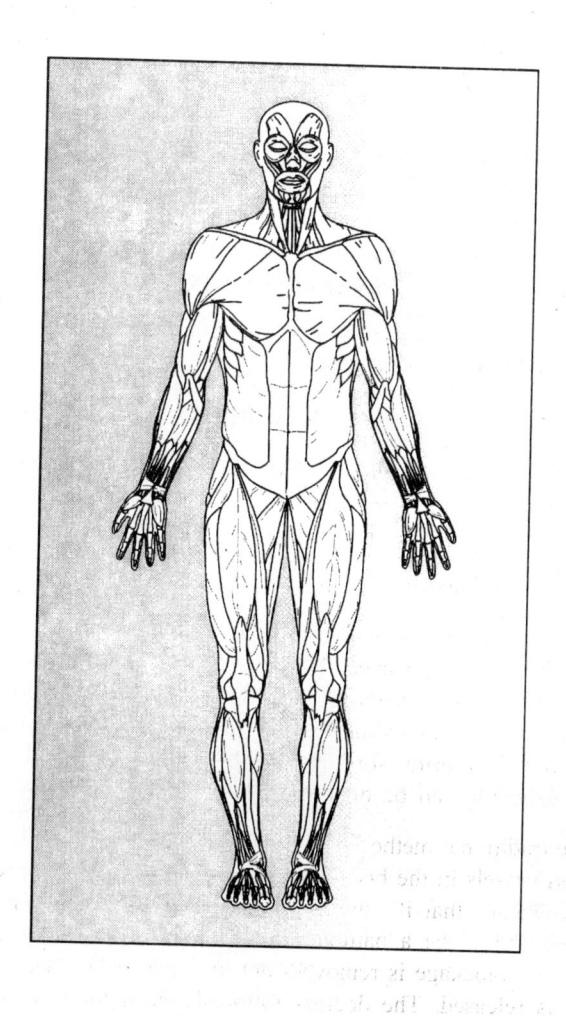

Marma gyana or the knowledge of the vital points of the body was an ancient Indian science, which was used by the great physicians for healing people. This science travelled from India to China and developed into the science of Acupuncture. Later this science travelled to Japan and developed into Shiatsu. This science was mostly used by rishies, Boudh Bhikshus for healing people. Later martial artists for winning used the knowledge of the vital points in the body over there opponents.

In ancient India, people used the knowledge of vital points in Kalaripayatu. This knowledge is still used for understanding the physical flow of the body. When a fighter gets hurt then traditional herbs and correct pressure on the vital points would release the block of flow of blood, thereby relieving the person of the pain.

Before understanding how the cure was done, it is important to know why do we get the diseases.

We get diseases due to two major reasons

- *Human Error : These include lack of hygiene, eating habits, intake of alcohol, cigarettes, drugs etc.*
- *Environmental Factors: Pollution, wounds and bruises, old age and genetic factors.*

Once the reason for the disease is understood the flow of the ch'i in the body is to be checked. Believing that the ethric body and the physical body of the person are not two but a part of the same individual helps in understanding the flow of energy. Doing a Aura Scan on the body can bring forth the problematic area if not then the physical checking can be done for getting the same results.

In the traditional method of healing, it is accepted that all the veins and blood vessels in the body have their endings at the hands and the feet. This means that if a particular part of the body is having pain then there should be a natural/ forced blockage in the flow of the blood. If the blockage is removed then the pain in the particular part of body is released. The doctors following the allopathic pattern of medicines are now accepting this concept.

Marma Gyana and Mudra

How to understand if there are any blockages or not

- ❖ Some part of body will be warm, cold, numb, dry, oily, hard, soft or discoloured compared with other parts of the body.
- ❖ The places where the above symptoms are present the Prana is leaking due to the blockage.
- ❖ Our body is made of the three dosas Vata, Pitta, Kapha. They are naturally present in the body in the form of the Five tatvas in the body. Even if one of the tatvas get disbalanced then the diseases are formed in the body. Due to the blockages in the water, blood, fat, bone marrow, excreta, urine the diseases take dangerous proportions.

After years of research and development, our great sages and rishies had found that the concept of diseases could be easily found from the Nadi Shodhana. Nadi forms the mirror image of the body's status be it sick or healthy. The major reasons for this is that in the body there are millions of veins which work as per the instructions of the Central Nervous System and have endings at some of the body parts.

These body parts form the image of the body itself. Then information regarding any diseases in the body is also passed on to these vein ends. If a person knows how to understand the information of the veins then he will be able to solve the problems of the patient.

This is the major reason the concept of Nadi shodhana is still used by both the doctors and the traditional healers. These nadis are the mirror image of the person body and show the problems of the body by just following the various patterns of pulsation in these nadis.

To prove this point lets do a experiment:

Just after waking up in the morning feel the pulse by placing your left index and middle finger on the vein of the right hand. Count the pulse for a minute and release. Note the reading on a piece of paper. Repeat the same process after relieving yourself and taking the bath.

Experiment this process before taking the food and after taking the food, count the pulse in the afternoon and in the evening. During emotional phases like sadness, anger, love, hatred etc. also check the pulse reading, as it will give lot of information.

In all the cases, we can see that there is difference in the flow of the pulse. Regular checking and noting of the pulse flows, we can easily diagnose the diseases and the tendency we have during a period of time.

The rate of pulse per minute of a healthy person during various stages of development

New born child	140
Till the age of 4 years	120-135
From 4 to 6 years	100
From 6 till 14 years	90
From 15 till 50	70
Beyond 50	75

Marma Gyana and Mudra

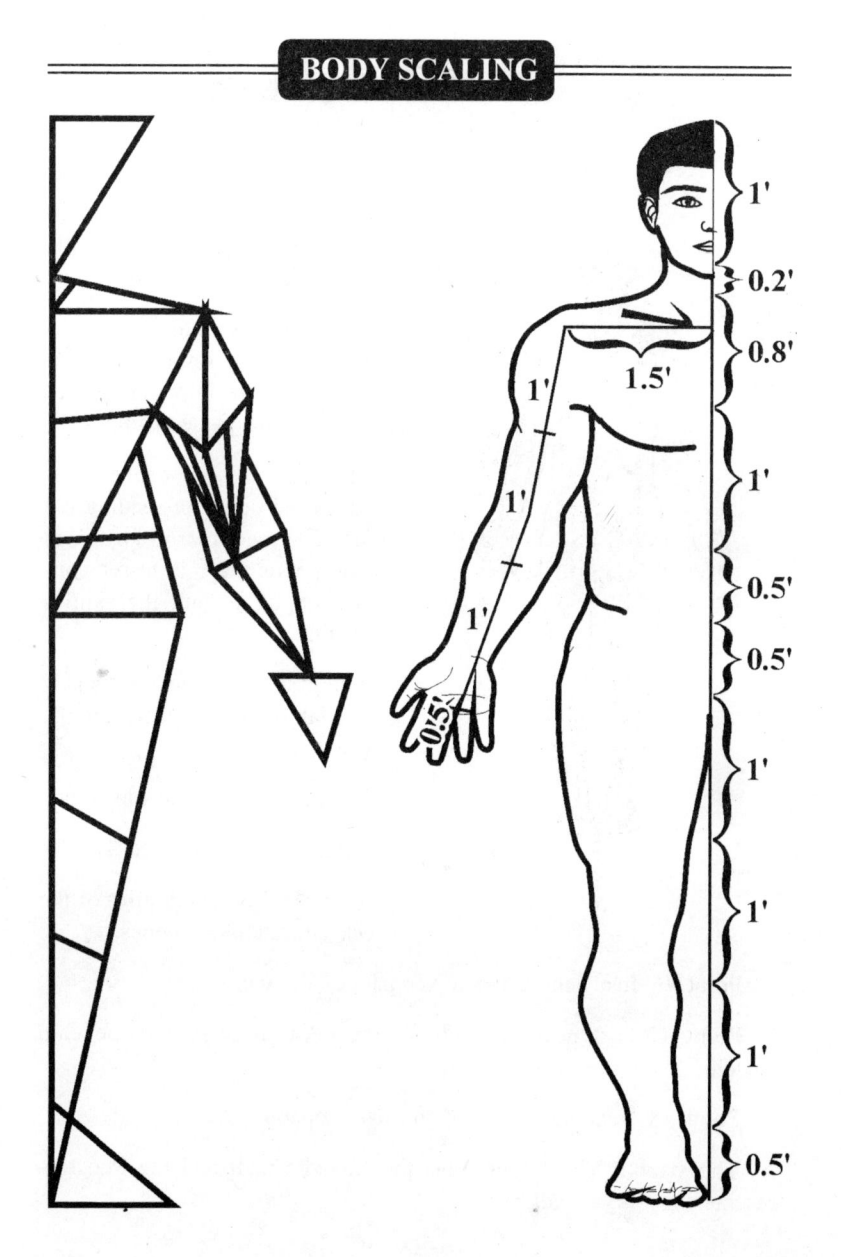

BODY SCALING

- 1'
- 0.2'
- 0.8'
- 1.5'
- 1'
- 1'
- 1'
- 0.5'
- 0.5'
- 0.5'
- 1'
- 1'
- 1'
- 0.5'

VITAL POINTS IN THE BODY

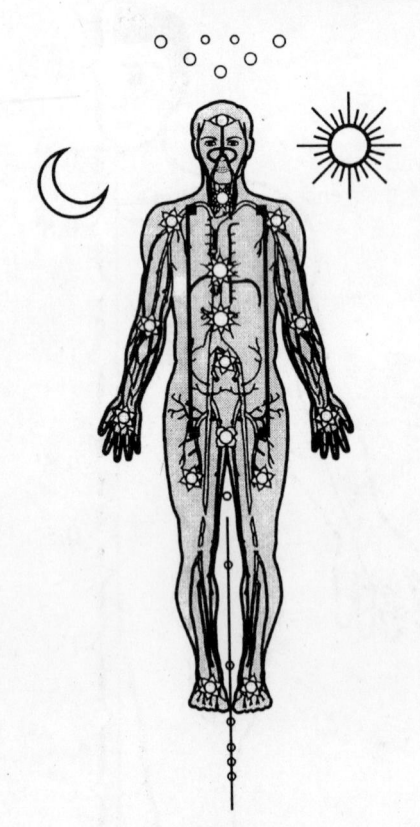

In the diagram, we can see the flow of the veins with the main minor chakras located at the various junctions of the body.

Eight centres have been encircled with the respective numbers showing the important places for taking the pulse readings.

Point #1 This is the most commonly used point for reading the pulse. The main reason for this is in the hands there is lesser condensation of fat and the skin is very thin.

Point #2 Just near the testis is the vital point for checking the pulse.

Point #3 Near the hip joints.

Point #4 Back of the ankle.

Point #5 Near the joint of the neck and shoulder bones.

Point #6 Just behind the lower part of the ear.

Point #7 Just near the joint of the neck muscles and the chin muscle.

Point #8 Near the joints of the nasal openings.

The symbol Moon represents the Chandra nadi and the Sun represents the Surya nadi.

The bracketed area shows the Major chakras and the other flowers represent the minor chakras. The circles flowing from the earth to the Mooladhara chakra represent the seven layers of human energy fields that have been explained in the **Aura Section.** Seven circles above the head of the person represents the seven energy fields which controls the birth, death, karma, relations, place, loka of origin and stages to nirvana.

The whole body is covered with a network of veins and nerves. Most of the veins and nerves have their endings at the fingertips and toes. Hand and feet represent the image of the whole body in itself. The flow of the energy also happens at both the hands and feet, the fingertips have the quality of drawing in energy, and the toes at the feet have the tendency for flowing out of the energy. This was known to our rishies and that is why we have the custom of touching the feet of elders for blessings. When a person blesses, he transfers the positive energy to the other through his fingertips and from toes the energy flows out to the fingertips of the person seeking the blessing and the whole energy is received by the crown chakra. This is the reason in temples and churches we see Lord is blessing with his hands and we bow down to receive the blessing.

This goes to show that the palms and the base of the feet form the mirror image of the organs in the body. Knowledge of the major points in the palms related to the organs in the body can help a sadhaka to remove the problem by pressing the related points.

HOW TO PRESS THE AREA OR THE POINT

- ❖ Use the thumb finger to press the related energy centres related to the body.
    - ✸ The thumb finger should be used in such a way that equal distribution of pressure is given to the area.
    - ✸ Never pressurise a area with the tip of the thumb.
- ❖ While treating others, both the thumbs can be used. Pressure should be exerted by one thumb over the other.

❖ While giving energy to the larger area index, middle and ring fingers can be used on the specific area.

HOW MUCH PRESSURE TO GIVE

❖ The points related to the organs that require healing are very sensitive to pain. So the pressure should be given upto a limit the person can withstand. Slowly the pressure should be increased.

THE ROLE OF THE NADIS FOR A SADHAKA

It is important for a sadhaka to know about the nadis and other vital points before he delves deep in to the realm of the meditation.

The knowledge of the nadis is helpful to the sadhaka in the following manner

❖ It helps the sadhaka to understand the flow of the energy inside the body

❖ It helps the sadhaka to control various emotional tendencies flowing inside the body before and during the process of dhyana.

❖ If a sadhaka is suffering from some disease or trauma then concentrating on the particular vital point during the process of meditation helps in solving the problems to a great extend. Regular practice with the nadi gyana can help heal the disease or the trauma.

❖ Once a sadhaka is well versed with the flow of the energy inside his body then he will be able to understand the flow of energy in another person, thereby helping the person to be healed.

❖ In this section, we will talk about the energy points in the palms and base of the feet. A sadhaka who sits for meditation will find it easier to concentrate on the said vital points by using his fingers.

FLOWS OF ENERGY IN VARIOUS PARTS OF THE BODY

Palms (Left and Right)

1- Energy flowing points   2- Minor chakra   3- Radiance minor chakras

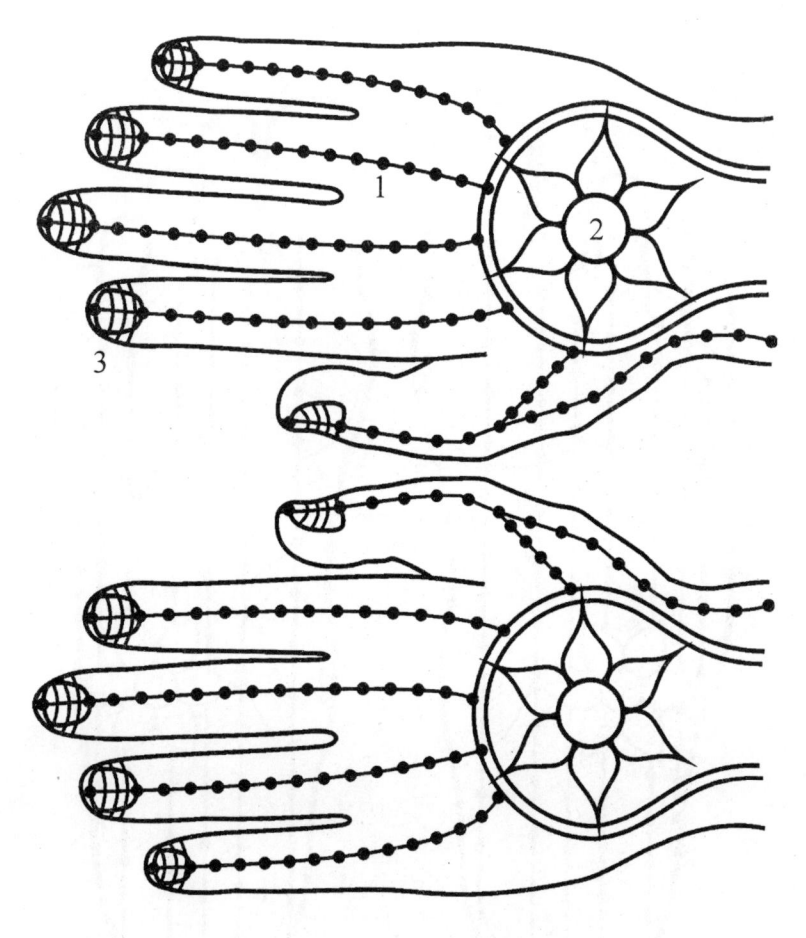

ENERGY FLOWS IN THE BASE OF THE FEET

1-shows the flow of energy and the energy points related with it. 2- Shows the minor chakra in the centre of the base. 3- Shows the radiance minor chakras.

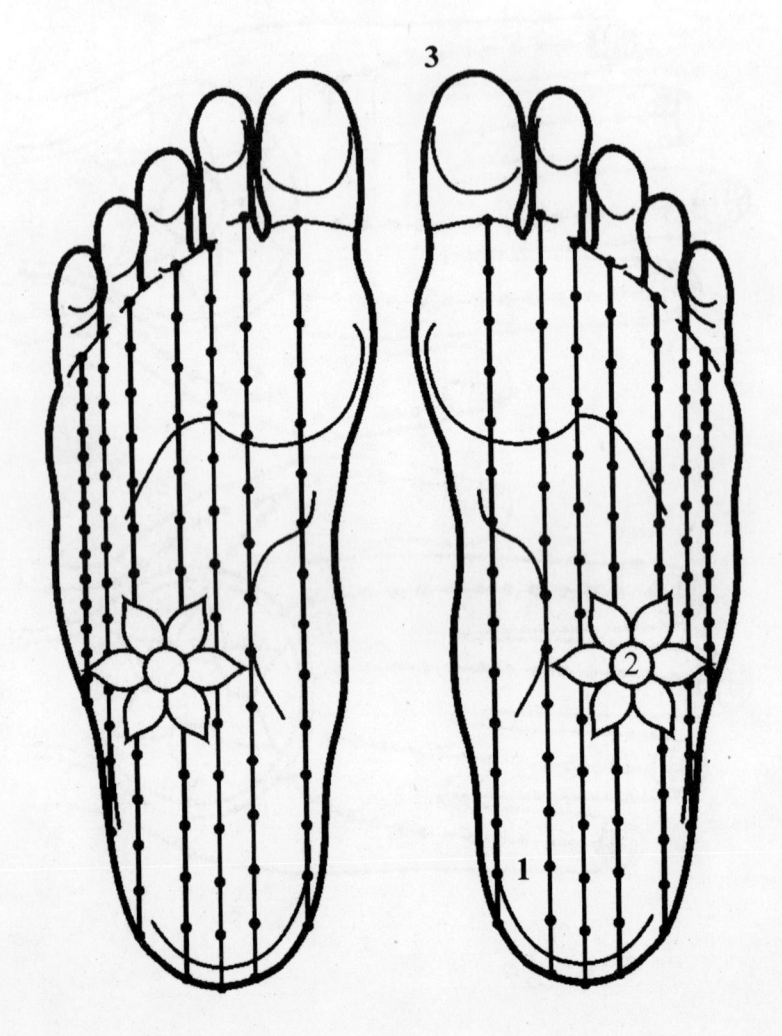

Energy flows in the Arms   **Energy flows in the legs**

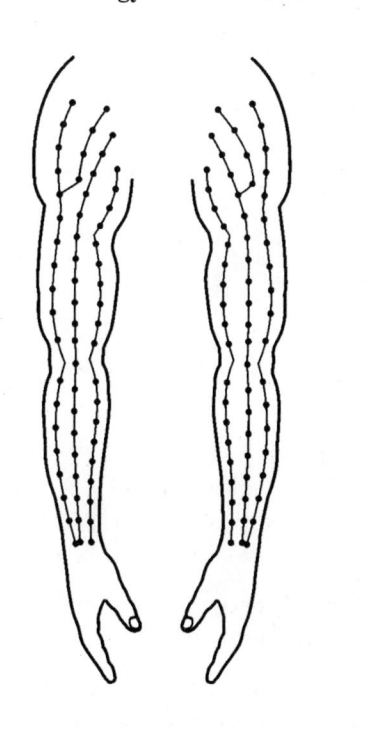

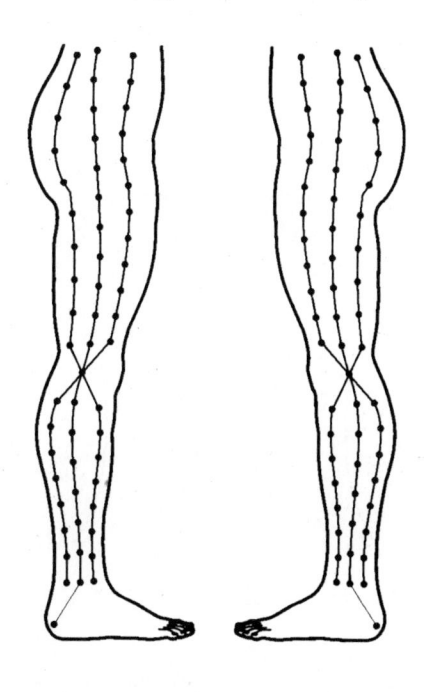

The flow of the energy through the points helps in passing the required strength to the arms and the legs. When a person is walking the strength required is calculated and it is passed on to the feet. The minor chakra and the Radiance chakra situated at the base of the feet calculate this energy requirement.

The same happens when a person is picking up a heavy load then the strength required for that job is calculated before the minor chakra and radiance minor chakras situated at the palm.

ENERGY FLOWS IN THE BODY

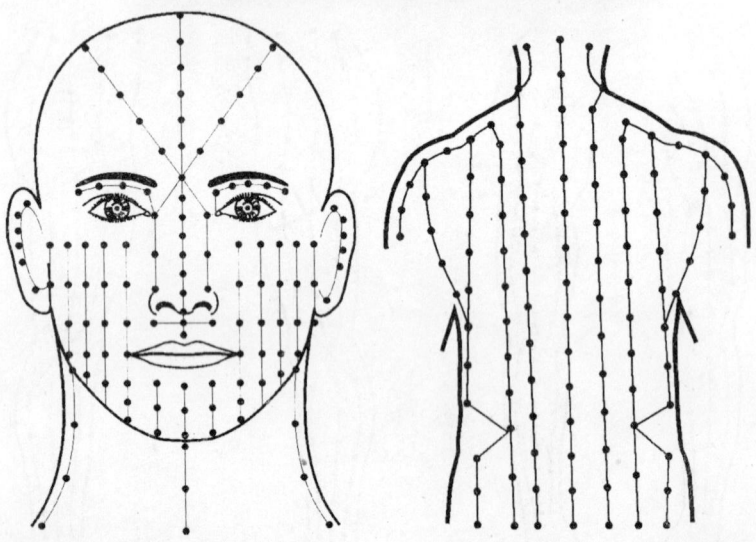

Flow of energy in the face

Flow of energy in chest and throat region

These diagrams show only the flow of the energy in the face and the chest region and do not show the major and the minor chakra, which are situated in the body regions shown above.

Flow of energy in the face shows the process of receiving and transmitting the signals sent from the brain to the various parts of the body. These signals are controlled by the minor chakras, which are located on either side of the cheek and the eye lobes.

Flow of energy in chest and throat region shows the sending and receiving signal points from the brain. Two major chakras (Vishuddhi and Anahat chakra) and their related minor chakras control this region.

The various energy points in the body shown in the above diagrams, which form the vital source of prana in the body.

Marma Gyana and Mudra

ACCUPRESSURE POINTS IN THE PALMS

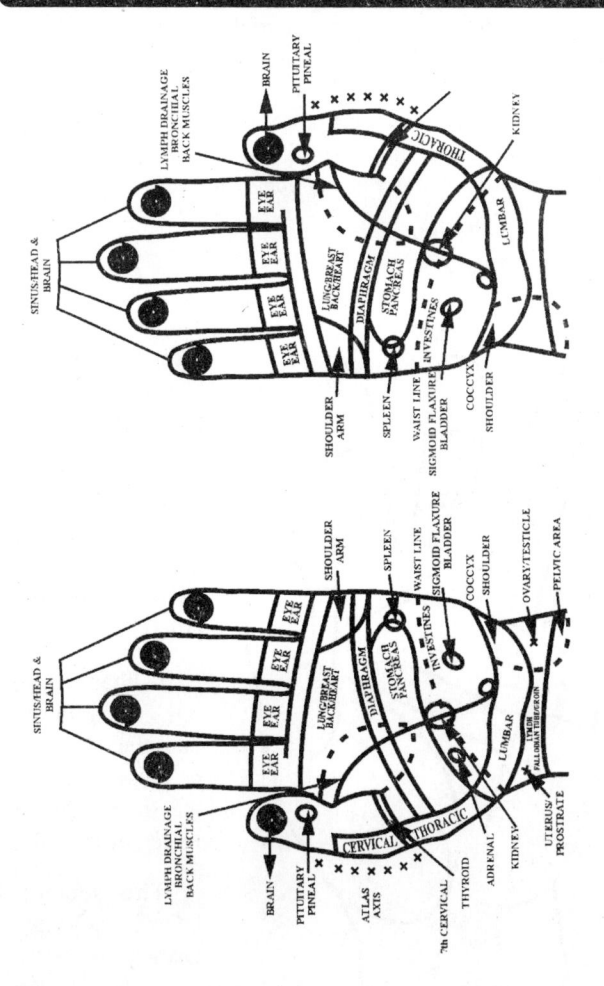

The body parts shown in the palm are related with the physical aspect of the body. If any of the shown part of the body is suffering from a disease then the shown position should be pressed for a period of five minutes at regular intervals till the pain is reduced.

MUDRAS

Mudras were used from time immemorial in Indian classical dances. Natya sastra has thousands of mudras, which have helped dancers to mesmerise the audience. Lord Shiva gave this science for the benefit of the human race. Mudras are like short cut keys for achieving success in material and spiritual world. In this section, we will cover some of the important mudras for achieving success in the spiritual world.

HAND MUDRAS

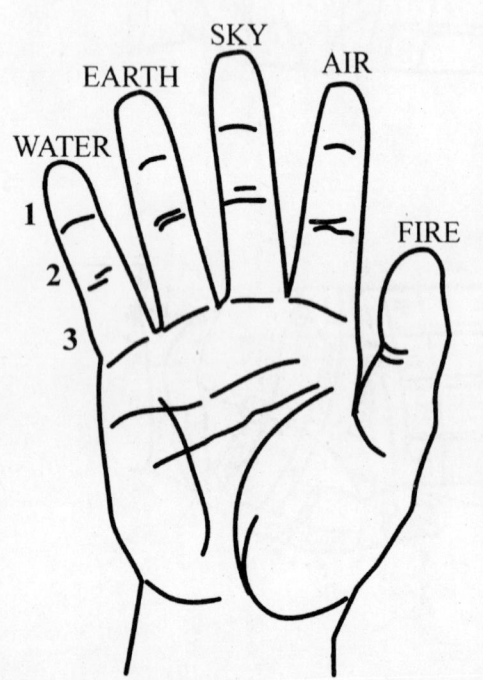

The palm is the true representation of the five tatvas and each finger on the palm represented one tatva.

In every finger there are three notches which helps the increasing/ decreasing/ balancing of the tatva.

If there is more of 'air' tatva in the body then the 1st notch should be pressed regularly with the thumb and the first finger of the other hand.

The second notch helps in balancing the air tatva in the body.

If there is less of 'air' tatva in the body then the 3rd notch should be pressed regularly with the thumb and the first finger of the other hand.

Marma Gyana and Mudra

APAN MUDRA

This mudra helps in rejuvenating the energy points in the chest and the throat points. Regular practice of this mudra helps in solving the sinus problems.

PRANA MUDRA

This mudra helps in increasing the energy in the body. People suffering from the heart disease, arthritis should regularly do this mudra, as this will solve the problems.

ADVAITAM MUDRA

This mudra helps in solving digestive problems, liver, kidney, and lung problems. It is important that the middle, ring, and little finger should press the palm hard and the thumb should be on the second notch of the first finger for getting full benefit of this mudra.

YONI MUDRA

This mudra helps in balancing the left and the right hemisphere of the brain. People suffering from psychosomatic problems will get benefit from this mudra. This mudra also helps in balancing the body temperatures. Regular practice of this mudra keeps sinus, cold, heat strokes, headaches at bay.

Marma Gyana and Mudra

SHAN MUKHKARNI MUDRA

This mudra covers and energises all the body parts and helps in reducing skin problems.

ASTRAM MUDRA

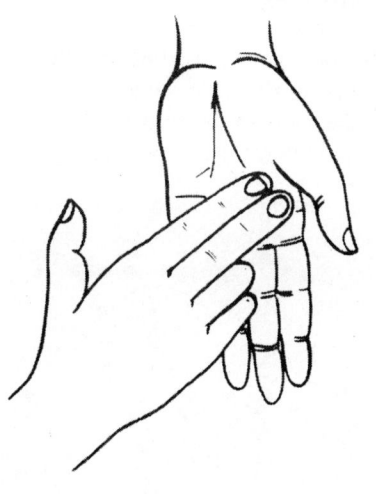

This mudra helps in reducing problems related with the reproductive organs. This mudra helps in increasing the virility in the males.

TRISHULA MUDRA

This mudra represents Tamasic, Rajsic and Sattvic gunas. This mudra helps in balancing the three nadis Ida, pingala and susmana.

GYANA MUDRA

This mudra is mostly used during the meditation and rituals. This mudra helps in allowing the sadhaka to reach levels of supra conscious within a short period of time.

GLOSSARY

Advaita	The concept of single god, non dual entity of the Universal Lord
Agni	Fire god, Fire
Ajna Chakra	Pronounced as 'Agya Chakra' situated in the centre of the bhu Madya or the centre of the eyebrows. It is the psychic centre of intuition.
Akasha	Etheric plane, sky
Amrita	Nectar of life
Anahata	The heart chakra located on the back of the heart.
Asana	Steady and comfortable position for doing meditative exercises and Sadhana.
Astanga Yoga	The eight fold path of yoga as shown by the great saint Patanjali.
Atma	Soul
Aum	The pranava mantra/ primordial sound. Pronounced as 'OM'
Bhakta	Devotee of the lord
Bhu Madhya	The centre of the eye brows the seat of the Anja chakra
Chakra	Celestial wheel which controls the entire body both physically and mentally
Diksha	Initiation
Gunas	The three qualities of matter the Rajo guna, Tamo Guna and Sato guna.
Guru	Spiritual master

Karma	The acts done for the material benefit is called karma. When a person uses this karma for the advancement of the spiritual development, it is called Karma Yoga.
Karmindriyae	The physical organs of action.
Lalana	A minor chakra responsible for the secretion of the amrita.
Manipura	One of the seven major chakras situated on the solar plexus.
Maya	Illusion
Nirguna	Without any material qualities.
Nirvana	The state of ultimate bliss, where there are no miseries, agony or any other material problems.
Prana	Cosmic energy that gives life to the physical body.
Sadhaka	A practitioner on the path of spiritual upliftment
Samadhi	The sadhaka in this stage experiences the cosmic union of Shakti with Shiva.
Sanyasi	A spiritual person who has crossed the material requirements and has devoted his life to the service and prayer of the universal Lord.
Shakti	Force, energy, power.
Shiva	The primodial lord worshipped by the Hindus. He is the lord of all the knowledge representing the highest level of consciousness.
Swadhisthana	This chakra is located at the pubic bone and is related with the physical benefits.
Vajra	Thunderbolt, nadi through with the body energy flows.
Yoga	The art of merging of physical body with the universal soul.

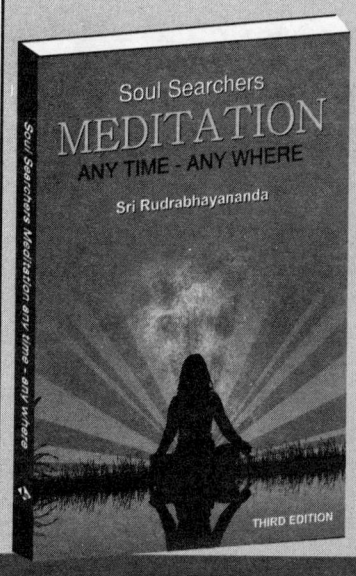

SOUL SEARCHERS
MEDITATION
ANY TIME-ANY WHERE
(3RD EDITION)

Sri Rudrabhayananda

ISBN : 978-81-319-0784-9
Price : Rs. 95.00
Pages : 208 I PB

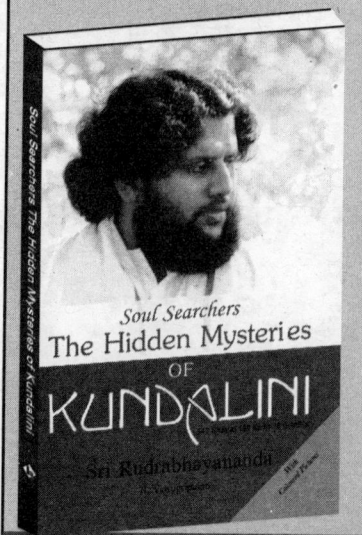

Soul Searchers
The Hidden Mysteries
of
Kundalini

Sri Rudrabhayananda
R. Venugopalan

ISBN : 978-81-319-0047-5
Price : Rs. 225.00
Pages : 460 I PB

Contact your nearest bookstore for a copy

B. JAIN PUBLISHERS (P) LTD.
1921, Street No. 10; Chuna Mandi, Paharganj, New Delhi-110055 (India)
+91 11 2358 0800   +91 11 2358 0471
info@bjain.com   www.bjainbooks.com

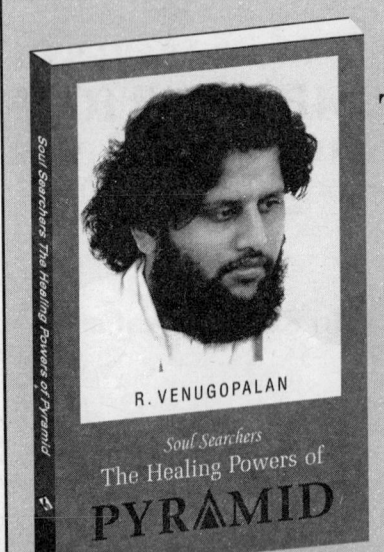

Soul Searchers
The Healing Powers Of
PYRAMID

R. Venugopalan

ISBN : 978-81-319-0178-6
Price : Rs. 90.00
Pages : 168 | PB

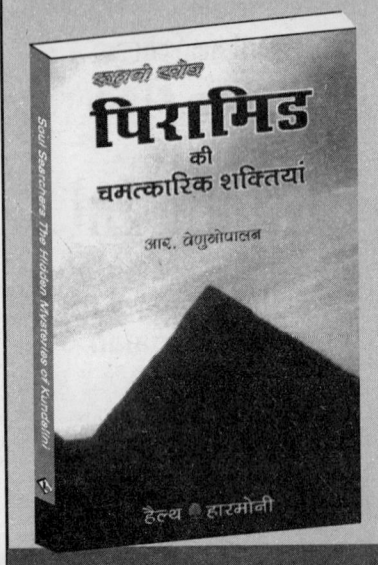

रूहानी खोज
पिरामिड
की चमत्कारिक शक्तियां

आर. वेणुगोपालन

Code : BV-5646
ISBN : 81-8056-042-2
Price : 125.00
Page : 192

Contact your nearest bookstore for a copy

B. JAIN PUBLISHERS (P) LTD.
1921, Street No. 10, Chuna Mandi, Paharganj, New Delhi-110055 (India)
☎ +91 11 2358 0800   📠 +91 11 2358 0471
✉ info@bjain.com   🌐 www.bjainbooks.com